THE FERRANTE
LETTERS

LITERATURE NOW

MATTHEW HART, DAVID JAMES,
AND REBECCA L. WALKOWITZ,
SERIES EDITORS

Literature Now offers a distinct vision of late-twentieth- and early-twenty-first-century literary culture. Addressing contemporary literature and the ways we understand its meaning, the series includes books that are comparative and transnational in scope as well as those that focus on national and regional literary cultures.

Caren Irr, *Toward the Geopolitical Novel:*
U.S. Fiction in the Twenty-First Century

Heather Houser, *Ecosickness in Contemporary U.S. Fiction:*
Environment and Affect

Mrinalini Chakravorty, *In Stereotype:*
South Asia in the Global Literary Imaginary

Héctor Hoyos, *Beyond Bolaño: The Global Latin American Novel*

Rebecca L. Walkowitz, *Born Translated:*
The Contemporary Novel in an Age of World Literature

Carol Jacobs, *Sebald's Vision*

Sarah Phillips Casteel, *Calypso Jews:*
Jewishness in the Caribbean Literary Imagination

Jeremy Rosen, *Minor Characters Have Their Day:*
Genre and the Contemporary Literary Marketplace

Jesse Matz, *Lasting Impressions:*
The Legacies of Impressionism in Contemporary Culture

Ashley T. Shelden, *Unmaking Love:*
The Contemporary Novel and the Impossibility of Union

Theodore Martin, *Contemporary Drift:*
Genre, Historicism, and the Problem of the Present

Zara Dinnen, *The Digital Banal:*
New Media and American Literature and Culture

Gloria Fisk, *Orhan Pamuk and the Good of World Literature*

Peter Morey, *Islamophobia and the Novel*

THE FERRANTE LETTERS

AN EXPERIMENT IN COLLECTIVE CRITICISM

SARAH CHIHAYA

MERVE EMRE

KATHERINE HILL

JILL RICHARDS

Columbia University Press *New York*

Columbia University Press
Publishers Since 1893
New York   Chichester, West Sussex
cup.columbia.edu
Copyright © 2020 Columbia University Press
All rights reserved

Library of Congress Cataloging-in-Publication Data
Names: Chihaya, Sarah, author. | Emre, Merve, author. |
Hill, Katherine, 1982– author. | Richards, Jill C., 1983– author. |
Marcus, Sara, 1977– author. | Brostoff, Marissa, author. |
Loofbourow, Lili, author. | Schiller, Amy, author. |
Swanson, Cecily, author.
Title: The Ferrante letters : an experiment in collective criticism /
Sarah Chihaya, Merve Emre, Katherine Hill, Jill Richards.
Description: New York : Columbia University Press, 2019. |
Series: Literature now | Includes bibliographical references.
Identifiers: LCCN 2019022531 (print) | LCCN 2019022532 (e-book) |
ISBN 9780231194563 (cloth) | ISBN 9780231194570
(trade paperback) | ISBN 9780231550888 (e-book)
Subjects: LCSH: Ferrante, Elena—Criticism and interpretation. |
Female friendship in literature. | Women in literature.
Classification: LCC PQ4866.E6345 Z6716 2019 (print) |
LCC PQ4866.E6345 (e-book) | DDC 305.42—dc23
LC record available at https://lccn.loc.gov/2019022531
LC e-book record available at
https://lccn.loc.gov/2019022532

Columbia University Press books are printed on permanent
and durable acid-free paper.
Printed in the United States of America

Cover design: Jennifer Heuer

She was trying to understand, we were both trying to understand,
and understanding was something that we loved to do.

ELENA FERRANTE, *MY BRILLIANT FRIEND*
(TRANSLATED BY ANN GOLDSTEIN)

CONTENTS

THE FERRANTE
LETTERS

INTRODUCTION

Collective Criticism

Nobody can remember exactly how it started. We all recount the beginnings of the project differently but agree on one fixed point: *The Ferrante Letters: An Experiment in Collective Criticism* officially began in late April 2015 at a bar in Brooklyn. It was that moment when spring flirts with summer, the wind antagonizing cherry trees in bloom. The four of us—Sarah Chihaya, Merve Emre, Katherine Hill, and Jill Richards—sat around a table, drinking and chatting. Some of us had never met before, so we made small talk first: where we lived, what trains we had taken to get there, the ordinary antics of our dogs, cats, girlfriends, husbands.

Then we talked about the authors we might like to read and write about as part of a project Sarah had proposed: a summer dedicated to writing criticism about the work of a single author; criticism that would take the form of letters first exchanged among the four of us, then published online. We named Mark Danielewski, Amitav Ghosh, Jane Gardam, Kate Atkinson. One of us—no one can remember who, and no one will admit to it now—suggested that we read the first four books of Karl Ove Knausgaard's *My Struggle*. There was a polite silence.

Then one of us—no one can remember who, though everyone would admit to lay claim to it now—suggested Elena Ferrante's Neapolitan Quartet, translated by Ann Goldstein. The novels tell the

story of a writer named Elena (Lenù), whose subject is the working-class neighborhood in Naples where she grew up and her long
acquaintance with Lila, the brilliant, troubling classmate she leaves
behind and returns to intermittently over the next fifty years.
Toward the end of *Those Who Leave and Those Who Stay*, the third
novel in the quartet, Lenù laments her separation from Lila and
imagines what might have happened had they gone on to middle
school, high school, and university together. "We would have written together, we would have been authors together, we would have
drawn power from each other, we would have fought shoulder to
shoulder because what was ours was inimitably ours," she writes.[1]
The idea of reading and writing about women reading and writing
together appealed to us. Ferrante was at once inside and outside all
of our individual fields of study. While we all work on contemporary
fiction, none of us had written about Ferrante before, and though
some of us are comparatists by training, none of us specializes in
Italian literature. Ferrante turned out to be the ideal object for our
experiment, neither too close nor too far from our lives as professional writers and scholars.

When our experiment first appeared online in the journal *Post45*
as "The Slow Burn," the organizing principles were simple. From June
to September 2015, we would read a book a month. We would each
write one or two letters per book, enough to keep us reading and
writing throughout the entire summer. We would stay productive—
summer in the academy is notoriously a time to be productive—
without burdening ourselves with unnecessary constraints. There
were no rules about what constituted a letter. It could be a confession, a character study, or a series of close readings, though they all
began with acts of address that picked out our intended respondents:
Dear Sarah, Dear Merve, Dear Katherine, Dear Jill.

Though our structures of address mimed a private exchange,
the public circulation of the letters instituted a unique set of norms

about how we would perform our entwined acts of reading and writing for a larger audience. Naming each other kept us responsible. It reminded us that we had an obligation to specific people not to fall behind, to keep our reading and writing on schedule and synchronized. It established expectations of vigorous citation and intertextuality. Each letter would build on the arguments of previous letters by agreeing, disagreeing, extending, and reframing. We would respond to one another with the knowledge that the ideas on offer were new, tentative—in retrospect, some were simply misguided. But we would be kind and careful with one another, deliberately so, and from one week to the next our kindness would replenish our trust in one another. "The solitude of women's minds is regrettable," thinks Lenù in *Those Who Leave and Those Who Stay*. "It's a waste to be separated from each other without procedures, without tradition."[2] "The Slow Burn" was a critical experiment that refused such waste by laying down first a procedure and then the beginning of a tradition.

What began as a pleasurable gamble emerged as a regimented practice of reading and writing. Its end was not the production of this book—that would come later. It was the cultivation of a distinct model of criticism: one deliberately oriented to the ongoing labor of thought; one that would not insist on a static argument but embody a flexible and capacious process. We would not be competitive, not try to one-up one another. The boundaries between our readings would stay permeable, "softer and more yielding," as Lila imagines in the frightening moments when she perceives that the margins between people are dissolving.[3] We knew that making ourselves permeable would not be easy. It is unnerving to have other peoples' voices clamoring in your head. But we believed that this would make visible the slow, fractured, and creative accretion of ideas that underwrites all acts of criticism, both inside and outside the academy.

Sharing thought in process invites vulnerability and participation. We hoped our project would make other readers want to interlope, to seize on the thrill of reading and responding to something that was not explicitly addressed to them. It did—others joined us, people who had been reading "The Slow Burn" and wanted to contribute letters of their own: Marissa Brostoff, Lili Loofbourow, Sara Marcus, Amy Schiller, and Cecily Swanson, whose letters are included in an appendix to this book. We began to create, through the form and performance of our criticism, a space where we could slip from classroom talk to late-night chatter without hesitations or apologies. That space has only expanded. In the years that followed that first summer, colleagues have taught our letters alongside the Neapolitan novels, using our epistolary form as models for class assignments. New iterations of "The Slow Burn" have appeared each summer, featuring different correspondents writing about Knausgaard's *My Struggle*, David Lynch's *Twin Peaks*, and Darren Star's *Sex and the City*. "The Slow Burn" transformed from one summer's experiment in reading and writing into a method. We call it collective criticism.

* * *

Every introduction is also an afterword: a story of how the book you are reading came into being and why. Our project was born out of a desire to reconcile shared pleasure with critical practice to produce an iterable model of reading and writing—a model that others could replicate through their prose or in their classrooms. The metaphor we used to describe our practice was conversation. Though we were not literally speaking to one another, our solitude of thought was touched by our projection of one another's voices. We became one another's ideal readers, respondents who we knew would write back attentively, enthusiastically, and respectfully, within a matter of days. Our practice was a proxy for the kinds of quasi-professional conversations we had all enjoyed—in classrooms and at conferences but also in coffee shops, bars, and around kitchen tables; over phone calls, email, text, and chat. We hoped to reanimate the vibrant activity of such talk as a dynamic written form available to a wider public.

Collective criticism is marked by a model of authorship that departs from dominant forms of academic production. Traditionally, the work of writing is counted and weighed as an individual accomplishment, especially when it is produced in professional increments. A book is attributed to a single author. Praise, prizes, job offers, promotions, and money (rare though it may be) are extended to her. Whatever conversations she may have had surface, if they do at all, in brief expressions of gratitude in a footnote, and the people who helped are relegated to a blur of names in the acknowledgments. Amidst such commonplace protocols for streamlining and standardizing academic writing, it is easy to forget that the words you commit to paper are yours, but they are not yours alone.

Collective criticism is also marked by a different temporality and set of technologies from scholarly publishing. We wanted to explore the possibilities afforded by online publications to bring to life the hybrid temporality of contemporary critical writing. Our letters were written both to be read in the very immediate present—by each other—and in the unknown future by readers of Ferrante's books. This differed from the standardized time of academic publishing. In the pages of prohibitively expensive journals and edited collections, debate about new books emerges in fits and starts over periods of months, years, or even decades. Arguments are selected for their relevance to the critical conversation, though that conversation often shifts or thins or grows stale between the time of writing, the time of publication, and the time of response. Momentum is difficult to build or sustain. It is easy to believe that you are alone with your thoughts.

Yet that feeling of solitude belies the rich and active social world of academic discourse. The hundreds of scholarly books released each year all emerge from individual minds but also from all manner of elaborations, questions, critiques, and riffs; from conversations inside and outside of institutional walls. When they are good, these conversations are both work and play, diligence and distraction. The blurred line between labor and leisure in these generative moments makes them hard to account for in the increasingly quantified rubrics of academic success and productivity. While it is implied that their affective pleasures should compensate the professional reader and writer for her time, attention, and the energetic responsiveness with which she regards other peoples' ideas, this particular kind of shared work often goes unacknowledged. *The Ferrante Letters* offers one model for encoding the intimate labor of conversation as part of scholarship. Our goal was to formalize the texture of togetherness to show that this, as much as putting one word next to another, is the labor of writing.

But what, precisely, does *togetherness* mean? What were we to one another? Interlocutors? Collaborators? Lovers, metaphorically speaking? The history of cowriting between women has often taken the idealized scene of exchange between lovers—desirous, euphoric, mutually fulfilling—as its model of work and intimacy. "From our first encounter, we have been unable to distinguish between the two," write Carey Kaplan and Ellen Cronan Rose of their long partnership as coauthors, a writing practice they describe as "lesbian." Though they were not lovers in real life, their writing was galvanized by the anticipation of talking to, and thinking with, each other. Drinks turned into dinners that turned into late night gossip that turned into words on the page. For Kaplan and Rose, their partnership reflects neither the "hierarchy and competitiveness" of heterosexual relationships nor the "anxious collaboration" between men that Wayne Koestenbaum describes in *Double Talk*. Instead, their emphasis falls on intellectual and emotional convergence, a "reciprocal, nonhierarchical yearning" rooted in "relentless fidelity to bodily as well as cerebral experiences."[4]

But the model of lovers, even polyamorous ones, never quite fit our relationship. From the beginning, friendship, with its flexibility, its productive conflict, its necessary individuation, has been our model of collective criticism. Like Lila and Lenù, we always remained "she and I," never metamorphosing (except for now, and only briefly, illusively) into "we." We began closer to where Sandra Gilbert and Susan Gubar arrive in their introduction to the second edition of *The Madwoman in the Attic*, a dialogue acknowledging "that behind the hyphenated yet superficially monolithic authorial entity known as Gilbert-and-Gubar, there are and always have been two distinct, if deeply bonded human beings, each with her own view of the world."[5] What was true of the beginning is truer now at the end: we have worked on this project for several years, our voices, rather than growing closer together, have grown more clearly distinct. Our reading and writing has fallen out of sync. Work, love, heartbreak, children, illness, and death have derailed each of us at different moments. As some of us have written more and some of us less about Ferrante, it became clear that the labor of writing this book had never been equally distributed. How could it have been? But learning how to acknowledge and respect that unevenness became part of our critical project.

Collective criticism as we have practiced it is different from the "we" model of collaboration. While our reading and writing has operated cooperatively, we have not, anywhere other than this introduction, collaborated on a single piece of writing. Part of this was just the nature of the epistolary project, but part of it was a principled refusal of a shared voice and its structural limitations.

Within the academy, collaboration has been co-opted by discourses of industry and interdisciplinarity, by the expectation that autonomous acts of reading and writing should make themselves amenable to "knowledge exchange." Yet collaboration between women still remains "a risky business," according to Elizabeth G. Peck and JoAnna Stephens Mink in *Common Ground: Feminist Collaboration in the Academy*. It is "often viewed suspiciously" in contrast to the heroic individualism of the single-authored monograph.[6] As Lorraine M. York has observed, "Collaboration, whether by women or men, has often been figured as female passivity, sentimentality, and weakness."[7] For women, particularly junior ones in precarious institutional positions, the kind of collaboration that would collapse us into a single entity rather than maintaining a lively sense of difference and individuality seemed both unnatural and unproductive—a lose-lose wager.

Where collaboration felt constrictive, collectivism offered more liberating possibilities for the roles and relationships we could inhabit. As Brent Edwards, Anna McCarthy, and Randy Martin argue, collectivism does not necessitate collaboration. In fact, it is most generative when it moves away from it. "It is precisely what seems *dépassé* about collectivism—its fragility, its frank avowal of interested affiliation, its conviction that the difficulties it brings to light cannot be avoided or rationalized away—that makes it so crucial today, in an age of accounting and quantification."[8] If today the avowal of interested affiliation is crucial to all scholars, then it has always been necessary for politically marginalized ones. In the United States, we see this emerge in the work of women of color feminists in the 1970s and 80s, including Audre Lorde, Kimberlé Crenshaw, and the Combahee River Collective. As Cherríe Moraga writes in *This Bridge Called My Back*, "one voice is not enough, nor two, although this is where dialogue begins."

In Italy, this observation has been crucial to the literary culture of postwar feminism as articulated by Luisa Muraro, one of Ferrante's influences, and the Milan Woman's Bookstore Collective. As Rebecca Falkoff has suggested, Muraro's theory of *affidamento*, "a practice of 'putting faith in' or 'entrusting' between women . . . would be the basis for a new symbolic order to counter patriarchy."[9] Second-wave calls for sisterhood relied on two premises: an equal rights platform that denied the specificity of sexual difference between women and men, and the fantasy of unity and consensus among women. In contrast, *affidamento* imagined that women could build relations independent of men, modeled on the ties between mothers and daughters. These relations did not always entail alignment. Nonalignment was key to figuring the idea of the political as an assortment of individuals rather than a falsely single voice.

Collective criticism offers another model for feminist praxis, a way of tying ourselves more closely together, not just as mothers and daughters but as friends, colleagues, mentors, and confidantes. It dislodges the fixation on individual productivity and its coldly quantified standards of academic success, refusing the culture of competition that defines many aspects of our profession. It enables a plurality of methods, an amplified confidence in our different approaches to interpretation and appreciation. It preserves the liveliness of conversation, in all its tangles and tangents, as a mode of writing that is both personal and professional instead of collapsing these exchanges into a single, linear intervention. It reasserts the desires that led us to become critical writers: to read with depth and feeling, to interpret with creative rigor, to share ideas generously rather than stake out positions possessively.

* * *

After training ourselves to read and write in the collective mode, writing as "we" in this introduction proved difficult. The first-person plural drained us of our shared sense of liberty and safety. It was hard to overcome artifice of collaboration. Our methods were too different; our styles too resistant to consolidation. We could not physically write together—in the same room, at the same time, looking over one another's shoulders, first one person, then another suggesting words. "The erasures, the transpositions, the small additions . . . gave me the impression that I had escaped myself and now was running a hundred paces ahead with an energy and also a harmony that the person left behind didn't know she had," recalls Lenù in *My Brilliant Friend* of writing with Lila.[10] If our goal for the introduction was to look back at our experiment with that same sense of harmony, then our first drafts failed spectacularly.

This failure revealed that collective criticism is not amenable to streamlining. It is more accommodating of our discontinuous styles, our individual habits of thought and feeling. The letters invited many forms of expression that fell between the personal and the professional—conversation, anecdote, autobiography, confession—knowing that even the slightest hint of the personal can court disdain and disapproval. "It intrigues me," writes Cathy Davidson, "that personal revelation seems to make some scholars queasy when it is done by someone they know but delighted when it is done in the past, by someone who is comfortably dead."[11] The queasiness is a kind of denial, a refusal to recognize that the production of criticism is subject to inequities and imbalances, crosshatched by race, gender, sexuality, and class. The personal recalls us to the uneasy fact that there are "selves behind these projects," as Jack Halberstam puts it, and that those selves are discovering "how to articulate desires" that may seem strange or illegible.[12]

Though autobiography and other forms of women's life writing have emerged as objects of scholarly interest, the autobiographical mode rarely migrates to the writing itself. It is perhaps easier to state the injunctions against it, which are often delivered as friendly or concerned advice from well-intentioned mentors. Literary criticism might be about the status of the personal, but it should not be overtly personal. Literary criticism might concern itself with the sentimental, but it should not itself be sentimental. Literary criticism might analyze the domestic, but it should not acknowledge the pressure that everyday domestic responsibilities exert on thinking and writing. Not everyone follows these rules, of course. In embracing the personal, scholars like Saidiya Hartman, D.A. Miller, and Stuart Hall have beautifully interlaced their objects of study with their styles of expression, revealing the seams where life and criticism meet. Yet within the academy, this freedom seems to be a late-career phenomenon, acceptable only once standardized forms of success have been established.

Our emphasis on conversation and collectivity differs from much autobiographically inflected criticism. We do not believe that our experiment in the *I* or the *We* is more honest or authentic than the declarative form of most academic writing. But we do believe it brings to life ongoing possibilities for transforming the personal into feminist praxis—a critical experiment with no defined end. There are husbands, boyfriends, girlfriends, and lovers in the mix. Pregnancy matters as more than just a personal concern. Young children, ailing parents, friends, and strangers require care. Race and ethnicity come into play in ways that do not neatly match up with any uniform sense of the "we." Life gets written and rewritten into arguments as intimacies are forged and dismantled, as the roles we inhabit shift and multiply. The gamble of *The Ferrante Letters*, like the gamble of the Neapolitan Quartet, is its willingness to enmesh literature and criticism in the web of lived relations among daughters, mothers, wives, colleagues, advisors, and friends.

We are not alone in asking these questions, either about the broad demand in academic and popular criticism for new models of engagement or about Ferrante's appeal to contemporary feminist collaborations. Our work arrives in a cultural moment bursting with woman-helmed critical collectives, from *Public Books* to *Avidly*, and it joins a thriving conversation about Ferrante across numerous cultural spaces and channels—from Emily Books, which introduced many American readers to Ferrante's work, to academic exchanges like the 2017 MLA Prose Fiction panel with Hester Blum, Christina Lupton, Pamela Thurschwell, Sarah Blackwood, Sarah Mesle, and David Kurnick, later published in *ASAP/J*. This contemporary blossoming of feminist collectivity across the varied worlds of critical writing only further demonstrates that, as our second-wave predecessors well knew, the gendered configurations of our labor practices and literary thought are still impossible to separate.

* * *

Although this introduction marks the end of our experiment, collective criticism lives on, both as a set of practices and as an ethos of critical subjectivity. Rereading the letters as we have organized them in the first half of the book, we can see the energetic circulation of ideas among the four of us over the last three years. We pass phrases and concepts back and forth without right of possession. We note and annotate and reannotate the same passages with generosity and cumulative appreciation and without concern for replication or exhaustion. The second half of the book grows out of the little seeds of argument we first planted in those summer letters, either with future-oriented intention or by casually spitting them out along the way. Each of these full-length essays on Ferrante, which look back on the series as a whole, emerges from the thoughts we first worked through together in our correspondence and then developed in our individual idioms. It is important also to note that while this is a book about reading Ferrante, it makes no claim to being *the* book on Ferrante. While the Neapolitan novels were the spark that first lit "The Slow Burn," *The Ferrante Letters* is ultimately an attempt to share the experience of reading together and to invite new readers into this togetherness.

Understanding together, understanding each other, made it possible to continue writing. We can see how collective criticism has cohered as an orientation—or perhaps a counterorientation—to the norms of our discipline. We've worked steadily through these years in shifts, according to our different academic and life timelines, weaving our labors together with shared patience, trust, and investment. This is the model that we propose as a prompt. Our experiment in collective criticism has been a mutually beneficial and revelatory process that has shaped our readings and reshaped each of our understandings of ourselves as readers and writers in turn. None of the essays could have found their final forms without this long process of sharing, talking, and writing. None of us are now the same writers, or critics, or friends, or women we were when we began it.

I

LETTERS (2015)

MY BRILLIANT FRIEND

Summer 2015
Brooklyn, New York
Sarah, June 22

Dear Readers,

Friendship and reading take time, but I tend to be pushy with both. I'm a voracious, perhaps violent reader of novels, and a voracious (hopefully not violent) cultivator of new friendships; I blaze through books in single sittings and similarly crave those day-into-night, coffee-into-beer conversations where you learn everything about a person in one heady rush. This isn't necessarily a good thing. Both of these impulses are surely born out of a brutish impatience to reach some certain knowledge of what will happen, to get to the end. It's hard to force myself to slow down and relish the meandering pleasures of getting to know a person or a novel.

And I suspect that this is true of many of us whose work it is to rapidly generate readings and writings. Summer, then, seems the ideal time to take up that challenge. Given this pause from the academic schedule, can we stretch this time out? Can we luxuriate in the unique pleasures of leisurely writing, of savoring a text, of conversing more deeply, of luxuriating in the very things that we rush through during the school year?

So, for the next few months, we at Contemporaries[1] will attempt to give ourselves—at least to some degree—the liberty of taking that time and extending those pleasures. "The Slow Burn" is an experiment in what I've been thinking of as slow-form criticism: readings that happen on the back burner while your mind is mostly elsewhere, that, in their extended simmering, develop a different richness and depth over time from a quick-fired review. In lieu of stand-alone articles, we will embark on a summer-long reading project—or, as we've been thinking of it, a good old-fashioned book club—by correspondence. The correspondents are a novelist, Katherine Hill, and three academics, Merve Emre, Jill Richards, and myself. Over the course of the summer, we will discuss Elena Ferrante's Neapolitan novels, as translated by Ann Goldstein: *My Brilliant Friend* (2011), *The Story of a New Name* (2013), *Those Who Leave and Those Who Stay* (2014), and the newly translated *The Story of the Lost Child* (2015).

This experiment in slow reading will be both long-term and collaborative, elements that are as essential to our project as they are to Ferrante's novel cycle. Just as Ferrante's novels examine two characters intertwined in a lifelong dialogue (about each other, themselves, and the world they live in), so too will our readings of them emerge out of conversations over time, as we write for and to each other. And along the way—as Ferrante's characters Lila and Lenù do—we will contemplate what it means to dwell with books, with the stories of our lives and others, both alone and together.

A presto—
Sarah

Dear Sarah, Katherine, and Merve,

I don't like love stories, as a general principle. It's not that they are too precious. It's the death or marriage trajectory of the couple form that I find particularly depressing, though it must be said, I have a very cranky attitude towards marriage. Elena Ferrante's *My Brilliant Friend* looks like a love story and is one, sort of. The novel has all the pieces of a coming-of-age romance: two female friends, difficult childhoods, education, a courtship, marriage, seemingly limitless social mobility, all against the shifting terrain of postwar Italy. But everything is somehow tilted at the wrong angle. Here the friend is not the natural given, off to the side. She is not that handy, lurking person with whom the future-bride, the Daisy or Estella or Emma, discusses the mysteries of her husband-to-be. In this novel, female friendship takes center stage, It is a social relation equally mysterious, difficult, and precarious as the bonds we most often, most exclusively, attribute to romantic love.

Lila and Lenù grow up together. They grow out of each other, increasingly unable to name which behavior first belonged to whom. They are perpetually in competition. It is an economy of two. In Lenù's words, "what I lacked she had, and vice versa, in a continuous game of exchanges and reversals that, now happily, now painfully, made us indispensable to each other."[2] In this social division of personality, L&L switch places within the familiar dyads. One girl is beautiful, the other is smart. One girl is slutty, the other is chaste. This divvying up of personality is a kind of balancing act, where the two girls exist at opposing poles. L&L are so perfectly matched, as though each girl were stepping into the negative left by the other. Then again, there is something fantastic, almost charmed, in the very real persistence of the delimited categories so often imposed upon adolescent girls: smart *or* beautiful; slutty *or* chaste. I think of *The Babysitter's Club*: Claudia is artsy, Kristy practical, Dawn the hippie, Mary Anne the shy one. So normalized, at such an early age, is this bizarre suggestion that amongst friends what makes you *you* has to bounce off everyone else in a claustrophobic pool game of limited personalities. L&L's mutual resentment manifests itself in sometimes vengeful ways, but it is also a frustration about this social directive to be only one thing.

The novel doesn't start like that. Lenù has to catch Lila, keep up with her, literally tail her, as though she might get away. Lenù wants to be Lila and so embarks upon a series of imperfectly mimicked behaviors. But she also wants to have Lila, to keep her, less out of possessiveness than survival. Over the years, this friendship is not a supplement to family or romantic love. It is almost an atmosphere, an intermediary between Lenù and everyone she knows, every place she knows, and all her imagined futures. There is antagonism here, even hatred, but it is all about maintaining the right balance to stay afloat so that the other one doesn't drift too far out of reach. L&L drag each other down and then bandage the wounds. They are vicious, sabotaging each other's chances for escape, then regretting it halfway through and changing course. All the while, the strange thing about Ferrante's prose is the way you sort of disappear into it, into Lenù's so often matter-of-fact narration. That confidential voice is so close to speech it feels like realism—this happened, then this, then that. But, here and there, the couple form that is L&L goes blurry and the sentences stick together in a cascading series of mutual entanglements: the intention behind this act, the regret at its consequence, the forgiveness for the intention, the resentment at the forgiveness, the guilt about the resentment, and on and on.

What is tricky is the way that, while these strings get tangled across the novel, there remains that symmetry of matched persons on the course of social mobility: Lenù goes to school and Lila marries rich. For Lenù, Lila's marriage is a catastrophe. If Lenù is only half of a person, and Lila cannot be had or kept, then someone else has to fill this gap. So Lenù embarks upon an increasingly desperate series of replacements. At the wedding, Lenù panics, in one of those cascading moments when the prose goes windy:

> I felt an urgent need to be caught up again by Nino, I didn't want him to start talking to my classmate exactly the way, until a moment earlier, he had been talking to me. I needed—in order not to rush to make up with Antonio, to tell him, in tears: yes, you're right, I don't know what I am and what I really want I use you and then I throw you away, but it's not my fault, I feel half and half, forgive me—Nino to draw me exclusively into the things he knew, into his powers, to recognize me as like him. (MBF, 327)

Lenù wants to be caught up and pulled in, as though a satellite orbiting a larger planet. The syntax here is weird, so that whoever exists on the other end of Lenù's proposition gets confusing. Nino or Antonio? Does it matter? What's funny about this quotation is that it shifts the drama of the friendship into a more familiar arena— the drama of romantic love. This is a scene we can recognize. The shift into the language of romantic love is partly tactical, because there isn't really a good language for friendship: best friend, work friend, friend of a friend, sex friend, ex-friend. To describe L&L, I am perpetually borrowing from another language that doesn't quite fit: seduction, eroticism, romance. But then the progression narrative is off, because, despite my hopes for a contrary denouement, L&L appear decidedly heterosexual. All the same, what I like about this bit, more than anything else, is the way that it entirely fails to tell a story of progress about feeling, as a child to adolescence adolescent coming-of-age where everything might fit together and make sense, leading towards the cumulative self that is the adult. For Lenù, settling on an account of how she came to be remains, at best, a compromise between this orbit or that one, depending on the person she is trying to convince.

In retrospect, all of this has been rather Lenù-centric. She is my favorite, of course. I am not immune to the gravitational force of Lila—that dazzling, magnetic personality that seems to live more and better than everyone around her. But Lila makes me wary. One is, it seems, perpetually guarding their fingers and toes around the Lilas of the world. The way that I can just pluralize Lila's name, as a type of magical person, then makes me wonder: What is it, about this particular friendship, that makes you pick a side? What would the story be like if it was told from the other end, from Lila's perspective? Utterly different, I expect, because Lenù is hardly forthcoming. Lenù has a number of stories about herself and Lila that are more currency than truth. I think of that moment when Lila shuts herself up in her parent's house, threatening to cancel her wedding. In a series of hypotheticals typical for *My Brilliant Friend*, Lenù imagines what she would do in Lila's place, what Lila might be capable of doing, what she most wants Lila to do, and then convinces her best friend to do the opposite, what she thinks Lila *wants* to be convinced to do—to marry Stefano. Practical, the brilliant friend, Lenù uses the version of their story that will work as a means to an end that someone else wants. By now we know that Lenù is a good talker. She is also a liar. "I reshuffled the cards that by now we knew well enough. I spoke of the before and the after, of the old generation and of ours, of how we were different, of how she and Stefano were different" (*MBF*, 311).

—Jill

Dear Sarah, Jill, and Merve,

I devoured these books the first time, the way I remember devouring books as a kid, the way Lila does, according to Lenù. It was that old feeling, the excitement of having a mind to which another mind is speaking from the page. Rereading them has been remarkably slow—and not just because Sarah encouraged it. Part of me is trying and failing to memorize the sentences, which build rapidly and by association—comma, clause, comma, clause—like the inveterately booming, inveterately corrupt city of Naples. The next part is trying to decipher what has happened here, how this book was made, why I have forced it on every woman I care about with little more than a lame jacket copy summary. *Italy. Friendship. Their whole lives.* No wonder so many of those women looked at me with blank hopefulness, wishing I would say something intelligent, give them a good reason, or even just a few more words.

"Just trust me," I have to tell them, inadequately. "You'll love it." And the fact is, everyone does.

Why?

Mostly, I think, because it is a book about deciphering that which is present and has always been around us: life, these people, our parents and neighbors, the world into which we are born, our maddening friends. It's all there already, our material, we just have to put it in order. So, in going back to the beginning, for the slow, searching reread, I can't help but think about the arrangement of this material—the order in which Lenù, who is writing it, presents it to us—which seems to be the order in which it presents itself to her.

I say *seems* because of course the writing is labored over, as all literature is. But in these novels, Ferrante accomplishes what Lenù attributes to Lila, that is, the effortlessness of voice:

> Lila was able to speak through writing; unlike me when I wrote, unlike Sarratore in his articles and poems, unlike even many writers I had read and was reading, she expressed herself in sentences that were well constructed, and without error, even though she had stopped going to school, but—further—she left no trace of effort, you weren't aware of the artifice of the written word. (*MBF*, 226–27)

It's an odd claim coming from Lenù, who is the one writing in just this way. But what is a writer if not a jealous, self-loathing creature who sees the world from her own narrow point of view? (Like Jill, I'm Team Lenù. Can you tell?)

Part of this effortlessness, no doubt, has something to do with authorial speed. Ferrante has said she wrote these novels very quickly, "as if under dictation,"[3] and that seems right to me. They proceed, diary-like, as though life has already been lived, and Lenù is just getting the events down. We devour them on first read because they demand it. The food just keeps on coming.

On second read, we take a little time to decipher. The life we are reading is both a remembered life and a recorded life, that of a contemporary Torinese in her sixties, looking back on a working-class girlhood in Naples. The episodes recounted, from Melina's madness to Don Achille's murder, from to Lenù's first period to Lila's wedding, are the seismic events of that life, the moments that pulse most intensely on the narrative map. They are the moments that, in light of everything that has happened to Lenù, to Lila, and in the world, the adult Lenù deems worth recording.

She has selected them, as every writer does, for a variety of reasons. Some adhere to our conventional understanding of key moments in a lifetime or a bildungsroman. Others have a certain personal intensity: The Kind of Thing You Remember. Still others are early clues to the world beyond the present-tense experience of childhood. They reveal in glimpses, much as the world is revealed to a growing child, the postwar neighborhood, Naples, and Italy, into which both Lenù and Lila were born.

This is where I think the artifice of the written word performs its most beguiling work. It *seems* as though Lenù is just telling us how it was, how it happened, how she felt—a chronological regurgitation of everything she remembers in an effort to figure it all out. But this narrative seeks a many-fingered truth—emotional, social, historical, political—that's too complicated to fall into place without some major authorial orchestration. How else could the structures of power be intuited in early childhood chills, enacted in grade school jealousies, and revealed to the (literally) myopic eyes of a nervous teenage nerd? Lenù keeps insisting she didn't understand certain events, that in fact she has never deciphered certain things, her narrative voice somehow the confused child and the awakening adolescent and the rigid adult all at once. But for all her limits, she's the one telling us everything. She's the one who's put it all together already, in this particular way, as it seemed or occurred to her. If Ferrante wrote these novels quickly, it's only because she knew exactly what she was doing.

"I liked to discover connections like that, especially if they concerned Lila," Lenù admits of herself at fifteen. "I traced lines between moments and events distant from one another, I established convergences and divergences" (*MBF*, 256). She could just as easily be talking about her sixty-something self, the author of this novel. Personally, I'd love to talk more about that self, and all of Lenù's overlapping selves, including her brilliant friend Lila: what they know, what they're wrong about, what they're honest about, how they lie.

—Katherine

Dear Sarah, Jill, and Katherine,

> *Burn* (n.): A manifestation of anger or frustration; usu. in phr. "slow burn," a display of slowly mounting anger; the act or state of gradually becoming enraged.
> —OXFORD ENGLISH DICTIONARY (2015)

* * *

As a child, I was often told not to do things out of anger. Don't speak in anger. Don't let your anger get the best of you. Whatever you do, don't go to bed angry, and if you do, in your anger, do not sleep well. None of this was particularly meaningful to someone with my temperament: someone for whom anger was both impossible to suppress and acutely motivating. I liked doing things out of anger and I did things well when I was angry.

I tell you this not in a spirit of confession but so that you may understand why I am drawn to the frame narrative that introduces *My Brilliant Friend*: Lila's sudden and silent disappearance from her home in Naples provokes in Lenù neither worry nor anxiety but hostility tinged with a desire for revenge. "She wanted not only to disappear herself, now, at the age of sixty-six, but also to eliminate the entire life she had left behind," Lenù observes. She continues: "I was really angry. We'll see who wins this time, I said to myself. I turned on the computer and began to write—all the details of our story, everything that still remained in my memory" (*MBF*, 23). We are meant to believe that the novel we hold in our hands is the product of Lenù's swift recourse to writing; a move that counters Lila's wordless abandonment of her life with the simmering of narrative prose. If Lila has sought to eliminate her entire life, Lenù's payback will be to restore it in its every last, painstaking detail.

What does it mean to write angrily? For me, the production of the novel's slow burn is just one endpoint in a long history of anger—not just Lenù's particular anger towards Lila but the widespread poverty and dispossession that made "our mothers, our grandmothers as angry as starving dogs." That this anger lodges itself differently in women that in men is, for Lenù, the natural order of things. Whereas the "men were always getting furious, they calmed down in the end; women, who appeared to be silent, acquiescent, when they were angry flew into a rage that had no end" (38). Anger is a never-ending infection; violence a disease that draws women together only to pull them apart as they scheme, scream, punch, pull hair, and draw blood.

Yet through her avowedly flat, antinostalgic relation of her childhood, Lenù seems to insist that we consider her productive anger as a distinct structure of feeling altogether. More reflective in its consideration of the past, and less childishly presentist than the anger of all those other women who lash out at one another blindly, Lenù's anger has been tamed by some force external to its point of origin. It is anger shaped into a very particular generic form; an anger taught to control its tone, to pace itself across more than 1,000 pages, to look back and assess its growth and development over nearly half a century.

Perhaps it's not surprising, then, that a distinctly literary education is what sets Lenù's anger with Lila apart from the novel's other female pairs. After all, who can bother to distinguish Melina from Lidia, Carmela from Gigliola, in Naples's never-ending "chain of wrongs that generated wrongs?" (MBF, 83). Whereas the other women feud pointlessly over men—crude and stupid men, without exception—Lila and Lenù's friendship begins by staking out the classroom as their battlefield, "challenging each other, without ever saying a word" (28). "Lila appeared in my life in first grade and immediately impressed me because she was very bad," recalls Lenù, in what is without a doubt one of my favorite sentences of all time (31). (I can only hope that one day my impish child will be sent home with a report card containing this very sentence.) Lila is very bad, but she is also very brilliant; a relentless and greedy autodidact who has taught herself to read from the dusty newspapers her father and brother use to wrap shoes in the Cerullo family's workshop. "The fact was this: Lila knew how to read and write, and what I remember of that gray morning when the teacher revealed it to us was, above all, the sense of weakness the news left me with," Lenù observes (XX). And Lila exploits that sense of vulnerability mercilessly, leaving no room for kindness. She thinks as violently as others fight:

> Her quickness of mind was like a hiss, a dart, a lethal bite. And there was nothing in her appearance that acted as a corrective. She was disheveled, dirty, on her knees and elbows she always had scabs from cuts and scrapes that never had time to heal. Her large, bright eyes could become cracks behind which, before every brilliant response there was a gaze that appeared not very childlike and perhaps not even human. Every one of her movements said that to harm her would be pointless because, whatever happened, she would find a way of doing worse to you. (*MBF*, 48)

Lila's bright, slitted eyes are her weapon of choice in the girls' games of literary one-upmanship, which are both delightful to behold and terribly disheartening. Delightful because Lenù's memories of learning to read, and even of learning to read in fierce competition with another person, can turn hushed and reverent— a brief respite from the anger and violence of the home, the school, the streets. When the girls buy a yellowed copy of *Little Women*, they sneak off to the church courtyard "to read it, either silently, one next to the other or aloud." They read it so many times that the book becomes "tattered and sweat-stained," loses its spine, comes unthreaded, falls apart. "It was our book, we loved it dearly," Lenù writes of her and Lila's conversion to literary worship under the auspices of Meg, Beth, and Amy, but especially Jo March, everyone's favorite bookworm turned successful author (MBF, 68).

The appreciation and manipulation of literary language thus emerges as a magnetic bond, one that Lenù believes sets the girls and their friendship apart from the anger of Naples as they grow older. Unlike the literal-minded Carmela, the moony Gigliola, or any of their bitter, feuding family members, Lila and Lenù alone possess "the capacity that together—only together—we had to seize the mass of colors, sounds, things, and people, and express it and give it power." This too is a competitive process but one that yields a shared way of looking at the world. In a sentence that might double as a description of Ferrante's own breed of slow burn realism, Lenù observes, "More effectively than she had as a child, [Lila] took the facts and in a natural way charged them with tension; she intensified reality as she reduced it to words, she injected it with energy." "But I also realized," she continues, "with pleasure, that as soon as she began to do this, I felt able to do the same, and I tried and it came easily. This—I thought contentedly—distinguishes me from Carmela and all the others" (130).

Yet disheartening because literary pleasure has its limits—it can't put food on the table or pay the rent. As such, it can never fully thwart the anger borne of deprivation. When Lila's father refuses to pay for her to continue her education, the girls channel their obsession with books into an obsession with wealth. "Things changed and we began to link school to wealth," Lenù observes. "We thought that if we studied hard we would be able to write books and that the books would make us rich." But even this stance of partial pleasure can't be sustained once the question of money looms.

Whereas Lenù continues to harbor dreams of writing throughout middle school and high school, Lila devotes herself to the shoe business. In attempting to modernize her father's faltering repair shop against his wishes, she roars and rages, falling into a fury that knows no bounds and respects neither the bonds of friendship nor family—just money. "I felt grieved at the waste," Lenù laments, "because I was compelled to go away, because she preferred the adventure of the shoes to our conversation, because she knew how to be autonomous whereas I needed her" (132). Eventually, Lenù's grief transforms into an uneasy sense of self-superiority, secured by her access to the institutions of higher education that Lila can only yearn for. "I was with boys and girls who were studying Latin and Greek, and not like her, with construction workers, mechanics, cobblers, fruit and vegetable sellers, grocers, shoemakers" (163). Lenù's invocation of their original childhood competitions in her frame narrative—"We'll see who wins this time," she says as she begins to write the novel (23)—may seem spiteful, but it is in fact a return to a purer scene of literary togetherness.

I suppose I see all of this competitive to-and-fro less as a love story, as Jill does, and more as a twinned *Künstlerroman*. *My Brilliant Friend* is the portrait of the artist as not one but two young women; a portrait limned by the convergences of language and the divergences of class. It is precisely this intertwining that makes it difficult for me to take sides or even to perceive clearly what each side may represent. I suspect I'm not the only one who assumed, when I started reading, that the title *My Brilliant Friend* was Lenù's homage to Lila's brilliance. Imagine my surprise when it turned out to be the other way around. ("You're my brilliant friend," Lila says to Lenù on the eve of her wedding, without a trace of anger. "You have to be the best of all, boys and girls" [*MBF*, 312].) But really it is—and it always has been—both.

—Merve

Tokyo, Japan
Sarah, June 26

Dear (brilliant) friends,

How real are we to each other?
This is a weird but perhaps singularly fitting question to ask, as we write from far-flung locations to each other (and to the mysterious, invisible denizens of the internet). And it's a provocative and sometimes painful one that Ferrante's been making me ask a lot lately about friendship, one that's demanded by the opening pages of *My Brilliant Friend*. Upon hearing of Lila's total disappearance, Lenù is flatly unsurprised for, as she writes, "[Lila] wanted to vanish; she wanted every one of her cells to disappear, nothing of her ever to be found. And since I know her well, or at least I think I know her, I take it for granted that she has found a way to disappear, to leave not so much as a hair anywhere in this world" (*MBF*, 21).

Lenù accepts Lila's magical vanishing act without batting an eyelash, as one of the things she knows best about Lila is that her friend desires complete disappearance, and furthermore, that she is capable of it. But this odd certainty gives the reader pause: ultimately, the true and most intimate sum of Lenù's knowledge about Lila is that her friend will someday attain complete *unknowability*. And tellingly, Lenù's phrasing here betrays the necessary fault line at the heart of any true friendship, the crack of doubt that lets the thing flex and shift and grow: "I know her well, *or at least I think I know her*." Lenù has known Lila for more than sixty years, for that vague time most easily periodized as forever. There is no doubt in this reader's mind that they *do* know each other well, perhaps better than anyone else. But that knowledge is necessarily incomplete and, like many of this book's proffered forms, it is deceptive—for, as I think the book proposes, perhaps friendship isn't exactly about knowing your friends at all.

At first, Lenù and Lila's friendship seems to fit a classic genre of literary friendship: the very human, sympathetically flawed narrator can't tell her own story without looking longingly at that brighter, scarier, more *alive* other, that brilliant friend that shines too bright, has an edge so keen she shouldn't get too close but can't resist cutting herself. You know: Nick to Gatsby, Gene to Phineas, Sal to Dean, and so on. These characters are dangerous to the narrator, to themselves, to the reader, and as a result, they usually die or collapse into themselves—because, we're told, perhaps we *shouldn't* aspire to burn so brightly, for people who do must end by immolating themselves in the blaze of their own terrifying brilliance, that hackneyed old Kerouac refrain about the person that burns, burns, burns like a Roman candle, et cetera.

Yet while *The Great Gatsby* or *A Separate Peace* or *On the Road*—these bro-love tales of masculine exceptionalism—suggest to us that bright-burning human fireworks like this might actually exist somewhere, Ferrante's brilliant friend[s] show[s] us the opposite. Rather, I wonder if Ferrante's point is to highlight the fact that *all* friendships—especially real, deep, true ones—are, on some level, built on fantastic projections. We don't get to know the real Lila (Lina to everyone else in the neighborhood) and can't ever, really. For as long as Lenù is our narrator, we'll be blinded by the too-bright blaze of her particular and singular understanding of Lila as her enigmatic and brilliant friend, her opposite, her better half. It's a weird depiction of friendship that offers a frightening revelation: that to some extent, perhaps all our friends are imaginary ones. But even if our friends are somehow unreal to us, it doesn't mean that friendship, and friend-love, aren't real or true. And even if this sounds shifty and makes me seem like something of a sociopath, I don't honestly think it's a *bad* thing. It's also kind of a beautiful thing—it's what lets us see our close companions through the bifocals of friendship (critical on top, rose-colored on bottom), to describe them in that particular nonerotic language of love that Jill evoked. It's the imaginary, malleable quality of our friends that allows us to shape them into desirable and aspirational definites, visions of personhood clearer than our own uncomfortable partial views of our misshapen, amorphous selves. Thus, a large part of Lila's magnetic draw is in the specificity of her depiction. Through the form-giving lens of Lenù's friendship and admiration, Lila is as magical and frightening as a mythological shapeshifter who shifts form with no warning, transforming with utter precision. Each of her stages is described in terms cleanly specific, and she is always the sharpest, clearest thing in a world of "things not identifiable, dark masses" (MBF, 55). Witness tiny Lila in elementary school, possessed of a certainty that attracts and terrifies Lenù:

> I saw in her, in her posture more than in her face, something that disturbed me and is still hard to define, so for now I'll put it like this: she was moving, cutting across the street, a small, dark, nervous figure, she was acting with her usual determination, she was firm . . . firm in the pain, firm in silence as a statue is firm." (MBF, 41)

Notably, another of Lenù's paradoxes: just as Lila's desire to be unknown is the most certain thing Lenù knows about her, what's "hard to define" is her very sense of clear self-definition. Later on, when she transforms from diminutive, determined gnome-child to graceful elfin beauty, she is described in equally clear and definite terms, as Lenù observes wonderingly that, "Lila had become shapely. Her high forehead, her large eyes that could suddenly narrow, her small nose, her cheekbones, her lips, her ears were looking for a new orchestration and seemed close to finding it. When she combed her hair in a ponytail, her long neck was revealed with a touching clarity" (MBF, 142).

This in opposition to the disturbing, baggy monster of Lenù's self-image: she imagines her own "cheeks like balloons, hands stuffed with sawdust, earlobes like ripe berries, feet in the shapes of loaves of bread" (*MBF*, 57). As adolescence sets in, she feels her alien body overcome by eruptions, swellings, and uncontrolled formlessness in her new form, which, she writes, "expanded like pizza dough" (112). We briefly and tantalizingly find out that Lila also suffers from a lack of self-definition analogous to Lenù's own, in the nightmarish vision of the dissolving margins that threatens her sense of self and other. And so perhaps it's this desire for *definition*, the purely imaginary idea that another human being *can* be clearly and beautifully legible—and thus more fascinatingly enigmatic to the illegible, imagining self, again the paradox—that feeds into the fantasy of the brilliant friend. This title is, as you all point out, bidirectional in its force: Lila is Lenù's brilliant friend, while Lenù is Lila's.

If this were a different kind of novel, we might get a kind of *Fight Club* twist at the end: Lenù *is* Lila, light is dark, formlessness is form, one or the other *actually* never existed, blah blah blah. But Ferrante doesn't seem interested such narrative tricks. Instead, we just have the original fact of Lila's disappearance, of her total elimination "without a trace." Whether or not she ever really existed and whatever that existence was *really* like, all that eventually matters is what Lenù writes about her, the clear and defined shapes she molds Lila into. And that, I think, is the simultaneously poignant and alarming truth about friendship—*real* friendship—that Ferrante draws out beautifully here. The friends we truly love are at once the most real people in the world to us and the least real.

Of course, this shifting nature of friend-reality also brings up a stylistic question: What is the status of realism overall in the novel? I'm intrigued by the way Merve framed Ferrante's style as "slow burn realism," thinking about the slowness and buildup of anger in her writing, something that links up with Katherine's questions about Lila and Lenù and "what they know, what they're wrong about, *how they lie*," and with Jill's interest in the novel's weird invocations of enchantment that violently resist categorization under magical realism. Perhaps it's the diaphanous and deceptive smoke screens of fiction that hover above the surface of seemingly defined things (events, people)—the speculative and phantasmagoric aspects of Lenù's recollection, the dissolving margins of Lila's visions—that are the *real* realism of Ferrante's account of friendship and its fundamental unreality?

But more on that next time. 'Til then, I remain

Your imaginary friend
Sarah

Bridport, Vermont
Katherine, July 1

Dear Brilliant Friends,

Can I just say what a pleasure it's been to write in solidarity with you three? Not that I thought we'd pull hair, like all those Neapolitan women Lenù is trying to escape, but it was possible we'd really hate each others' readings. Yes, I know, there's still time for that—but until then, I'm going to keep thinking of us as collaborators and coauthors, riffing on each others' ideas until the summer ends.

I wrote last time about pacing, but I left out one curious line: Lenù's insistence, in such a fast book, that "I was a slow reader, I still am" (*MBF*, 68). She offers this as an admission of weakness, but to know Lenù, a classic Virgo, is to know that it's probably also a humble brag. It's as though she's cautioning us to resist her own narrative speed, another of the book's many lies. Whatever her meaning, I'm now thinking of this slow burn project as a way of standing in solidarity, not just with each other but also with her.

Solidarity is a significant theme in these novels both personally and politically. I assume we'll talk more about the political variety when we get to the second and third volumes, and, building on Merve's argument, the extent to which political anger motivates Lila (such a Leo). *My Brilliant Friend* hints at this with Lila's epiphany, as expressed by Lenù, that "there are no gestures, words, or sighs that do not contain the sum of all the crimes that human beings have committed and commit" (154)—Walter Benjamin's documents of civilization have nothing on gestures, words, and sighs.

So while communism is certainly in the ether of this Neapolitan childhood, for the most part, *My Brilliant Friend* concerns itself with personal solidarity: Lenù's role in brokering Stefano's hand for Lila,

Lila's tutoring of Lenù in Greek. Such gestures secure a friendship. Despite the pain of competition and unknowability that you three have so cleverly pointed out, these acts of solidarity allow us to feel that this is on balance a good relationship, based on mutual regard and shared hopes. We root for Lenù and Lila to stick together, whatever the costs.

But stick together in what? In some perfect childhood moment? In some shared imagined future? Lenù certainly wants to have it both ways:

> We were twelve years old, but we walked along the hot streets of the neighborhood, amid the dust and the flies that the occasional old trucks stirred up as they passed, like two old ladies taking the measure of lives of disappointment, clinging tightly to each other. No one understood us, only we two—I thought—understood one another. . . . There was something unbearable in the things, in the people, in the buildings, in the streets that, only if you reinvented it all, as in a game, became acceptable. The essential, however, was to know how to play, and she and I, only she and I, knew how to do it. (MBF, 106–7)

It's Lenù and Lila against the world here, together: coauthors of an alternate history as well as an alternate destiny, walking in a present in which they are twelve-year-olds and old ladies at the same time, a purely fictional proposition. And that's as it should be, because if all friends are imaginary (yes, Sarah, you've convinced me), then what is a friendship but a shared fiction, an atmosphere (good word, Jill) that exists only because both parties believe in it? The same could be said of a romance, or a marriage, or indeed any relationship between two people—but for everyone's sake, I'll keep it topical. The bond is threatened only when the fiction is, when one person withdraws her belief. Lila's disappearance at the beginning of the novel is precisely this kind of threat. You can disappear for stretches in a friendship, but you cannot disappear *without leaving a trace*. Not without killing the twelve-year-olds. Not without killing the friendship. Lenù is writing in revenge (absolutely, Merve), but she's also writing in resuscitation, as a way of keeping the wounded fiction alive.

I'll be the first to admit that the thought of an old friend vanishing is just about the most frightening thought imaginable. With my closest friends, I too have the old lady fantasy, which has evolved from something distant and formulaic involving rockers on a porch to the much more familiar, physical intimacy of piling onto a couch with our memories (so Gemini). Of course, we argue over the memories, in those inevitable flare-ups of coauthorship: what happened that one time and why; who each of us has been; what, in the end, was important. In that sense, the old lady fantasy isn't that different from a great Saturday afternoon right now.

But you need the friend there to make it fun. Lenù asks similar questions throughout *My Brilliant Friend*—"What was I like, really? What would she, sooner or later, be like?" (133)—and they are always somehow tinged with dread. Without her coauthor to speak her words back to her, challenge her, and elaborate upon what she knows, the memories are subject to all the errors of a single, unchecked perspective. The novel Lenù is writing is as much a fiction as the friendship; but unlike the friendship, it is the work of Lenù alone.

Okay, but I lied a little bit there. Really, it's the work of two Elenas: our fictional narrator, Elena Greco, and our fictional author, Elena Ferrante, the pseudonym that stands in for the writer of these books. We have to talk about that, don't we—what it means, as a writer of fiction, to be a fiction yourself?

Your coauthor,
Katherine

Semiliye, Turkey
Merve, July 6

Dear Jill, Katherine, and Sarah,

Do any of you own a copper pot?

I don't—I'm a miserable cook. But many Turkish women I know take great pride in cooking with copper pots. Here is what I have learned from them: that cast iron is stubborn, for it holds heat overlong; that steel is a middling conductor, a play thing for children afraid to burn their fingers; and that only copper is volatile enough to reward real culinary mastery. Only copper warms and cools decisively, thoroughly, so that whatever one exposes to it can be manipulated with the utmost precision. And only copper is beautiful in its own right and, as such, is prohibitively expensive to buy and to maintain.

The copper pot that emerges in the last third of *My Brilliant Friend* is many things to many people. To Lila, it is a prophecy, one that visits her late at night after Marcello, her wealthy and threatening suitor, has left the house. As she relates the incident in a letter to Lenù, Lila was "washing the dishes and was tired, really without energy, when there was an explosion." Startled out of her exhaustion, she turns to find that her family's "big copper pot had exploded." But "exploded" does not begin to describe how dramatically the pot's form had altered. "It was hanging on the nail where it normally hung, but in the middle there was a large hole and the rim was lifted and twisted and the pot itself was all deformed, as if it could no longer maintain its appearance as a pot" (*MBF*, 229).

Energy can neither be created nor destroyed; it can only change from one form to another. This is Lila's mystical interpretation of the exploding copper pot. It is, a receptacle for the slow and diffuse deformation of the Cerullo household: Marcello's violent insistence that Lila marry him, her parent's anger at her refusal, her brother's hostility, the fog of sexual desire that follows Lila wherever she goes. It is precisely the conversion of social entropy into material destruction that terrifies Lila. To Lenù, she writes, "It's this sort of thing . . . that frightens me. More than Marcello, more than anyone. And I feel that I have to find a solution, otherwise, everything, one thing after another, will break, everything, everything" (*MBF*, 229).

If you reread Ferrante's description of the copper pot aloud—go ahead, try it—you too may linger on the energy compressed into the middle clause. *Lifted* and *twisted* hiss like a geyser about to erupt, and *itself* directs this hissing from the middle of the sentence to the middle of the pot. It is as if the words Lila uses in her letter enact the very conversion she fears, shaping the spectral evil of the neighborhood into the actual sounds of a pot crumpling in on itself. (Whether this is the work of Ferrante or her translator, Ann Goldstein, I can't be sure, but either way, it's delightful.) I think this is the quality in Lila's writing that Lenù later describes as seductive: Lila's ability to transfigure the evil of village folklore—exploding pots, captive girls, tyrannical fathers, violent lovers—into language that is vivid, everyday, and yet still enchanted.

But like I suggested in my last post, language can only take you so far. To Lila, money is far better at giving shape to life than language; at preventing people and their families from dissolving into nothingness. Thus Lila frees herself from Marcello by attaching herself to Stefano, a stilted little man who owns a grocery shop, a bright red convertible, and, at Lila's urging, invests generously in her father's shoe business. "The fundamental feature that now prevailed was concreteness, the daily gesture, the negotiation," Lenù observes. "It was, in short, wealth that existed in the facts of every day, and so was without splendor and without glory" (*MBF*, 249). And whereas that wealth had once weaved its way into Lenù and Lila's fantasies of literary production, now Lila latches onto a more tangible and strategic form of seduction: fashion. By arming herself with "a new hairstyle, a new dress, a new way of making up her eyes or her mouth," she encourages Stefano to "seek in her the most palpable symbol of the future of wealth and power that he intended: and she seemed to use that seal that he was placing on her to make herself, her brother, her parents, her other relatives safe from all that she had confusedly confronted and challenged since she was a child" (265).

When Lila's "beauty of mind" ends up in "her face, in her breasts, in her thighs, in her ass," Lenù steps in, armed with a more sophisticated understanding of how to do things with words (MBF, 277). To Lenù, the exploding copper pot is an irresistible metaphor for her friend, one that she returns to time and again to grasp Lila's transformation from the "tense, aggressive Cerrulo" into a "princess," a "diva," and, ultimately, Stefano's wife (265). Volatility, manipulation, mastery over the other elements—all the properties of copper emerge as the character traits that define Lila, once she begins to make herself over for Stefano.

Like any amateur novelist, Lenù's compulsive return to the pot-as-metaphor is a touch transparent, a little heavy handed in its proud self-consciousness. The pot was "always lying in ambush in some corner of my mind," writes Lenù. Yet it is an unforgettable image all the same, one that helps us track the plot's climax and denouement. The pot makes its final fated appearance on the day of Lila's wedding, when Lenù washes Lila in a "copper tub full of boiling water," which "had a consistency not different from Lila's flesh, which was smooth, solid, calm" (312). Instead of an unstable and old copper pot, there is a new copper tub. The danger of explosion, it seems, has disappeared with the appearance of Stefano and everything he owns. And the pot, like Lila, has consolidated itself, forming a "solid vision, without cracks" of the world that money will allow her to create.

In part, Lenù's obsession with finding a literary form to contain the new Lila is an act of deflection; she is unwilling to shape her own confused desires into something intelligible to herself or communicable to others. "I made no attempt to find a form for my emotions," she confesses after her first, fleeting sexual encounters with Nino and his father leave her hot and bothered and more than a little ashamed. But it is also, as Katherine pointed out, an act of solidarity and intimacy. After all, Lenù claims she does not yet know about Lila's experiences of "dissolving margins"; her sense of "a pressure so strong" that it "broke down" the "outlines" of the people she loves, making herself and everyone around her "softer and more yielding" to the violence of the neighborhood (176). While there is much that Lenù may not know about Lila, as Sarah has persuasively argued, there is also a mysterious telepathy at work that electrifies all that unknowingness. After all, what is friendship if not the ability to intuit each another's shifting boundaries—to give words to those sensations that we, as individuals, are not yet able to name?

—Merve

Bonjour, bonjour, bonjour!

Okay, maybe this is incredibly trivial, but before we're done with *My Brilliant Friend*, can we talk about how hilariously insufficient the cover blurb on this (Europa) edition is? In case you've forgotten/didn't notice, the oddly bland snippet—a misleading quote plucked from James Wood's otherwise quite compelling 2013 *New Yorker* profile of Ferrante—describes the novel as "a large, captivating, amiably peopled bildungsroman [sic]."⁴ For lack of a better critical question: WTF?

This description brings a range of incongruously affable visions to mind (the most persistent of which, to my Disney-warped mind, is the opening musical number of *Beauty and the Beast*, hence my salutation to you today). The blurb suggests a kind of gentle, pleasant, conventional realism, and a narrative of gentle, pleasant, conventional character development, a semisweet literary blancmange that goes down easy and doesn't trouble the stomach. But what could be further from the truth? With the exception of "captivating," every descriptor here is off-mark. As Jill points out in her post, "Bildungsroman" is the most obvious red herring—while there certainly are elements of *Bildung* in Lenù and Lila's shared story, it's an often-mysterious tale of unclear and sudden transitions that, at times, refuse elucidation and push back upon themselves. Think of Merve's evocation of the terrifying and sudden deformation of the copper pot: these character changes can be explosive, unsolved mysteries. On that note, don't even get me started on "amiably peopled": how could any of the characters that grow up steeped in this miasma of poverty, madness, and resentment be particularly amiable? The novel is populated with compelling liars

(Lenù!), screamers, madwomen, fighters. And, because I'm peevish and persnickety, let me also just say that even "large" is a relative claim (in his piece, Wood weighs it against Ferrante's shorter previous works); at 331 pages, *My Brilliant Friend* can feel downright compact in the lingering shadow of the maximalist novel and alongside the hulking weight of Knausgaard's oeuvre.

In short, this blurb tries to sell us a friendlier, more digestible Ferrante than the one we find inside the cover. And once you've actually read the book, the misleading quality of the blurb is rendered even more apparent by its superimposition on the peculiar cover image, which is possessed of its own strange deceptions. The book's style on the whole is a bit like its disorienting packaging: it may look like a familiar brand of realism at first glance, but the longer you look, the more it becomes something of a surrealist assemblage. Take a closer look at the picture: it seems from a distance like an unremarkable vintage photograph of a wedding party by the Neapolitan shore. Upon closer examination, though, it is oddly scaled and strangely doctored; the little girls' dresses gleam under an unearthly light that's surely not the sun; the figures all feel flattened and pasted onto a blurry, generic backdrop, against which the groom's ominously black silhouette cuts too sharply. The whole thing feels overexposed and unnatural. If you look at it too long, you start to feel the visual overload of looking at a Magic Eye: how do these confusingly layered figures relate to each other? Who are they? Where are they going? In short, the questions the novel itself provokes. It's at once extremely clear and extremely puzzling, creating a vertiginous divide between the purported reality of the photographic medium and the unreal, *too* clear, *too* bright quality of its processing.

Similarly, while on one hand the novel embraces a kind of visceral realism, its very viscerality makes it a phantasmagoric realism as well. Ferrante's accounts of Lenù's experiences are *so* hotly vivid that they make one feel like the novel's real life experiences actually play out in a fever dream. Rather than recounting the facts of events, Lenù offers us her grotesquely torqued, imagined versions of them; for example, the criminal neighborhood czar, Don Achille, is depicted most memorably as a fleshy, composite monster in young Lenù's eyes (and older Lenù's recollection), as, "For years I saw his body—a coarse body, heavy with a mixture of materials—emitting in a swarm salami, provolone, mortadella, lard, and prosciutto" (*MBF*, 36). Though we later see that he's just a middle-aged man, it's impossible to dispel the primary image of the meat-monster; it has become as much a part of the reader's sense of Ferrante's Neapolitan reality as he is part of Lenù's. Around the same time, Lenù is:

> overcome by a kind of tactile dysfunction; sometimes I had the impression that, while every animated being around me was speeding up the rhythms of its life, solid surfaces turned soft under my fingers or swelled up. . . . I had a bad taste in my mouth, a permanent sense of nausea that exhausted me. . . . It was an enduring malaise, lasting perhaps years, beyond early adolescence. (*MBF*, 57)

This is Lenù's grotesque, fantastic experience of her world, and from this early point onwards, it is ours as well. Ultimately, rather than realistic depictions of people, things, or places, palpable, embodied dream-visions like this are what actually structure the reader's real world of Ferrante's impoverished Naples. While the quotidian events related in the novel (local vendettas, marriages, teenage affairs) might by themselves indeed be the stuff of some parallel "large, captivating, amiably peopled bildungsroman," Ferrante's particular reckoning warps them into something much odder and darker.

Thinking about the kind of world that "large" and "amiably peopled" novel of development might bring into being, versus the malignant and fantastical world of Ferrante's book, might offer some hint as to why the latter might necessitate her particular brand of weird realism. The novel offers, after all, a world built on absence rather than presence, the opposite of any facile expectations of historical or material reality: we must always remember that its point of origin is Lila's total disappearance. Rather than describing what is there, Lenù shapes a world out of what is *not*. We see this in the paucity of detailed physical description in the novel; for example, we know that Lenù's mother lends her a significant silver bracelet, but we have no idea what it looks like. Even a childhood fetish object like Lenù's doll is described in the barest, repetitive terms: "She had a plastic face and plastic hair and plastic eyes" (*MBF*, 30). This curious lack of physical detail relates not only to Lila's pending self-erasure but also gestures towards the poverty of the neighborhood (after all, the only special thing about Lenù's doll is her *plastic* face, compared to Lila's sawdust-filled cloth doll). However, this seemingly nonchalant lack of concern with material detail allows Ferrante to evade both the traps of describing either the personal effects of impoverishment (think Zola's naturalist poverty porn: the roughness of a burlap shirt, a moldy baguette crust on a café counter) or the cathartic dramatization of emptiness and want. In lieu of either of these modes of physical description, we get these descriptions of *feelings* and *visions* that are palpable, often disturbingly so.

And perhaps that's one of Ferrante's ways of getting at class here, sneakily, weirdly, unpredictably. Just as Merve points out that money and writing substitute for each other in L&L's shared imagination, so too do Lenù's materializations of imaginative interpretation stand in for actual things. The world is over-full of physicalized emotions, filling in the hollows of material lack. Yet this volume comes to an end with a sudden overflowing of those hollows, with Lila's marriage to wealthy Stefano, and the abrupt appearance of all manner of worldly goods. But if the dark, fantastic imagined world of *My Brilliant Friend* is suddenly supplanted by the real material one, what will happen to Lenù's mode of telling as the story moves forward in *The Story of a New Name*?

—Sarah (not a particularly amiable peopler of this blog)

THE STORY OF A NEW NAME

Commie Camp
Jill, July 14

Dear friends,

I borrowed one of those yellow legal pads, to write down the names of the people that wanted to talk. In the hubbub after the panel, I forgot to return it, of course. A day or two later, the pad was re-purposed, this time as a coloring book for the children of persons attending Feminism and Anti-Capitalist Organizing, Part II. Someone else, probably me, spilled water on what appears to be a tax calculation sheet tucked into the last pages, most likely from an end-of-year book sale, given the notebook's original source. There were a few blank, nonwrinkled pages left, so mid-week, in my tent, having abandoned a dance party, I started sketching out the bones for this post. But I was tired. There were too many panels and too many people. Dear friends, not much writing got done at what had been affectionately termed "commie camp"— basically a week-long conference and report-back on global uprisings—in the mountains outside Seattle where reproductive labor was communized and costs were few. It was a reunion of sorts, with far-flung leftists and the Oakland comrades, my most brilliant friends.

So I don't feel entirely self-indulgent starting with the autobiographical, in this case. The funny thing about being around so many people, mostly left communists, anarchists, antistate socialists, radical queers, Marxist feminists, and the like, is the way that so many things get passed around and back. Or what's funny, I guess, is the way that this basic mode of sharing appears sort of magical, like the stars were aligning in a given object, a notebook, say, that could then make visible the crisscrossing of social relations that circulated around it. On the Metro North home, as I was flipping through the legal pad, it did seem sort of magical—the tax sheet, the crayon drawings, the stack of names to be called on, some incoherent notes on feral teenagers, looting selfie sticks, Prosecco riots, and the overthrow of corn lords.

This sense of charmed intersections, somehow accrued in a single object, had other, less happy vectors. There were ghosts in the constellations, wound up in everything else: banished persons, serial rapes, police repression, sex work crackdowns, denunciations, persons lost to suicide and murder and AIDS. At that meeting, the one with legal pad as coloring book, everything was sad, sad, sad, or that was what, in a fit of melancholy, I texted Eli, back on the East Coast. I was sitting through this meeting of mostly women, talking about different kinds of violence and persons lost, about death threats and accountability processes, thinking about how easily a sense of shared trauma creates intimacy, on the street or in similarly lived histories, and how horrible it is, really, that these ties grow out of such cruel soil. There is a danger, I think, in romanticizing that trauma or making the violence too beautiful, as a story we tell about ourselves.

All this brings me back to Ferrante's Neapolitan novel cycle, which is, more than anything else, I think, a chronicle of the

gendered intersection of intimacy and violence amidst the backdrop of Italy's Creeping May. In *The Story of a New Name*, the wider
political context begins to emerge as a backdrop that perplexes
Lenù. Amidst the mansplainers holding forth at a party, she
wonders, "what were Gaullism, the O.A.S., social democracy, the
opening to the left; who were Danilo Dolci, Bertrand Russell, the
pieds-noirs, the followers of Fanfani; and what had happened in
Beirut, what in Algeria"?[5] There is much to say on this score—I want
to return to that party later. However, here, in this last *My Brilliant
Friend* post, I want to take a second pass at a few things, to chew
over them a bit more, really. I want to begin, again, with how magical, how supremely beautiful, almost charmed, Ferrante makes the
poverty and desperation of Lenù's childhood appear. It is such a
pleasure, this book, to read. But recall, early on, when Lenù sets
the reader straight: "I feel no nostalgia for our childhood: it was
full of violence." The declarative is misleading in that it feels like
the truth. But then the sentences get longer, as though explaining.
They tilt, so that it is not so much childhood but just life that is like
that, violent. The matter of violence unsticks from childhood and
becomes nothing special, certainly nothing to cry about. As Lenù
continues, stitching together the head that cracked like a melon
on the stairs and those grandmothers tearing at each other's hair,
there are tiny animals sneaking into the neighborhood from abandoned trains and Swamps—the imagined. Frogs, salamanders, and
flies infecting all of these persons through water and air, as though
mutual aggression were some sort of interspecies plague. In this
prose, what looks normal, or at least recognizable, gets mangled
into enchantment so deftly, so quietly, that you are not sure how
you got there or really where you are at all. It might seem like
magic, and it pretends to be, sometimes. But this kind of vertigo
is more aptly understood as desperation: that mixture of unpredictable, dangerous, and combustible that results from having no

other choices and nowhere else to go. Nevertheless, it's a thin line here between the magical and the desperate. This is writing like an oil slick—slippery, thick.

Sarah described this effect as a fever dream, which is exactly right, I think. It is not magical realism in the mode of García Márquez, for example, where the world is somehow enchanted, filled with yellow butterflies. There is a doubleness in Ferrante, so that the magical is only a kind of scrim—a fever dream, a game, a childhood misunderstanding—that makes the unenchanted world palatable. Consider, for instance, the moment that Katherine took up in her last post:

> We were twelve years old, but we walked along the hot streets of the neighborhood, amid the dust and the flies that the occasional old trucks stirred up as they passed, like two old ladies taking the measure of lives of disappointment, clinging tightly to each other. No one understood us, only we two—I thought—understood one another. . . . There was something unbearable in the things, in the people, in the buildings, in the streets that, only if you reinvented it all, as in a game, became acceptable. The essential, however, was to know how to play, and she and I, only she and I, knew how to do it. (*MBF*, 107)

The game is magical and the game is imaginary. The game is a way of coping. It is a made-up story, very beautiful, almost romantic. There is something unsettling about the ways that this cruelty can become so beautiful, but then I wonder: Why assume that lives touched by desperation should be entirely stark, black and white, without ornament? Isn't this as much of a paternalistic imposition as the fantastic or beautiful? Why is the realism of poverty, violence, desperation necessarily, *naturally*, understood as a matter of the subdued—the prosaic, gritty, spare, austere?

As we move into the next volume, *The Story of a New Name*, Ferrante's realism changes slightly. If *My Brilliant Friend* was slippery, the reading like an accelerated flight, *The Story of a New Name* feels like picking through tiny, dry stones. The second book is even more violent, maybe, but the game looks different:

> So, caught between Nino's impatience and her husband's complaints, instead of regaining a sense of reality and telling herself clearly that she was in a situation with no way out, Lila began to act as if the real world were a backdrop or a chessboard, and you had only to shift a painted screen, move a pawn or two, and you would see that the game, the only thing that really counted, *her* game, *the game of the two of them*, could continue to be played. As for the future, the future became the day after and then the next and then the one after that. Or sudden images of massacre and blood, which were very frequent in her notebooks. She never wrote *I will die murdered*, but she noted local crime news, sometimes she reinvented it. In these stories of murdered women she emphasized the murderer's rage, the blood everywhere. . . . It was as if she wanted to take the power away even from the realistic possibility of violent death by reducing it to words, to a form that could be controlled. (*SNN*, 343)

In *The Story of a New Name*, Lenù finds Lila's notebook, so that we have two accounts of every event. The notebook offers a second narration of what happens, from Lila's eyes and then filtered through Lenù. But the notebook also becomes a place to imagine other endings, to stave off the reality of having nowhere else to go and no way out.

One critique of the ultraleft, across its various manifestations, is that the imagination of a world beyond or after capitalism is utterly unrealistic, impossible, totally fantastic, a science fiction for children, et cetera, et cetera. The end of capitalism is, in one well-worn phrase, more impossible to imagine than the end of the world. I started this post with the seemingly magical connections accrued in that yellow legal pad, not really to query the status of an object as artifact, but to push on the lines between what gets to be called real and what is fantastic. It is not all that supernatural that stationary might be used by different persons temporarily living together. What is significant here and in Lenù's belated reading of Lila's notebook is the way that the thinking of other futures and the persons within them can happen together, as a conversation, the voices drawn together in a set of papers passed back and forth. Looking at this particular yellow notebook, I think of corn lords, magical animals, and filigreed street games, the alleys transformed into checkerboards. Anything can be called a game or a fantasy if you want to belittle it. I guess I'm more interested in the process Lenù describes: the ways that the boundary between what is real and what is fantasy might be constructed and reinvented between people, like some massive and precarious sandcastle. Lenù's mixed metaphor is all two-person board games, but I like the idea of building something together and then taking part of it down to start over with what is left: a room churned out here, a moat collapsed, everyone wrist-deep in wet sand, still figuring it out.

—Jill

First Car, Metro North, Between New Haven and New York
Merve, July 20

Dear Katherine, Sarah, and Jill:

As it happens I am on my way back from New Haven, where I ate lunch at a café next to two older women with light purple hair and excellent posture; two women so absorbed in their discussion of *The Story of a New Name*, they didn't realize I was listening.

"I couldn't stop reading," one confessed to the other. Quietly at first, and then with mounting excitement, she began rocking back and forth in her chair as she recalled to her friend the novel's many plot twists. "When Stefano hits Lila . . . ! When she miscarries . . . ! When she sleeps with Nino . . . ! When he gets her pregnant . . . ! When she leaves Stefano the first time . . . ! When she leaves him again for good . . . !"

Her friend nodded and murmured, "Such drama in this one. Such drama."

Perhaps it's only natural that these ladies who lunch should gravitate to Lila's story line over Lenù's. After all, hers is by far the more sensational of the two: an unhappy marriage, a summer affair, a child possibly born out of wedlock, the descent back into poverty. Lenù, by contrast, is an excellent student, marries into a respectable academic family, and writes a successful novella about losing her virginity one night in Ischia—all well and good but not exactly edge-of-your-seat drama.

The imbalance between the story lines marks a departure from the first novel. ("Such drama in this one. Such drama.") Whereas, in *My Brilliant Friend*, Lila and Lenù shared enough to keep their narratives of childhood hinged to one another, in *The Story of a New Name*, the divergence of their adult lives raises the problem of genre. Why tell two such distinct stories within one novel? How can Lila's

ferocious commitment to "playing for all or nothing," chasing the
ups and downs of love lost and found and violently shattered, coex-
ist alongside Lenù's reluctance to be "drawn beyond the limits" of
what is appropriate?

I think we can find an answer to these questions in the frame
narrative of *The Story of a New Name*. It is different from the frame
narrative that opens *My Brilliant Friend*—one which takes place
not in the present moment of writing but in the spring of 1966,
at a time when "our relationship was terrible," Lenù confesses.
Lila has entrusted Lenù with a box containing her personal
notebooks, and although she has asked Lenù not to read them,
Lenù does anyway. What she finds is a biographical account of
Lila's life to date: her childhood suffering, excitement, and fury
as the youngest member of the Cerullo family; her adolescent
satisfaction at becoming Signora Carracci, wife of the wealthy
grocer; and her subsequent desire to shed her oppressive new
name and find love with Nino Sarratore.

The frame narrative offers us both an ingenious recap of *My
Brilliant Friend* and a tantalizing reveal: there is a fictional ur-text
that precedes the novel we hold in our hands. Its author is not
Lenù, it's Lila, and by all accounts, including Lenù's own, it is the
better version of the story we have been reading all along. "Her
words were very beautiful," Lenù writes of Lila's notebooks. "Mine
are only a summary." Lila's narration emanates the "same force of
seduction that Lila had given off since she was a child" (*SNN*, 16).
Her descriptions of social life are thrilling, hypnotizing, humbling;
her history as an multilingual autodidact is enshrined in dozens
of Latin, Greek, and English translation exercises. The pages are
littered with isolated words in dialect, in Italian, and conversations about books and films and communism transcribed directly
from life. There are even small drawings of "twisted trees, humped,
smoking mountains, grim faces." If Lenùs words are only an inert

"summary," then we might think of Lila's notebook as an irrepress-ible paean to what Bahktin once called "novelness"—a keen sense of language as dialogic, alive, and ever-shifting; revolutionary even.

And yet, for Lenù, Lila's compulsion to treat "every person or thing with ruthless accuracy" is unbearable. For Lila is not just a beautiful writer. She is a natural writer: a writer whose prose spares no one, not even Lenù, in her descriptions. "What to say of the liberty she had taken with me, with what I had said, with what I thought, with the people I loved, with my very physical appear-ance," Lenù laments. "She had fixed moments that were decisive for her without worrying about anything or anyone" (SNN, 16–17). So exasperated, Lenù commits an act of symbolic murder. One eve-ning, she takes the box of notebooks to the Solferino Bridge and pushes them over the edge, "as if it were her, Lila in person, plummet-ing, with her thoughts, words, the malice with which she struck back at anyone, the way she appropriated me, as she did every person or thing or event or thought that touched her."

We are encouraged by Lenù to see Lila's exacting prose as an ethical violation of her subjects, the worst sin a writer can com-mit. But it's hard not to interpret Lenù's homicidal projection as petty, snide, and self-rationalizing; something akin to what one mean girl might do if she read about herself in another mean girl's burn book.

Indeed, once Lenù erases Lila's words, she sets out to write over them, to tell her version of everything contained in Lila's notebooks. But to compete with Lila, it isn't enough that Lenù tell Lila's story—that she recreate the "tempestuous happiness" that one finds in "novels, films, and comic strips . . . a furious confusion of evil and good that had befallen her and not me." She must tell her own story, too. Like Lila's notebooks, which contain everything in Naples, Lenù's rewriting of these notebooks will also contain multitudes: well-plotted sexual intrigue but also descriptions of

the neighborhood, an account of her education, existential rumina-
tions on humankind's place in the universe, and so much more. And
all the while, she will insist that none of what she has produced—
none of her dazzling, compulsively readable prose—measures up to
Lila's now unrecoverable literary labors.

This is a very old authorial trick. Create a fictional-text-within-
a-fictional-text as the horizon of aesthetic sublimity to which the
novel you are reading will aspire to but which it will inevitably fall
short of. Many of the novels that I would describe as narratively
seductive (If on a Winter's Night a Traveler, The Master and Margarita,
Atonement, Written on the Body) bait their readers with this promise
and always leave their readers wanting more. But Lila's erasure
by Lenù completely forecloses the possibility of us ever encountering the text behind the text we are reading. It is not just that
Lenù's erasure of Lila is so cruel, so complete, so annoyingly self-
deprecating; it is that Lila's writing is displaced so forcefully by
Lenù's words, making recovery a pipe dream. Now the only way
we can get to Lila is through Lenù. Is this the model of female
solidarity we were hoping for?

But more importantly, who cares about solidarity? I don't mean
this in the sense that solidarity isn't an important issue for us to
debate. I mean it in the sense that we—me, you three, others like
us—have been well trained to sniff out the bread crumbs of radical feminist thought that Ferrante has scattered throughout her
novels. But those violet haired ladies at lunch? I think they're just
in it for the drama; the sheer thrill of how the events and emotions
in The Story of a New Name build up, one on top of the other, only to
topple over on the next page. Maybe, in this way, they get closer
than we can to the spirit of Lila's notebooks. And maybe that's
okay, too.

—Merve

Dear Sarah, Jill, and Katherine—

Have you ever tried to erase yourself? When I was a child, I used to sit in a dark bedroom, Paula Cole's "Me" on loop, and try to imagine my way out of myself. It seems funny in hindsight, but at the time, it was a very serious exercise. I would start by imagining that my ten-year-old hands weren't my hands, my face not my face, the weight of my body an illusion I could throw off if I concentrated hard enough. From there, things would take a turn for the gravely existential. What if I wasn't me? What if I was nothing? A more promising thought would occur: What if I was someone else, only I didn't know it? Often that someone else was Leonardo DiCaprio's girlfriend—remember, this was 1996—but sometimes I tried scattering myself amidst a group of people: my family, my three best friends, the entire universe of nerdy ten-year-old girls who were sitting in their bedrooms at this exact moment, trying to dissolve with me.

You might protest that these childish games bear little resemblance to the forms of erasure we find in *The Story of a New Name*, the most dramatic of which is Lila's desecration of her wedding photograph. What the exploding copper pot was to *My Brilliant Friend*, the wedding photograph is to *The Story of a New Name*: a perfectly ordinary object onto which Lenù confers extraordinary powers of art and allegory. It first appears in the window of the dressmaker's shop, a portrait of Lila in her wedding gown, ankles bared and crossed, a pair of Cerullo shoes peeping out from under her hem; a portrait alluring enough to attract film directors and fashion designers and to make her husband Stefano violently jealous. It also attracts the attention of Marcello and Michele Solara, two local Camorristas who have financed the shoe store that Stefano will soon open in the commercial center of Naples. The Solaras do not see Lila's photograph as a wedding portrait; they see it as an advertising opportunity. Against Stefano's wishes, they demand to install Lila's image—and, by extension, Lila—in the shoe store, at the heart of their growing business empire.

If the Lila of *My Brilliant Friend* grasped onto money as the only bulwark against disorder, the Lila of *The Story of a New Name* has nothing but contempt for the "worthless metal, [the] waste paper" that lines the cash register of Stefano's grocery. Money has let Lila down. A rich husband is no less likely than a poor one to beat his wife, to mangle her sense of self and piece it back together it as it pleases him. Marriage, like money, is also a form of ownership, something that Lila realizes when she locks herself in a hotel bathroom on her wedding night just before her husband rapes her. "She was bothered by the idea that the ownership of the nice new things was guaranteed by the last name of that particularly individual who was waiting for her out there," Lenù writes, imagining herself into Lila's honeymoon suite, into Lila's consciousness, for that one horrifying night. "Carracci's possessions, she, too, was Carracci's possession." A fancy car, a spacious apartment, a wedding dress—none of these things can protect Lila or any other woman from the fact that "our fathers, our boyfriends, and our husbands could hit us when they liked, out of love, to educate us, to reeducate us."

To follow the novel's money trail is to see that Carracci's possessions are also the Solaras' possessions. As Stefano is in debt to the Solara brothers, and as Lila is his possession, she emerges as collateral in the fight between Stefano and the Solaras. Or at least, her photograph does, which, for her, amounts to the same thing. "They used me," she says to Lenù. "To them I'm not a person but a thing. Let's give him Lina, let's stick her on a wall, since she's a zero, an absolute zero." But Lila will not see herself pinned and wriggling on a wall, an erotic testament to the power of men with money. She will quite literally preempt Stefano and the Solaras' erasure of her by erasing herself first:

> She cut strips of black paper, with the manual precision she had always possessed, and pinned them here and there to the photograph, asking for my help with slight gestures of quick glances. . . . The body of the bride Lila appeared cruelly shredded. Much of the head had disappeared, as had the stomach. There remained an eye, the hand on which the chin rested, the brilliant stain of the mouth, the diagonal stripe of the bust, the line of the crossed legs, the shoes. (*SNN*, 119)

At first, Lila's avant-garde art project recalls other attempts at female erasure. Consider Kurt Seligmann's *Ultra-Furniture*, a stool supported by three slender and detached female legs, each one identical to the next. Consider also Willem de Kooning's Woman series, particularly the charcoal drawings that he erased with great brutality throughout the 1950s, and Robert Rauschenberg's total negation of de Kooning's woman for his *Erased de Kooning Drawing*. Erasing women is a popular trope, so blatantly does it link the idea of the feminine to categories like "abstraction," "archetype," and "anonymity." Broken into her component parts, the erased women of art can be anyone or anything to anybody.

Yet the visual association I find most compelling comes not from the male avant-garde, but from a female commercial artist, one who has also arranged herself carefully so as to highlight the line of her leg, the diagonal stripe of her bust, and the brilliant stain of her mouth: Angelina Jolie's much-parodied bared leg at the 2012 Oscars. Like Lila's surrealist photograph, the paparazzi snapshot of Jolie on the red carpet, leg askew and arms akimbo, is a statement of bodily presence—taut, angular, nude, and undeniably badass. Its aesthetic logic also relies on a kind of erasure; the leg must stand on its own, separate and separable from the rest of her body, which recedes quietly behind the lines of her black sheath. And like Lila's photograph, Jolie's pose risks misinterpretation. "You've erased yourself deliberately and I see why: to show the thigh, to show how well a woman's thigh goes with those shoes," Marcello congratulates Lila after he sees what she has done to her photograph. Sex may sell, but Marcello is wrong about Lila's intentions, which are not commercial in the slightest. He does not see, as Lenù does, that what Lila wants is to "present her own self-destruction *in an image*"—to transform the unmaking and remaking of women into an aesthetic form, a carefully stylized parody of what men expect women to do in life.

But the question remains: Why erase yourself? What becomes visible once the self retreats into the background? Just before Lila begins to erase herself, Lenù notes how her attitude toward the other women in the community has changed. Whereas Lila once played the role of the haughty bride, capable of using money to transcend her origins, now, more than usual, "she had an involved way of talking. She chose emotionally charged words, she described Melina Cappuccio and Giuseppina Peluso as if their bodies had seized hers, imposing on it the same contracted or inflated forms, the same bad feelings. As she spoke, she touched her face, her breast, her stomach, her hips as if they were no longer hers, and showed that she knew everything about these women." By making the isolated parts of her body the focus of the painting, Lila shows how easily these could be the legs, the bust, the lips of any woman. This is as much a savvy advertising technique ("Imagine Yourself in the Product") as it is a gesture of collectivity, one akin to Lila touching her breasts, her stomach, and her hips as if they no longer belong to her. Any woman could break the way that Lila has. And in Naples—in the world at large—many of us do.

Ultimately what erasure makes visible is an alternate model of community, one that Lenù, still in thrall to the chatter of the leftist intelligentsia, will fail to appreciate throughout the novel. If *My Brilliant Friend* gave us a partnership of two, Lila and Lenù, brought together by a shared commitment to literary education, in *The Story of a New Name* partnership has broadened into a community. It is a community defined not by the intellectual's heady triumph over violence but by an inescapable form of violation: the capacity for the female body to be broken at a man's will. The photograph is both a testament to that cruel bond and an act of resistance—the spark of Lila's rebellion against her marriage. How fitting, then, that in the middle of the novel, just before Lila embarks on her affair with Nino, the painting spontaneously bursts into flames, emitting "a rasping sound, a kind of sick breath" before destroying its own image of self-destruction.

For this is how the revolution begins—with a spark.

—Merve

Forio d'Ischia
Katherine, July 30

Dear Sarah, Merve, and Jill,

Already, I've lied to you. I'm not in Forio, I'm back in Princeton, but I began this slow post in Ferranteland, on Ischia, where *The Story of a New Name* takes its lengthiest and most decisive turn, so Forio, where I spent three nights, is where I've chosen to drop my pin.

Now, in compensation, I'll be honest: I have built my entire summer around Ferrante. Not only am I rereading the Neapolitan novels and little else, not only am I writing about them and little else, I have also made Matt read them so that he will talk to me about them all the time. We even went to Italy. To see friends who had invited us to northern Lazio, yes. But also to go south, to Campania, to track down the real places of these books. I had to see the Piazza dei Martiri, where the Solaras have their shoe shop. I had to eat pizza and *sflogliatelle*, the traditional ricotta pastry Gigliola's father makes so well. I definitely had to go to Ischia. I had to try to find the old neighborhood, where everything begins, the one place in the series that is perennially, and conspicuously, unnamed.

Why this obsession with setting? On the one hand, the novels cry out for it; everything about them suggesting autobiography, and through autobiography, history. Surely Elena Ferrante is Elena Greco, both of them born in Naples, both of them novelists, the author a mystery, the character a novelist who draws explicitly from life. And surely that means there's also a real Lila, a real Nino. Certainly, there is a real Corso Vittorio Emanuele, where the Galianis have their house full of books. There is a real Maronti, on Ischia, where Lenù finally succumbs to Donato Sarratore's advances. There is even a real San Giovanni a Teduccio, where Lila lives with Enzo and works with sharp knives and sickening fat in

Bruno Soccavo's sausage factory. The novels are completely littered with place names, all of them, with the exception of that sneaky neighborhood, easy to find on a map.

So off we went, first to our B&B, off the Piazza dei Martiri, where "every crucial development in [Lila's] war had occurred" (SNN, 345): the fight with the rich boys, the defacement of the wedding photo, the afternoon romance with Nino at the shop. The shop of course is fictional, but the real piazza, with its central monument to the martyrs of various anti-Bourbon uprisings, is exactly where the elegant Alfonso would want to be. In a city decked with hanging laundry and warring traffic, it's a rare car-free zone, almost Parisian in its upkeep, currently home to Ferragamo, Armani, and a Feltrinelli bookstore prominently displaying *L'Amica Geniale*.

We went looking for Lenù's high school, too. We knew from *My Brilliant Friend* that it's off Corso Garibaldi. She commutes by bus, but we figured it should be possible to walk, as she does the day she follows Nino to Corso Novara, which eventually takes her home. This detail, along with Rino's description of the sea being "in the direction of Vesuvius" seemed to place her native neighborhood to the north of the train station. Was the old one Secondiglio, the new one Scampia, both notorious Camorra districts? Subsequent research has zeroed in on Rione Luzzatti, to the east of the train station and much closer to the center, but we didn't know that then. Focused on the north, we peered down the sweltering boulevard, spied an overpass but no tunnel, debated hailing a cab to take us to a *stradone* or even just some apartment block up north, but ultimately chickened out. Naples was so hot in July even our eye sockets were sweating, no wonder everyone flees for the beach.

We joined them, following Nino to Ischia, specifically Forio, where he and Bruno rent their summer place. Islands, we were forced to remember, are crowded, and in July this one was packed.

Our room was hot like the Cerullo-Carracci house, so at night, we opened all the windows, risking the disfiguring mosquito bites poor Lenù is so desperate to avoid. At the southwestern beaches, it was easy to imagine Lila swimming. The beach slopes down, the water is powerful and quickly deep, even just a few laps could strengthen the limbs. Maronti, though, surprised us. We thought it might be quiet, but like every other beach on this island, it's now end to end with colorful chairs and umbrellas, €15 per couple per day. Sex here, even at night, would not be a secret affair.

But what, after all, did we expect? This is always what happens in the real places of fiction: there remain elements that don't quite scan. Often there's a gap in time, but just as often there's a gap in perception. The physical has been translated into words, then translated back to the physical, which looks and feels a little different to every reader, and to every character, too. For us, Maronti is a nice place to read Ferrante and have a meal. For Lenù, it's the site of a cataclysmic betrayal:

> I thought: yes, Lila is right, the beauty of things is a trick, the sky is the throne of fear; I'm alive, now, here, ten steps from the water, and it is not at all beautiful, it's terrifying; along with this beach, the sea, the swarm of animal forms, I am part of the universal terror; at this moment I'm the infinitesimal particle through which the fear of every thing becomes conscious of itself; I; I who listen to the sound of the sea, who feel the dampness of the cold sand; I who imagine all Ischia, the entwined bodies of Nino and Lila, Stefano sleeping by himself in the new house that is increasingly not so new, the furies who indulge the happiness of today to feed the violence of tomorrow. (SNN, 289)

The only way to feel this is to read it. It may help to have seen a beach once in your life, but in the end, it doesn't matter which one.

Still, there's something to be said for literary tourism. We saw, first-hand, how powerful Naples is, a whole world in that sprawling, convulsive, specific city: rich and poor, streets that rise and fall, a volcano that faces the sea. We learned the map a bit, too, and walking it, passing all kinds of people, we found ourselves thinking much more about the giant supporting cast of these books: Gigliola and Michele, Pinuccia and Rino, Ada and Stefano, Carmen and Pasquale, Enzo, Antonio, Alfonso, and Nino, all of whom, sooner or later, will get to have their turn.

So far, we've been talking about the Neapolitan novels almost entirely as the story of a friendship. And it is. But it's also, significantly, the story of all of these lives, and of the city in which they live.

—Katherine

Brooklyn—Toronto—Brooklyn
Sarah, August 9

Dear all,

I guess I'll start with Sebald:

In August 1992, when the dog days were drawing to an end, I set off to walk the county of Suffolk, in the hope of dispelling the emptiness that takes hold of me whenever I have completed a long stint of work. And in fact my hope was realized, up to a point; for I have seldom felt so carefree as I did then, walking for hours in the day through the thinly populated countryside, which stretches inland from the coast. I wonder now, however, whether there might be something in the old superstition that certain ailments of the spirit and of the body are particularly likely to beset us under the sign of the Dog Star. At all events, in retrospect I became preoccupied not only with the unaccustomed sense of freedom but also with the paralyzing horror that had come over me at various times when confronted with the traces of destruction, reaching far back into the past, that were evident even in that remote place. Perhaps it was because of this that, a year to the day after I began my tour, I was taken into hospital in Norwich in a state of almost total immobility. It was then that I began in my thoughts to write these pages.[6]

It was in a state of almost total immobility that I began to slowly write *these* pages some time ago, in the aftermath of a vague midsummer malady. The cat, sadly sprawled next to me and heaving dramatic sighs of deep feline melancholy, looked like my brain felt: deflated, overheated, weighed down by the humidity. I lay there and tried to think about Ferrante, or even not-think—feel?—about Ferrante, and heaved dramatic sighs of deep human melancholy.

And so, as I often do, I thought/not-thought about Sebald for a few reasons, none of them particularly scholarly: it was more this feeling in the body that led me back to him, after our summer of Ferrante. Before I go on, let's be clear—I'm not going to make any particularly responsible or rigorous claims here about Sebald and Ferrante as they relate to each other or the European Novel or Postwar History or Translation or Canonization or anything academic, really (it may be August, but IT'S STILL SUMMER, DAMN IT). This is *not* comparative literature. There will be no close readings. It's just some confused thoughts and feelings, stemming in some ways from Katherine's provocation to think about place over/with/under character, that I think have something to do with Ferrante, and something to do with how places have selves, and something to do, in some obscure way, with the idea that every new name is a story at once necessary and impossible to tell.

To start with a facile and incredibly obvious observation: names and places are problems for both Sebald and Ferrante. Both are deeply invested in the *where* of their stories, and the stories of their wheres, if that makes sense. This is a tension that plays out in very different ways between them. Sebald's narratives move through an accretion of places at human paces (by foot, by train or car, at the speed of memory), and as he moves through them, their names take on meanings, start to signify embedded histories. His writing on place has both descriptive and narrative depth to the point of vertigo (in his first novel, *Vertigo*, and beyond). While Ferrante—as I've written before—doesn't go in for deep description of this type, her Naples is just as thickly imbued with hauntings and stories, more of a dense miasma than Sebald's geological strata.

But, different as they are, both authors' books create a sense of place that's so affectively resonant, so immersive, that you can practically feel it in the body. The urge that Katherine followed to go to Naples—to go to Ferrante—resonates with a similar urge I and others have to go to and with Sebald: it's a *thing* to do the walk that he does in *The Rings of Saturn*, the meandering loop around the flatlands of Suffolk that fills his unnamed narrator with such malaise, so much a thing that director Grant Gee made a whole documentary about people doing it.[7] But why do we want to do this? Surely it is a perverse desire that demands that we go to a troubled place to inhabit the bad feelings (both Sebald's "freedom" and "paralyzing horror") we get from a text—a strange kind of affective inhabitation, worlds away from than the reliquary amusement park delights of more conventional literary tourism.

We want—or at least, I want—to go to Sebald's Suffolk or Ferrante's Naples, because it feels as though we've already been there, and more, because we need to feel in our own bodies what the place makes us feel, its particular character and texture. Despite, or perhaps through, their vagaries and abstractions, both authors create uniquely palpable geographies in their books: I dwell in Ferrante, uncomfortably but wholly, in a way that I haven't dwelled in a novel for a long time. Since Sebald, probably. It's a strange feeling, this dwelling *in*, different from the way that other absorbing texts might ask us to live *with* or live *as* certain character. Perhaps because of this power of place over person, character, in both cases, is often something of a problem; we see things through Lenù (or through the shifting "I"s of Sebald's multiply focalized narratives), but we don't get full access to these narrators, who offer a cautious and, in Lenù's case, deceptive version of intimacy.

This is where names come in. The desire to get inside the physical landscape of the text feels somehow aligned with that same confusion of *whose* place—or whose body—we would occupy there. I think my own temptation to go on the Rings of Saturn walk has something to do with the fact that the places are fixed (named, over-full with stories) and the walking self is not—so of course, I want to go to the places to feel for myself what that mysterious and unknowable self felt there and thus get a little closer to it. After all, the central "I" of *The Rings of Saturn* or *Austerlitz* is not exactly W.G. Sebald, and even less so the Max Sebald that the people who knew him describe. To identify Sebald's "I" as Sebald himself is both irresistible and impossible. There is at once a coy invitation and a coy rejection of identification here. A similar logic operates with Ferrante; while we imagine that Elena Greco might look in some ways like Elena Ferrante, the alignment of Elena F. with Elena G. at once flirts with identification and denies it. Both are authors who are named and not named, which we can and can't identify (with).

In Ferrante, this authorial confusion ties in to a broader confusion about the significance of names (or if they have significance at all). In some cases, no matter what a thing or place or person is named—or if it is named at all—those new names accrete and maintain the form of some original shape. For example, whatever she's called, Elena Greco is still Lenùccia from the neighborhood, still sly Lenù the deceptive narrator, still Greco the brownnosing star student. Lenù collects names like she collects accolades, thinking that they all help define her more clearly, an accumulation of signs that all point to the same thing. This is boring. What I find more intriguing is the status of the unnamed, whether person or place (or author): the thing that cannot be pinned down to a singular self.

Sebald often plays with the act of unnaming or the refusal to name (as in his defamiliarizing narratives about Stendhal and Kafka in *Vertigo*). In Ferrante, too, the unnamed or unnameable are the most fascinating objects of interrogation: the things that either have too many names or too few. The most significant of these things is Lila herself. People constantly try to define her nominally, but none of her new names really seem to stick—she is, after all, a disappearance waiting to happen. She, like Lenù, has many names—yet unlike Lenù/Lenùccia/Elena/Greco, these names are not cumulative. They are discrete versions of her, ones that seemingly don't fit together: the legal fiction of Raffaella Cerullo; remote Signora Carracci; Cerù the factory worker; the neighborhood Lina that everyone else sees but doesn't understand; the increasingly inaccessible and imagined Lila we see through Lenù's eyes alone. Yet none of these names are exactly real or proper to Lila herself, as she painfully expresses to Lenù as they carefully obliterate her portrait:

> Her new designation at first [had not] made much of an impression: *Raffaella Cerullo Carracci*. Nothing exciting, nothing serious. In the beginning, that "Carracci" had been no more absorbing than an exercise in logical analysis, of the sort that Maestra Oliviero had hammered into us in elementary school. What was it, an indirect object of place? . . . Lila, as usual, hadn't stopped there, she had soon gone further. As we worked with brushes and paints, she told me that she had begun to see in that formula an indirect object of place to which, as if *Cerullo Carracci* somehow indicated that Cerullo *goes toward Carracci, falls into it, is sucked up by it, is dissolved in it*. . . . Raffaella Cerullo, overpowered, had lost her shape and had dissolved inside the outlines of Stefano, becoming a subsidiary emanation of him: *Signora Carracci*. It was then that I began to see in the panel the traces of what she was saying. (*SNN*, 123-24)

The new name—Signora Carracci—grotesquely absorbs the old one, but that old one didn't even seem to contain Lila fully itself. Again, I think back to the images of Lila/Lina as the fairytale changeling, this time in a sad rather than alarming light: she has a new body, a new identity, a new story for every new name, but none of them reveal her true nature, none of them are her secret and true name. Rather, it seems safer and better to have none, such that she can be possessed by no one. It brings to mind yet another Sebald resonance, the peculiar story of the magical creature Baldanders ("soon another," itself a nonname), who transforms endlessly into, among other things, "a mighty oak, a sow, a sausage, a piece of excrement, a field of clover, a white flower, a mulberry tree, and a silk carpet."[8] Baldanders, like Lila, has a certain power in this indefinability, yet Sebald's reading of him (following Thomas Browne) is that "in this continuous process of consuming and being consumed, nothing endures. . . . On every new thing, there lies already the shadow of annihilation," an idea we might also see in Lila, whose many transformations are preludes to an ultimate erasure.[9] And indeed, even as a child, Lila herself seems to know the coexistent power and the sadness of the unnamed, or the nonnamed; remember, while Lenù gives her doll a human name, Tina, Lila cryptically calls hers Nu—a letter? A negation? A sound without meaning? A powerful nonname.

And finally, to loop back loosely to places, *the neighborhood* itself is the other unnamed and powerful thing at the heart of these vaguely and specifically Neapolitan novels. Herein lies the big difference between wanting to do Sebald's walk, and go to Ferrante's Naples. For while Sebald's places are clearly identified, described, even photographed, and thus are inextricably bound by their names or histories, Ferrante's primal place is evasive—it is, as we've noted before, both as real and unreal as Ferrante herself. As Katherine notes, we don't know exactly where it is or even exactly what it looks like, and yet it is the story's magnetic heart of darkness; it always draws Lenù back, no matter where she goes. It is at once like Lenù, a thing that seems like it stays the same despite external changes and reconstructions, yet it is also possessed of a

Lila-like changeability, as it morphs into a different and incomprehensible space every time Lenù leaves and returns, a changeability that perhaps masks, like Lila, a dark void, "the shadow of annihilation." *The neighborhood* is nowhere and everywhere, named and unnamed, asking the question: Do its readers and characters dwell in it, or does it dwell in us?

—Sarah . . . if that's even my real name.

THOSE WHO LEAVE AND
THOSE WHO STAY

New York, New York
Katherine, August 20

Dear All of You,

It's probably time we admitted that this is really just one novel we're reading. Not that formal definitions matter so much. I've never liked the ornery "Is this a novel?" conversation, about books that break with some tradition. But formal questions have always interested me, particularly when they drive a narrative.

I'm thinking of Lenù and Lila as a single novel not merely because the volumes proceed chronologically; or because the pages, with some notable variation, generally retain their powerful, declarative style; or even because the narrative centers on a single speaker, friendship, and social world; but also because the resonant symbols we first encounter in *My Brilliant Friend* never really leave us. Three-quarters of the way through this saga, I can't stop thinking about the degree to which so many of them are symbols of corrupted shape and form: Lila's visions of dissolving margins, her experience of the exploding copper pot. In both cases, a shape or entity that has been, to some degree, fixed, loses its shape, much to Lila's horror.

The horror is compounded in *The Story of a New Name*, like a dreaded oracle come to pass. On their honeymoon, Stefano rapes Lila, literally violating her form. "What are you doing, be quiet, you're just a twig," he tells her, recalling Ovid, Roman poet of rape and change, "if I want to break you I'll break you." And she's not the only one to lose her shape: "He was never Stefano, she seemed to discover suddenly, he was always the oldest son of Don Achille. . . . The father was cracking his skin, changing his gaze, exploding out of his body" (*SNN*, 41–42).

Later, after Lila's love affair with Nino, comes pregnancy, and this, too, is a realization of her worst nightmare (and maybe also mine):

> She had the impression of having become large and inflated inside rather than outside, as if within the wrapping of her body every organ had begun to fatten. Her stomach seemed a bubble of flesh that was expanding because of the baby's breathing. She was afraid of that expansion, she feared that the thing she was most afraid of would happen: she would break apart, overflow. (*SNN*, 372)

Lenù, meanwhile, has always been drawn to changing forms. Escaping the confines of the neighborhood and Naples, growing tan and blonde at Ischia, even, to some extent, the violence of childbirth—each of these experiences leaves her ecstatic. Her career and domestic trajectory have been superficially orderly, but her heart yearns for something wilder. Near the beginning of *Those Who Leave and Those Who Stay*, shortly after the publication of her first novel, she finds herself skipping her own book event in favor of a radical political meeting, where she looks with envy upon the happy, aggressive women in attendance: "Now that I have some money, I thought, now that I'll earn who knows how much, I can have some of the things I missed. Or maybe not. I was now too cultured, too ignorant, too controlled, too accustomed to freezing life by storing up ideas and facts, too close to marriage and settling down, in short too obtusely fixed within an order that here appeared to be in decline."[10]

Lila values that order. She wants it, desperately, for Lenù—never mind what Lenù might want for herself. In *The Story of a New Name*, while Lila is still with Stefano, she forcefully underwrites Lenù's education because, "She expected from me what she would have done in my place. She really wanted me fixed in the role of someone who spends her life with books" (*SNN*, 93). Later, when Lenù demands Lila's opinion of her second novel, with its workers and Camorrists and its Spaghetti Western ending, Lila breaks down sobbing on the phone.

> You mustn't write those things, Lenù, you aren't that, none of what I read resembles you, it's an ugly, ugly book, and the one before it was, too. . . . Don't make me read anything else, I'm not fit for it, I expect the best from you, I'm too certain that you can do better, I *want* you to do better, it's what I want most, because who am I if you aren't great, who am I? (*TWL*, 272–73)

It's a demand that arises from her own experience of chaos, within marriage, within the violence of the neighborhood. I keep recalling Emily Dickinson: "After great pain, a formal feeling comes." Lila's pain can be alleviated only by order: by personally devoting herself to Gennaro's early education; by the routine of factory work in San Giovanni a Teduccio; by her later work with computer systems, "transform[ing] everything into diagrams and holes" (*TWL*, 262); and by her vicarious comfort in Lenù's success. Though Lila is fiery, and always moving, freezing life might actually seem like a pretty safe bet, but only because she hasn't read Dickinson, whose formal feeling ends with a mass death in snow. After all, it is Lila, not Lenù, who turns back in the tunnel; she is the one who stays.

Competitive friends so often want what the other one has. Whatever Lila might think, Lenù finds her domestic situation with Pietro increasingly untenable. They are a poor match erotically, leaving her perennially unsatisfied, and they are a poor match intellectually, arguing constantly over politics. Worst by far, he won't even read her fiction.

The fiction is another source of dissatisfaction. Lenù spends the period following her first novel's publication on the all-too-familiar pendulum between grandiosity and self-doubt. A positive review fills her sails; a negative review sends her reeling. She feels embarrassed at the public's reaction to the "dirty parts," then learns to talk about them in terms that justify her choice—"I spoke of the necessity of recounting frankly every human experience, including . . . what seems unsayable and what we do not speak of even to ourselves" (*TWL*, 64)—then comes to rethink them yet again. All along, she can't shake the feeling of exposure, or of posing:

> Whenever I saw the book in a window, among other novels that had just come out, I felt inside a mixture of pride and fear, a dart of pleasure that ended in anguish. . . . I knew what great literature was, I had done a lot of work in the classics, and it never occurred to me, while I was writing, that I was making something of value. But the effort of finding a form had absorbed me. And the absorption had become *that* book, an object that contained me. Now I was there, exposed, and seeing myself caused a violent pounding in my chest. (*TWL*, 53)

Reading this, each time, causes a violent pounding in my chest, too.

But I bring up this debut novelist moment not (only) to tell you it's so true but also because it highlights Lenù's longstanding obsession with form, dating back to her good student years. Having spent the vast majority of her life upholding the well-constructed sentence, she finds her adult self thinking of her first novel as "frivolous and very traditional." For her second effort, she wants to move away from it, toward a form with more political significance, "one that would contain the tumult of the present" (TWL, 248). Yes, yes, yes—as you might remember, I'm working on a second novel, too.

Anyway, the spaghetti Western Camorra novel fails, a devastating moment for Lenù and me both, but another effort, a story-essay hybrid on the creation myth and the hubris of man, finds a prestigious publisher in France. So Lenù's writing career is finding its way, not by adhering to forms but by breaking them, and much to her own satisfaction.

No wonder she runs away with Nino, that brooding Marxist boy who keeps turning up, who washes dishes, and who defends her time to that selfish Casaubon, Pietro: "I thought: Something great is happening that will dissolve the old way of living entirely and I'm part of that dissolution" (TWL, 418).

She has seen herself on the shelf, contained, and she has exploded out of that containment with Nino—always Nino—as her muse. If Lila's efforts to right what's wrecked recall Dickinson, then Lenù's desires put me in a Rilke frame of mind. Faced with her own, living torso of Apollo, she knows she must change her life.[11]

We've been reading this novel too long to feel that Lenù's triumphant first flight will end happily—and yet, how could we read on if we were not hoping, just a little, that it might?

Bursting from my borders,
Katherine

Dear friends—

At a dinner party some weeks ago, I declined a glass of wine and told my host that I was four months pregnant. "I bet you've read all the baby books," sighed the younger woman sitting next to me, a woman who knew very little about me except that I liked to read. I demurred. I disliked baby books, I told her, as well as mommy blogs, maternity clothing, baby showers, and all other sentimental scenes of motherhood. What were they but false promises, cheerful and hallucinatory flashes intended to distract women from the unpleasant facts of what was to come: the drudgery and boredom of childcare, the visceral unfairness of pregnancy?

I must have raised my voice, because the younger woman shrunk back. "I don't think everyone feels that way about their children," she said primly.

The flip side of sentimentality is rage, and many of the parenting books I have read this summer are indignant, vengeful, frustrated, or unsettling tales about what Rachel Cusk has called the "mythic snare" of motherhood: that a child will forever "live within the jurisdiction" of her mother's "consciousness," wrenching a woman from her former self so violently that her understanding of "what it is to exist is profoundly changed." Cusk's *A Life's Work* is on my shelf, where it leans on Adrienne Rich's *Of Woman Born*, Jenny Offill's *Department of Speculation*, Elena Ferrante's *The Lost Daughter*, and the final two books in her Neapolitan series, *Those Who Leave and Those Who Stay* and *The Story of the Lost Child*.

Beyond just the existential pangs of maternity, these books all wrestle with the politics of childcare. There exists, in fiction and reality alike, a transparently unequal division of labor between those who leave in the mornings (usually men) and those who stay at home during the day (usually women). For women who stay at home, and for those who make a living by writing, a dilemma presents itself: how to reconcile the demands of childcare—the feeding schedule, the midnight cries, the incessant need to minister to another human being—with the unbroken time and seclusion one so often needs to put pen to paper?

I like to joke that if Ferrante had written a parody of *What To Expect When You're Expecting* it might go something like this:

1. You can be one of two types of pregnant women. You can be a woman like Lenù, a woman who "feels light" and unburdened by pregnancy, a woman who experiences "no breakdown in [her] body, in mood, in the wish to be active." Or you can be a woman like Lila who turns green, sickly, aged, and bitter, morphing into a prisoner in her own expanding body. "The body suffers, it doesn't like losing its shape, there's too much pain," Lila warns Lenù, and her warning is a near perfect mirror—three clauses, three commas—of Lenù's rapturous physicality.

2. The first type of woman will never understand the second type. The inverse is also true. To Lenù, Lila's warning doubles as an invitation to masochistic communion, a chance for the two women to share an experience of pain that transcends the many experiences—education, marriage—that have divided them over the years. Lenù's unwillingness to accept Lila's understanding of maternity, and Lila's unwillingness to acknowledge Lenù's, seems a form of betrayal: a denial of something that both woman perceive as essential to their sense of self.

3. Which type of woman you are is, in part, a choice, a matter of willful thinking, not physical reality. When Lenù rejects Lila's invitation to suffer together—"It was a wonderful experience," she says of giving birth—her rejection is also a refusal to believe that motherhood is the "fabrication" of

one's "very own torture." She ignores the aches and pains and revels in exaggerated sentiment, convinced that her "sense of physical and intellectual fulness" has made her "bold" and "expansive." "Each of us narrates our life as it suits us," Lila responds passive aggressively. Here one can almost see Lila slitting her dark eyes and waiting for the other shoe to drop.

4. The other shoe will always drop. Lenù's baby shrieks, shits, vomits, and refuses to breastfeed. Lenù feels inadequate, useless, and pained. At some point, she begins to hate her husband for not suffering as she does, for not rising in agitation when the baby gives off a sense of unhappiness. She hates him for going to work when she must stay at home. She hates him for saying things like, "Someone who really has to write will write anyway, even if she has a baby." You, too, will feel ashamed and you will feel abandoned, "ugly and old before [your] time." You, too, will resign yourself to the idea that this is the way things are supposed to be.

5. Money is the only way out. Money most often takes the form of cash paid to a housekeeper/nanny/cook. For Lenù, money assumes the guise of a wealthy mother-in-law, one who arrives at the house with an armful of radical feminist tracts and tries to "rekindle" her "frozen mind" and her "frozen gaze." She does not want to read these tracts. She does not want to read anything, nor does she want to commit words to paper because, even with money, writing seems to require far greater expanses of time, and a far greater clarity of purpose, than she can summon.

6. Rarely will your children perceive you as an autonomous human being—a person with a past, a person with desires separable from their own existence, a person capable of being wounded by their thoughtlessness.

7. Eventually, you will abandon your children to save yourself. Bon voyage!

I could go on like this, but it occurs to me that it might be dangerous to do so. No matter how opposed to one another they may seem, sentimentality and indignation are equally capable of constricting the imagination. Both are intense, absorptive modes of feeling, and both are prescriptive in their own ways. If the preciousness of diaper ads, stork-shaped cupcakes, and staged baby photos advertises pure bliss, unsullied by the grime of exhaustion and self-estrangement, then outright resentment at the inequalities of childcare also produces a vision of parenting stripped of possibility. What if your partner wants to do as much as you or worries, as mine does, that you won't let him do enough? What if you have friends who are more intimately involved in your lives than family and are eager to raise your children alongside you? What if the new rhythms of parenting teach you how to write differently or to write better?

The most gripping passages in *Those Who Leave and Those Who Stay* are the passages that formalize the constriction of the writerly imagination, first by sentimentality and later by rage. In her sentimental mode, Lenù's perception of her body's fullness prompts her to wax poetic, to spout nonsense. When she states during a speech that she feels "as happy as the astronauts on the white expanse of the moon," Lila criticizes her for her rhetorical flight of fancy. "Sometimes it's better to say nothing," Lila observes, "to stand with your feet firmly planted in the troubles of the earth" (*TWL*, 234).

Rage, on the other hand, is terse and invective. Nearly two years after she gives birth, Lenù reads for the first time Carla Lonzi's manifesto *We Spit on Hegel*, one of the founding texts of Rivolta Femminile, or "Female Revolt." To capture her overwhelming emotional response to Lonzi's critique of Marxism, Lenù compresses Lonzi's elegant sentences and paragraphs into militant commands. "Resist the waste of female intelligence. Deculturate. Disacculturate, starting with maternity. Don't *give* children to anyone. . . . Restore women to themselves" (*TWL*, 280). Her experience of reading Lonzi feels empowering to her, but what about our experience of reading Lenù reading Lonzi? If sentimentality is enshrined in pretty idiocies, rage is spitting orders at one's reader.

Yet in the middle of these emotional bookends are long, anguished meditations on the daily ethics of childcare, passages which are neither purple nor piqued in their representation of motherhood. Between sentimentality and rage, the style of Ferrante's prose is unpredictable and ever-changing; not the fragmented starts and stops of Offill and others but sharp turns from one manner of feeling to the next. There are run-on sentences of baby talk, coos and gurgles and silly nicknames crafted to appease a colicky newborn. There are sentence-long paragraphs of self-doubt, which sometimes dissolve in tears but just as often emerge into tranquility and acceptance. There are alternating bouts of euphoria, anxiety, depression.

Here, then, is everything that is impossible to contain in one extreme feeling or another. Here are all the possibilities of parenting and writing, treading water somewhere in the middle.

—Merve

Oh Nino, why are you such a tool? Nino is a real goober, though it's really Enzo who gets me. To Enzo I say, you are boring and not particularly bright, stop being a martyr. Pietro you too, with all that intellectual strutting, the self-absorption justified by an overwrought sense of injury, as though the world has done wrong to you, you especially. And Juan, that's rape, not sexual liberation, you fool. To Rino I say, you are so mean, so incompetent at everything besides cruelty. To Stefano, I hate you, I hate you, I hate you.

Looking back, the men don't come off particularly well in the Neapolitan cycle, though it might be more accurate to say that no one goes through unscathed. All the same, I find myself talking to the men more than anyone else, most often in the declarative. This isn't a categorical claim about Ferrante's treatment of men. The women can be just as cruel and stupid. It's more about how I can't imagine myself talking to Lenù and Lila. Instead, while reading, I imagine myself *being* them, in every case.

This is all somewhat embarrassing to admit. It is certainly not a very professional mode of reader response that I'm describing— that is, talking to characters, giving them advice, insulting them, sometimes out loud, in public places, where people will stare at you. When I teach novels, much of my energy is geared towards persuading students to avoid these moments of identification. To students I say, I don't want to hear that you really love Clarissa or that, if you were on the *Patna*, you would have definitely jumped. Talking to characters, imagining what we would have done in their situation, and comparing their lives to our own, in the world of academic literary criticism at least, is looked down upon as an overly subjective, immature model of reading. It is not the thing to do.

This sense that talking to characters or comparing oneself to a character overmuch is a juvenile reading strategy compounds a second anxiety of mine. In general, when I write about a book, I have already finished the book in question. Indeed, most of my argument will hinge on some sort of development that we can only understand in retrospect. Across this summer, I've been writing about Ferrante as I go along, not knowing how things will turn out. Writing while reading, without knowing how the story will end, involves making a number of assumptions. Most pointedly, due to the general doucheyness of the male characters, I've assumed that Lenù and Lila will eventually shed their respective beaux. I've assumed that this shedding will involve some realization about feminism and, most likely, a kind of political awakening to what Mariarosa calls the revolution. Halfway into *Those Who Leave and Those Who Stay*, I am getting ready to be wrong and that itself generates a particular mode of reading. For now let's call it a freighted, anxious kind of waiting.

This kind of reading and writing, as one goes along, is happening in conversation with you all, with other women, some who are dear friends, some who I haven't met, a number of whom I have lived with or turned to in moments of crisis for couch-surfing and other forms of care. I am learning about the meantime of these other lives, in distant and nearby cities, amidst the reading and writing on Ferrante, as I go along. The writing about Ferrante then becomes a gloss for all these other things that I would like to convey but don't quite have the words. There are shadow narratives, about me and to these other women, underneath the stories that I tell about Lenù and Lila, so that the Neapolitan cycle blurs a bit into the background, as a merely enabling fiction. All these things I want to say, I think, I will say about Lenù and Lila. Some of them I will say on other mediums, with less prying eyes. If "The Slow Burn" is a companion to the Neapolitan cycle, I like to think of the email threads scheduling these posts as another literary form altogether, a companion to the companion, a spiderweb of dumb GIFs, summer schedules, revolving encouragements, friendship, trauma, care.

This blurring, between the fictional world of the novel and the spiderweb of our extended email correspondence, of our various summers, is perhaps what always happens but more often gets covered up. Normally I would just skip over the fact that this writing, here, now, is in a humid, airless room in my railroad apartment. I would not mention that there is a heat wave in New Haven and I have a nonfunctional air conditioner. I would not mention that my dog is panting with her whole body or that as I type I can hear the false echo of another click-clacking that is my girlfriend typing in the other room, because she is visiting me for a spell before returning to the city where she lives for the start of the semester. Instead I would just skip to the compounded metaphor, as though it came out of nowhere: the thing about heat is that, for me, it makes everything seem like a spell, like the in between. During this heat spell, I am perpetually waiting for the time of day that is less hot or trying to find the room that is less hot. Spaces get mapped out in my brain differently, according to respective temperatures. At this moment, the Neapolitan novels feel like the meantime and the meantime feels like a heat wave at the end of the summer. Is that merely a result of the particularities of my experience, here, now? If I was writing after having read that fourth novel, would my argument be entirely different? Right now, how I feel about these novels, about the cycle really, cannot really snap into place, so I end up describing that meantime or what it feels like here, now. In many ways, it feels like the passage that Lili noted:[12]

> The heat was unbearable. **I found** myself against a background
> of posters dense with writing, red flags, and struggling people,
> placards announcing activities, noisy voices, laughter, and

a widespread sense of apprehension. **I wandered** around, looking for signs that had to do with me. **I recall** a dark-haired young man who, running, rudely bumped into me, lost his balance, picked himself up, and ran out into the street as if he were being pursued, even though no one was behind him. **I recall** the pure, solitary sound of a trumpet that pierced the suffocating air. **I recall** a tiny blond girl, who was dragging a clanking chain with a large lock at the end, and zealously shouting, I don't know to whom: I'm coming! **I remember it** because in order to seem purposeful, **as I waited** for someone to recognize me and come over, **I took out my notebook** and wrote down this and that. But half an hour passed, and no one arrived. (*TWL*, 68; bold mine)

What I'd like to point out is not Lenù's recording of the scene, but the way that this recording, with its litany of first-person recollections, looks so different from another account of Italy in the 1970s, this time taken from Nanni Balestrini's *The Unseen*:

When we arrive there's a long procession filling the platform and it's moving up the stairs of the metro no one's bothering with tickets and in the carriages there are flags and the long poles for the banners someone has a go at singing but the mood is grim threatening we reach the university in the square in front of the university there's a tide of people but not just students not just young people all ages are there old people too there are workers in overalls with red kerchiefs round their necks the demonstration is already there drawn up ready to go the stewards in front kerchiefs masking half their faces and the heavy sticks with small red flags tied on there's a dull rumbling sound then a shout and a slogan launched murdered comrade you'll be avenged everyone together a roar and the demonstration sets off.[13]

For Balestrini, there is this sense of immediacy, of a *we* melded together, if only in a single moment. Ferrante won't give us that. The persistently mediating term, "I recall," makes the political scene a pointed memory, forever apart. While reading, I had understood this moment of Lenù's narration as a kind of gelatinous middle, a meantime that will eventually speed up, somehow, into the present-tense of Lenù's life, into Balestrini's "we." I had thought that surely Lenù will, at some point, come to recognize herself somewhere, if not amidst the students, then amidst the communists or the Florentine women. But then maybe there is something wrong with this progress narrative that ends in a unified "we" as it can be found in another book, so easily, so confidently narrated by a man. In any case, this is all speculation, so my judgment remains suspended, too.

Reading the posts by Merve and Lili, I try out these different endings. I am perpetually talking to and with characters as I wait in line, when I'm doing the dishes. Sometimes I talk to you all too, my friends and coauthors and the tiny handful of people I can count on as readers, as I try to position this response in relation to what you have already written or said. I curse at the characters, at Nino and Pietro, and perpetually, obsessively return to a handful of bent pages, like the moment when Lila says to Professor Galiani, just before the chapter breaks off, "We made a pact when we were children: I'm the wicked one" (*TWL*, 68).[14] It's a lie, according to the facts we have, but Lila believes herself. Or she believes the promises she's made to herself and to others, about who to be, as a reality more pressing than any words actually exchanged, any promises made, on Lenù's part. It is one of those moments that I see as blurred, subject to what Lila would call dissolving margins, not for her, but for us, the readers. I am confident that, at that moment, Lila believes every word that she says as the rock-hard truth. Funny, that blurring. It is so promiscuous. Looking backward, I realize that there must be seasons in these novels, but in my imperfect memory, one prone to melding what is fictional and real, all of it, everything, seems to have taken place during the hottest day, at the end of a long summer.

—Jill

NJ Transit, the quiet car ("Speak Softly"), circa Secaucus.
Sarah, September 1

Fellow readers, burning bright:

A long time ago, Merve asked us all a very scary question:
"Have you ever tried to erase yourself?"
That question has stalked me ever since, but I've been too afraid
to answer it in writing. In the intervening weeks, I've talked around it
in person to some of you, often shyly framed by talk about Ferrante.
(Incidentally, how many of our real life, real friend conversations
this summer have been like this?) These conversations happened
in fits and starts, over drinks and coffee and some embarrassingly
public tears—the hideous leaky-faucet kind you try to ignore and
talk through. I thought it was a question only to be answered in this
closed manner: a personal nonreading unimportant in the scope
of this ongoing literary discussion. But last week, when Lili told us
about her sister's self-erasure, her writing and unwriting, her letter
demolished some final retaining wall I'd been maintaining between
critical reading and personal feeling.[15] Perhaps that wall was wrong
or impossible to keep up in this conversation. Perhaps we cannot
help but ask intimate questions and tell intimate stories in these
public/private letters because they speak to the void at the heart of
Ferrante's whole saga: as Jill just reminded us, Lila is always already
gone. Her loss is what shapes this world and powerfully shapes our
reading of it, such that it can so easily reach out into our own lives.
And I've come to realize (nonacademically, with not a little critical
shame) that for me, the centrality of Lila's disappearance is the idea
in these books that I keep writing back to in my posts, because a
longing for utter erasure is my point of origin as well.

* * *

I cannot remember a time when I didn't want to disappear. I don't think it matters so much here, in this particular para-academic context, to say why, or what attempts were made to do so, if blame can be placed, et cetera. Suffice to say, the desire for self-obliteration is one I know well. Failed experiments at it left scars internal and external that I think will never completely fade. Pardon the coyness and cliché, but this is hard writing—this is writing that hurts. But Ferrante, for me, was *reading* that hurt; she has driven me to this point.

I see now that this is why these books have spoken to me in simultaneously captivating and terrifying tones all summer, for I recognize in myself Lila's formative fantasy of total disappearance. I think that's why I have *felt* Lila all along, sought her out from the very first pages, from that initial vanishing act. The reason I yearn for Lila, I want to be allowed to identify with her, is that she accomplishes what I spent so many years longing to do: she *unselves* herself. Recall the title of the first section of the first book: Eliminating All the Traces. The magic trick here is not the simple obliteration of suicide (the dream of no-longer-being), but rather, the genuine fascination of *never-having-been*:

> It's been at least three decades since she told me that she wanted to disappear without leaving a trace, and I'm the only one who knows what she means. She never had in mind any sort of flight, a change of identity, the dream of making a new life somewhere else. And she never thought of suicide, repulsed by the idea that Rino would have anything to do with her body, and would be forced to attend to the details. She meant something different: she wanted to vanish; she wanted every one of her cells to disappear, nothing of her ever to be found. (*MBF*, 20)

It is a dream I dream too, that is closer to the feelings of my youth, whose strange abstraction I could not comprehend then, even as I felt it; one that still rubs up against my mind in certain wobbly moments. Never before had I read so clear an articulation of this strange and singular desire. I feel possessively that, more than Lenù herself, "I'm the only one who knows what she means."

Yet, despite the fact I long for Lila-ness, and am chock-full of judgment (of the political, authorial, and petty personal varieties) for Lenù, there is something that always keeps this impulse towards disappearance in check. Framed by the Neapolitans, we might call it a certain Lenùccian ego; call it a desire for recognition that counters the slip into oblivion at every step. For I, like Lenù, also fear a certain flip side to disappearance: the fear of being sloppily, shoddily obscured, semi-forgotten, half-remembered. When I think about Lenù's personal anxieties of erasure, I see a woman's figure in pencil on newsprint, incompletely rubbed away; what is left spreads to mar the rest of the page, blurred, dirty and grey, gross shreds of blackened rubber clinging to the surface. Compare this to the shocking and total erasure of Lila's disappearance; this to me is the image of a white page seemingly never marked, whose whiteness itself marks a mysterious absence, an aching and significant void. Perversely, in its absence, the figure missing here *cannot* be forgotten, even if it was never known. One may desire the power of the latter image, but the fear is that the messiness of the former is actually the inevitable aftermath of any real-life attempt.

I don't want this to be a soul-searching, publicly tearful final revelation about myself as a depressed person or a reader or a site of female erasure, or, you know, whatever. *All* of this is still, for me, about Ferrante; these feelings well up from the cuts her books have made on me. These are simply the imagined visions I return to, again and again, as we near the end of this quartet, of this project, of Lenù and Lila's lives. The question that lingers is still the same, though stated in more definite terms. Not "will we," or "might we," or "are we afraid that we'll," but rather:

How will we disappear?

So let me just leave this here, a little pile of feelings-rubble on the construction site of a proper argument—it may be incomplete, as this whole project inevitably is, but I promise, there is one.

* * *

Let me start over again with the magic words, the fetishes, the oft-repeated incantations. The words we've puzzled over these last several weeks in public and private conversation, that we cannot define, that we cannot relinquish:

Solidarity
Dissolving margins
Erasure

From the beginning, we have invoked these terms in different ways, without pinning them down. They are the states of body and mind and body politic that we have talked around all summer as we've traced the delicate webs of feeling that Lenù and Lila weave. These abstractions are the connective filaments of their shared and separate lives. Those webs, like the ones Jill describes of spoken and unspoken things telegraphed between our readings, are what we call friendship. They are also sometimes indecipherable from what we might call animosity, or jealousy, or even flat-out hatred. These words all have different valences, yet they vibrate together in some weird frequency, which is perhaps what gives these novels, or in Katherine's reading, this one long novel, their disturbing, thrumming energy.

Looking back, I wonder if the central puzzle is the term that seems perhaps the least mysterious in theory but can be the most mysterious, dreamt-of, and longed for in practice: Solidarity.

> The heat was unbearable. **I found myself against a background** of posters dense with writing, red flags, and struggling people, placards announcing activities, noisy voices, laughter, and a widespread sense of apprehension. I wandered around, **looking for signs that had to do with me.** I recall a dark-haired young man who, running, rudely bumped into me, lost his balance, picked himself up, and ran out into the street as if he were being pursued, even though no one was behind him. I recall **the pure, solitary sound of a trumpet that pierced the suffocating air.** I recall a tiny blond girl, who was dragging a clanking chain with a large lock at the end, and zealously shouting, I don't know to whom, I'm coming! I remember it because in order to seem purposeful, **as I waited for someone to recognize me and come over**, I took out my notebook and wrote down this and that. But half and hour passed, and no one arrived. Then I examined the placards and posters more carefully, hoping to find **my name, or the title of the book.** (*TWL*, 68)

I return to a passage that both Lili and Jill have read and marked in order to read and mark it somewhat differently. The "I," of course, is Lenù, reluctantly but irresistibly sucked into a demonstration in Milan. Lili asked us to consider Lenù's questionable motivations for writing. Jill highlighted the "I" clauses: *I found, I wandered, I recall.* I, in turn, ask you to consider the desire for clear (read: selfish, self-asserting) singularity that renders this scene of collaborative political action so unsettling to Lenù. The density of the background overwhelms her; the signs don't speak to her particular Lenitude; she seems to envy the purity of the single trumpet among the "suffocation" of the madding crowd; as always, she wants to others to recognize her by name, as the famous author Elena Greco. Lenù is inexorably drawn to the *idea* of the demonstration, the *idea* of dwelling in this moment in solidarity with others, but at every turn it repulses her.

Solidarity to Lenù is both a dream and a nightmare; she wants to join in, but she is too afraid to relinquish her unique self to give in to the triumphal *we* that Jill highlighted in Balestrini. To her, that "we" is irreconcilable with the solitude of independent being or, more specifically, the desired solitude of the autonomous female being. For increasingly, as she walks through the mass of protesters looking for a familiar face or name (her own), Lenù finds it particularly hard to articulate the women from the mass or from each other. She sees men in passing and notes them individually as "handsome, ugly, well-dressed, scruffy, violent, frightened, amused," yet the women she sees "stayed close together . . . they shouted together, laughed together, and if they were separated by even a few meters they kept an eye on each other so as not to get lost" (*TWL*, 69). Only a few individuals "by themselves or at most in pairs," move amongst the groups of men, and they are marked by their hard-won distinction from the other women: "they seemed to me the happiest, the most aggressive, the proudest." It is 1968 and while Lenù struggles to absorb "the lesson from France," she is deeply terrified by the idea of losing the distinctly singular, *female* self she has worked so hard (albeit confusedly) to keep cleanly defined and bounded, in order to join the massed bodies of implicitly male solidarity.

So surely it's not too much of a stretch to say that *solidarity* slides in the mouth, on the page, into two other troubled terms for Lenù and Lila: solitude, solidity. Forgive this language game, and remember what Lenù told us early on: the game is everything. *Solitude*, in Ferrante's world, is another fervently desired but unattainable thing. The neighborhood, we have seen, is everywhere, sees everyone. And more broadly, you are not alone while you are connected to anyone, while you come from anyone, while you remember anyone, while you love or hate anyone. In short, while you are human. And Ferrante's psychological genius unfolds in the very paradox of this idea: "No one is alone" is a comforting platitude, but it is also, if you think about it, really a horrifying revelation. After all, in *The Story of a New Name*, we saw the original nightmare monster, Don Achille, erupt through his son Stefano's skin with an unexpected brutality. And in *Those Who Leave and Those Who Stay*, Lenù is more occupied than ever before not only *with* other people, but *by* them. When pregnant, she is afraid that her mother "had settled in [her] body," bursting out of some hiding place in her, warping her leg and her mind (*TWL*, 237). Similarly, Nino "was not fleeing his father out of fear of becoming like him: he *already was* his father and didn't want to admit it" (88). Lenù herself is increasingly full of these emotional squatters (a word she uses for the imagined figure of Lila, always occupying some hidden control center of her mind)—not only her mother and Lila, but Gigliola, Pasquale, Enzo, others. For the first time, we see her slide seamlessly and dizzyingly, into the first person (again, a Sebaldian feeling dogs me) when narrating the experience of others.

We are never alone: those we come from, those we love and hate and fear dwell always inside us. Yet—and here is the paradox—these are the very people who make us our unique and singular selves. We cannot be properly our own selves without them, yet that is perhaps all we want. Solitude, then, seems like an impossible dream in Ferrante's world—but only if you need to retain a conventional sense of self. Thus, Lila's desire for erasure starts to make a strange and perfect sense: the only way to be both in solidarity (to be everywhere, to be everyone) and to achieve perfect solitude (to be alone, to be without one's constant inhabitation by ghosts) is perhaps to dissolve the self completely. This is where the second slippery term springs to mind: *solidity*. Lila is the most clearly defined character at various points, yet she is also the most willing to embrace phase changes and transformations, at once the most and least solid of forms. Thus, both her magical changeability and her lifelong nightmare of slowly dissolving margins—perhaps migraine or madness or something more mystical—might both be incomplete, primitive stages on the way to her ultimate desire and destiny, the sudden "elimination without a trace." Maybe her proximity to the void is what makes Lila at once the most empathetic character (who feels other minds; around whom others dissolve) and the most remote one, that distant figure nobody can comprehend or touch, she who refuses to leave traces for anyone to hold onto ("I'll come look in your computer, I'll read your files, I'll erase them" [*TWL*, 29]).

Lenù, on the other hand, fears a lack of solidity beyond anything else. Hence, on one hand, her innate conservatism—but also, in wilder terms, her phantasmagoric anxiety about physical expansion (remember, the "expanding pizza dough" of her adolescent body). She's always anxious about lack of definition, and therefore resists melding with others at every turn for fear that any incursion might be a blurring of the self. And even when she recounts others' stories, she is an anti-empath; the one time she really *feels* someone else (while stoned), she actually passes out: "[Mariarosa] became furious, then stopped talking and burst into tears. I couldn't find a single word of comfort. *I felt* her tears, it seemed to me that they made a sound sliding from her eyes down her cheeks. Suddenly I couldn't see her, I couldn't even see the room, everything turned black. I fainted" (*TWL*, 289). To maintain her singularity, Lenù seeks individual form through her books ("the effort of finding a form had absorbed me. And the absorption had become *that* book, an object that contained me" [53]), through the articulation of set phrases and beliefs, through the definition of her relationships—culminating, I think, in that final flight to Nino. All of these attempts at definition, of herself and of others, speak back to her own terror at the idea of spreading and becoming indistinguishable from the external world, whether the "we" of the demonstration, or the nightmarishly malleable surfaces she hallucinated about in My Brilliant Friend. I wonder if this resistance to uncontrolled expansion and the loss of self explains, in part, why she persistently and violently overwrites Lila: she must contain Lila and Lila's story neatly within her own in order to contain herself.

Both of these anxieties—the fear of others spreading into you or you spreading into others—are edged with a kind of pleasure, though, a dangerous seduction. Perhaps the real, terrifying magic spell of these novels is the uncertainty about whether we are going to expand into everything or dissolve into everyone/no one, for one of these ends seems inevitable for us all; perhaps our various identifications with Lenù or Lila have to do with which of these ends we fear—or desire—most.

* * *

When the four of us began this whole enterprise, we met in person to talk about our projections and anxieties about writing together. Over pasta and wine, we worried about the idea of reading books together, long-term: What if we all came up with the same ideas? How would we distinguish our voices as writers? What if we weren't original enough? It turned out that none of these concerns came to anything, though of course we all fell into certain patterns of reading and even raised the same questions or terms or ideas. We never thought the same things or repeated each other. It seems so obvious now: of course we wouldn't, we are different people. And yet, that anxiety was so strongly felt. Why?

These are, of course, the very same fears that Lila and Lenù express in their different ways—the fears of pollution and codependence that inevitably accompany intimacy of any kind. Considering Lila and Lenù, considering us, considering this venture and the novels it springs from, I wonder if there is a way to be *confident* in solidarity—in a personal way (and in a political one too, I think) but not subsume each other; to experience an intellectual and emotional togetherness that feels the giddiness of being overwhelmed with feeling but does not itself overwhelm. If there is a way to truly be with one another, and infiltrate one another, and communicate deeply, but not get lost in other minds. If there is a way to both be your friend and be yourself and not betray either. If there is a way to dissolve margins but not give in to the seductions of madness or self-obliteration. Perhaps that is the most defiant challenge of these novels to their characters and to their readers.

Today is the first day of September, a day overburdened with significance this year. It is, as any student knows, always a symbolic end of freedom (this year it's my actual first day on campus) but, most importantly, this September first is the release of the fourth Neapolitan novel, *The Story of the Lost Child*. The heat is breaking; the spell Jill wrote of is almost over. I started composing this letter in a late August late afternoon, on that aching cusp between writing time and teaching time that reminds us of what we lose and what we gain with the structured arc of fall semester. The summer and "The Slow Burn" are both cooling, and our time here together is coming to an end. But, my brilliant friends, I hope that even after Ferrante, we can continue in some small way to live in each other harmoniously, to treasure the traces we've left in each other, to keep each other from disappearing.

Yours, *truly*,
Sarah

THE STORY OF THE LOST CHILD

Cambridge, Massachusetts
Merve, September 16

Dear friends—

Seven hours, thirty-two minutes, and fifty seconds: this is how long it took me to read *The Story of the Lost Child*. In that time, I did not get out of bed. I forgot to eat. I forgot to go to the bathroom. I repositioned myself once, to cry briefly, noisily, and then again to soldier on to the last page. By the time I finished, I was exhausted, sated, and yet, much to my own surprise, disappointed by where I—and where Lila and Lenù and Naples and the modern world as such—had ended up.

Why was I disappointed? It's never easy to pin down how and when disappointment begins, but let me try by beginning at the end. I don't think I'm spoiling anything for anyone when I reveal that the last five pages of *The Story of the Lost Child* are given over to a short epilogue; one subtitled—or more accurately, cotitled—"Restitution."

Like many epilogues, "Restitution" is set apart from the 1,668 pages of narrative that precede it, first by the physical space of two blank pages and then by a statement of disbelief addressed to Lenù's imagined reader. "I can't believe it myself," Lenù writes, as if she already knows that we too will not believe what she is about to tell us:

> I've finished this story that I thought would never end. I finished it and patiently reread it not so much to improve the quality of the writing as to find out if there are even a few lines where it's possible to trace the evidence that Lila entered my text and decided to contribute to writing it. But I have had to acknowledge that all these pages are mine alone. . . . Lila is not in these words.[16]

Sarah has insisted throughout this summer that Lenù is a prolific liar, and I can't shake my sense that the epilogue is the biggest lie of all. Every sentence rings false. Did Lenù really think that her story "would never end"? Can we trust her claim that she has "patiently reread" the manuscript "not so much to improve the quality of the writing" as to sniff out Lila's contributions to it? (We know that Lenù is a diligent reviser as well as a professional editor at a small literary publishing house.) Least believable of all is her final pronouncement that "Lila is not in these words." Lila's influence—her words, her ideas, her fierce and heartbreaking presence—is everywhere. That Lenù doth protest too much seems undeniable. The real question is: why?

All of these lies are, in one way or another, lies about the labor of writing. Planning, drafting, rereading, revising, collaborating—each of these steps is crucial to the process of producing a work of narrative art. As various characters have shown us time and again, writing is difficult, time-intensive work that never takes place in a sealed chamber of individual genius, though sometimes we may wish it did. Even more frustrating, perhaps, is how much of this hard work goes unacknowledged. Words are highlighted, deleted, changed. Sentences are crossed out. Entire pages and chapters are scrapped. It is tempting to feel a sense of shame about the whole enterprise, a psychic disruption akin to what Lenù feels when she sees her (now fat, now balding) ex-lover Nino for the first time after many years: "He gave me the impression of wasted time, of useless labor, that I feared would stay in my mind, extending into me, to everything" (SLC, 470).

Lenù would have us believe that there was no wasted time, no useless labor in the production of her greatest work of art. In a sense, this lie is a form of restitution, a recompense for injury or loss. Lenù's insistence on her self-possessed, romantic genius is designed to set off all the injuries and losses we know she has suffered in order to write the story we have just finished: the violence of her childhood, the indignities of her adolescence, her failed marriage, her tense relationship with her children, her humiliation at the hands of Nino, and ultimately, her loss of Lila's friendship after Lenù writes the story of their lives in her last novel, A Friendship.

But there is another, form of restitution at play in the epilogue. One day a package arrives for Lenù. Inside are Tina and Nu, the dolls that Lenù and Lila dropped into a neighborhood cellar nearly six decades and 1,668 pages ago in the opening scene of My Brilliant Friend. For Lenù—as for us, her readers—the dolls are the origin point not only of her story but of her friendship with Lila. These were the dolls, Lenù recalls:

> that Lila had pushed me to go and retrieve from the house of Don Achille . . . and Don Achille had claimed that he hadn't taken them, and maybe he had imagined that it was his son Alfonso who stole them, and so he had compensated us with money so that we could buy others. But we hadn't bought dolls with that money—how could we have replaced Tina and Nu?—instead we

bought *Little Women*, the novel that had led Lila to write *The Blue Fairy* and me to become what I was today, the author of many books and above all of a remarkably successful story entitled *A Friendship*. (*SLC*, 475)

By the end of the story, the dolls have been returned to their rightful owner. With this act of restitution, all 1,668 pages of Lenù's story can be compressed into a dizzying one sentence journey from the beginning of her life (and the beginning of *My Brilliant Friend*) to the end of her life (and the end of *The Story of the Lost Child*). It is as if nothing else had happened in between; as if the disappearance of Tina and Nu singlehandedly led Lenù "to become what I was today, the author of many books" and cast Lila into obscurity, caused her to disappear. More blatantly than Lenù's half-hearted protestations at the beginning of the epilogue, it is the causal and counterfactual leap at the end of the epilogue that delivers what seems like the greatest and most distressing falsehood of all: that nothing we have read over 1,668 pages ever happened.

And of course, *it didn't*. This is not autobiography or autofiction—a ridiculous and untenable category. This is fiction that has always called attention to its own construction as fiction through such short-cuts, repetitions, references, and doublings. In the epilogue, however, it's just more obvious than it ever was before. To begin and end with the dolls seems too neat, too transparent an example of a literary device. We know that Lenù has used this device before in *A Friendship*, which she tells us begins with the loss of the dolls and ends with the loss of Lila's daughter Tina. Many readers know too that Ferrante has used the same pairing of doll and daughter in her novella *The Lost Daughter*. To feel disappointment or betrayal at the obviously constructed nature of the epilogue—and by extension, everything that came before it is—is to perceive with a sudden jolt of recognition just how much work, how much labor, has gone into the writing of these novels. It is to embrace the exact opposite of what Lenù wills us to believe about her writing process in our final moments with her.

I don't pretend to understand why my sense of disappointment (or betrayal) has lingered. As I write this paragraph, I find myself renewing it, feeling it more acutely in the process of trying to pin it down. Maybe it's because I can't remember the last time I derived such pleasure from reading a novel that I forgot it was a novel—the last time I let myself believe in a kind of immediate, intimate relationship between the writer, the written word, and my absorption of it. That configuration may sound mystical or childish, but reading Ferrante has made me feel a little like a child again; a child for whom the workings of the world (and books and people) are infinitely mysterious and confusing and may remain as such. "Unlike stories, real life, when it has passed, inclines toward obscurity, not clarity," Lenù writes. The treatment of the unknown in all four novels is what compensates us—as readers—for the betrayal of the pat ending. For me, such obscurity has been, in its own unexpected way, a form of restitution.

—Merve

New York, NY
Katherine, September 18

Dear Friends,

As our hot summer of Ferrante stretches on, inexhaustibly, into fall, I know I'm not the only one still seeing her everywhere, even in places she doesn't really belong.

This one, though, is not a stretch.

Last weekend, for the first time ever, two Italians met in the US Open Final. Flavia Pennetta and Roberta Vinci have been friends since childhood, growing up in neighboring cities in the heel and later rooming together in Rome. In 1999, they teamed up to win the girls' doubles championship at the French Open. When they faced off as kids, Vinci always won. As adults, Pennetta has the edge. This was undeniably the biggest match of both of their careers.

Pennetta won, but Vinci hugged her so close and smiled and laughed so hard during the trophy ceremony that you might've thought their roles were reversed. "You have to know," Pennetta told the crowd, "we know each other since we are really young. . . . We spend so much time together, we can write a book about our life."

Really. She said *book.*

Another thing about these women: they're adults. At thirty-three, Pennetta is the oldest first-time major champion in the Open Era, having played her best at the moment when her body should've been breaking down. She announced her retirement immediately following the match.

Back in Ferranteland, Lenù and Lila are adults, too. They know things of the world. They are known. They both have names that precede them. But with knowledge and name come other losses: innocence, potential, various kinds of mutability and flexibility, and eventually, always, the body itself.

The name. The body. Two of the most formidable tyrants of adulthood. Can we resist them? In a world of greater injustice, should we even try? There are so many questions that play out in the long match of Lenù v. Lila, but I keep coming back to these.

Lenù, the earthy, curvy, lustful one, is also the one who wants to be known. She is desperate for her name to outlast her. Lila, the narrow pragmatist, would rather work surreptitiously, speak obliquely, and then just disappear. Lenù embraces sex and pregnancy and childbirth. She even renews her romance with her mother as she nurses her in her final sickness. Lila has no use for sex, hates pregnancy, and saves her most crippling anxiety for the kinds of violence she can't control. These two are, as sportscasters love to point out, a study in contrasts.

"What to do then?" Lenù asks as she struggles to write a balanced tale, one that honors both of their truths. "Admit yet again that she's right? Accept that to be adult is to disappear, is to learn to hide to the point of vanishing? Admit that, as the years pass, the less I know Lila?" (*SLC*, 25).

Pregnant together in 1980, their counterpoints come into sharp relief—sharper still when the historic earthquake strikes that November. Naples has been torn apart and our girls are huddled in Lenù's car, where Lila tells her, for the first time, about her visions of dissolving boundaries:

But, even now as I pondered the wave of Lila's distraught words, I felt that in me fear could not put down roots, and even the lava, the fiery stream of melting matter that I imagined inside the earthly globe, and the fear it provoked in me, settled in my mind in orderly sentences, in harmonious images, became a pavement of black stones like the streets of Naples, a pavement where I was always and no matter what the center. I gave myself weight, in other words, I knew how to do that, whatever happened. Everything that struck me—my studies, books, Franco, Pietro, the children, Nino, the earthquake— would pass, and I, whatever *I* among those I was accumulating, I would remain firm, *I* was the needle of the compass that stays fixed while the lead traces circles around it. Lila on the other hand—it seemed clear to me now, and it made me proud, it calmed me, touched me—struggled to feel stable. She couldn't, she didn't believe it. However much she had always dominated all of us and had imposed and was still imposing a way of being, on pain of her resentment and her fury, she perceived herself as a liquid and all her efforts were, in the end, directed only at containing herself. (*SLC*, 179)

Lenù, who writes—airy calling—feels solid. Even her personal life, even geologic disaster, even the violence of the Years of Lead cannot undo her stability, for she can always marshal it into orderly sentences. She can always put herself at the center. Lila, on the other hand, Lila who dominates, who negotiates, who *acts*—she is the one who feels liquid.

It's a high point for Lenù, who takes pride in her stability, and in her ability to comfort her ailing friend. Her game, for the moment, seems better. She can survive with this game. She can win.

I can't help invoking the language of tennis because, like tennis players, these two watch each other constantly. They battle, but from a distance, as though life has erected a net between them that they are rule-bound not to cross. Lenù takes the earthquake match, but the rivalry endures. Soon Lila is back to dominating and to exposing the weaknesses in Lenù's game:

Eh, she said once, what a fuss for a name: famous or not, it's only a ribbon tied around a sack randomly filled with blood, flesh, words, shit, and petty thoughts. She mocked me at length on that point: I untie the ribbon—*Elena Greco*—and the sack stays there, it functions just the same, haphazardly, of course, without virtues or vices, until it breaks. On her darkest days she said with a bitter laugh: I want to untie my name, slip it off me, throw it away, forget it. (*SLC*, 455).

Suddenly, Lenù's solidity seems not so solid after all. How can *Elena Greco* be the fixed needle of the compass when she's only a body—a sausage, really!—that will inevitably be consumed? By this point in the story, Lila has been wholly battered by life: Tina gone, Rino and countless others dead. Yet her nihilism preexists personal tragedy. It feels truer than Lenù's comparatively blessed life, truer even than Lenù's art.

All along, Lenù has feared that Lila is the real writer, the one secretly excelling at the thing by which Lenù has made her name. In middle age Lila spends an enormous amount of time in the library, researching Neapolitan history, an activity Lenù can only imagine as a prelude to a book, a work of genuine, mature genius. And what if that were true?

In that case her book would become—even only for me—the proof of my failure, and reading it I would understand how I should have written but had been unable to. . . . My image as a writer who had emerged from a blighted place and gained success, esteem, would reveal its insubstantiality. . . . My entire life would be reduced merely to a petty battle to change my social class. (*SLC*, 459)

Here's another tennis truism: Lila is in her head. While I think we mostly have to understand this as a manifestation of Lenù's self-doubt, it also highlights the inescapable selfishness in the quest to make one's name.

For her part, Lila denies writing anything at all: "To carry out any project to which you attach your own name you have to love yourself, and she had told me, she didn't love herself, she loved nothing about herself" (*SLC*, 462). This, too, is probably too strong, but it's a sentiment that generates tingles in this lengthy pseudonymous work.

In the end, Lenù endures, in name and body both. Lila's name endures only to the extent that Lenù betrays her. She has written about her, first in *A Friendship* and now again in the books we are reading, something she promised Lila she would never do.

But can we really be upset about that betrayal? Without it, we'd have no Neapolitan cycle! Everybody wants to be Lila: the genius, the resister, the living principle. But here at "The Slow Burn," let's admit again that we are not. We are the self-loathing Lenùs, and so is everyone who writes about Ferrante and attaches her name to the work.

So what, then, about Lila's body, which endures so much abuse over the course of the Neapolitan novels—as indeed all bodies do, if they live long enough? Like Tina, she might be anywhere. But unlike Tina, we sense that she must be alive, that she has merely taken off her ribbon and taken her exit, after so much grueling, thankless work.

Perhaps it is a stretch to see Ferrante in the all-Italia US Open. After all, Pennetta's retirement was taken in victory, with her old friend cheering her on. Lila's is the opposite: the game over, the friendship too. Lenù is the one left with the trophies, and what hard-earned trophies they are: the successful novel, the cheap and ugly dolls.

—Katherine

New Haven, CT
Jill, September 21

Dear everyone,

"I'm afraid that the last part has only the appearance of good writing."[17] That's our real-life author, Elena Ferrante, in a recent interview. She is talking about her earlier novel, *The Days of Abandonment*. The interviewer's follow-up question is, "Do you think this anxiety of yours has something to do with being a woman?"

Ferrante sidesteps the question. She talks about how, as a girl, she thought that a great book had to have a man as its narrator. Even her female heroines would imitate the men, their freedom and determination like the freedom and determination of men. Ferrante didn't want to write like Jane Austen; she wanted to write like Flaubert or Tolstoy. And then, abruptly, at the end of her answer: "That phase lasted a long time, until I was in my early twenties, and it left profound effects." *What effects, Elena? What happened after? A phase implies punctuality, that this phase of writing like the men came and went, so what next?* Our author does not say.

What Ferrante doesn't say is *Yes, I worry about being a bad writer because I'm a woman, because insecurity and worrying are womanish things.* Or, *I worry about being a bad writer because I exist in a largely male canonical tradition that positions female authors as imposters or upstarts.* One answer picks up on the condescension that can be read into the question, the other views it sympathetically. I like Ferrante for side-stepping, but that's neither here nor there.

What is more significant about that moment, the stated fear that past writing is bad writing, is the way it refracts a major plotline in the novels. In *The Story of the Lost Child*, the fictional Elena, for our purposes Lenù, worries about being a bad writer too. Lenù also worries about being a bad mother and a bad feminist. In some way, in the world of the novels, these roles seem to exist as part of a zero-sum game. Lenù leaves Italy to publicize her novels but then worries that she is abandoning her children (good writer! bad mother!). While caring for her children and lover (good mother!), Lenù lets her work slide, perpetually putting off the writing of a new novel (bad feminist! bad writer!). There is a devastating scene near the end of the book when Lenù's daughter Elsa pulls some of these earlier novels from the shelves and starts readings them aloud, ironically, maliciously, to combined effect (bad mother! bad writer! good feminist!):

> I had stressed certain themes: work, class conflicts, feminism, the marginalized. Now I was hearing my sentences chosen at random and they seem embarrassing. Elsa—Dede was more respectful, Imma more cautious—was reading in an ironic tone from my first novel, she read from the story about the invention of women by men, she read from books with many prizes. Her voice skillfully highlighted flaws, excesses, tones that were too exclamatory, the aged ideologies that I had supported as indisputable truths. Above all she paused with amusement on the vocabulary, she repeated two or three times words that had long since passed out of fashion and sounded foolish. (SLC, 458)

If Lila calls Lenù a bad mother, and Elsa suggests that she is a bad writer, it's really Nino who hits the nail on the head vis-à-vis political action more generally: "He teased me good-humoredly for always taking, in his view, a middle position. He made fun of my halfway feminism, my halfway Marxism, my halfway Freudianism, my halfway Foucault-ism, my halfway subversiveness" (SLC, 394).

I think of these passages whenever I see the Neapolitan cycle named a feminist epic. For me, the evaluation (feminist!/not feminist!) is not a particularly productive entryway into this zero-sum game. Lenù makes many choices, and some of them do not align with even the most general framework of a feminist or radical politics.

Lenù does not participate, except in a half-hearted spectatorial way, in the radicalisms of the 1970s. She claims to like "subversive words, words that denounced the compromises of the parties and the violence of the state" (*SLC*, 85), but not political actions, not demonstrations or meetings themselves (85). She escapes into the couple form, into a singular, almost contained relationship with Nino that makes the police, the checkpoints, the murders, mere "paving stones on which we marked the time of our relationship" (87). After learning that Nino has been lying about his separation from his wife, Lenù acknowledges a particularly sharp discrepancy between her words and her actions:

> Although I now wrote about women's autonomy and discussed it everywhere, I didn't know how to live without his body, his voice, his intelligence. It was terrible to confess it, but I still wanted him, I loved him more than my own daughters. At the idea of hurting him and of no longer seeing him I withered painfully, the free and educated woman lost her petals, separated from the woman-mother and the woman-mother was disconnected from the woman-lover, and the woman-lover from the furious whore, and we all seemed on the point of flying off in different directions. (*SLC*, 101)

Very early in this series, I complained that fiction for and about young girls, in the mode of *The Babysitters Club*, allowed for a limited economy of character types: the smart one, the pretty one, the artistic one. Here is the same problem, though set in the terms of adulthood. To be the woman-mother is to give up the woman-lover and the woman-writer, and vice versa, on all sides.

This is a problem the novel cycle does not solve. So it is not all that surprising then, that when we talk about the end of the Neapolitan cycle the words that keep getting invoked are these ones: *betrayal* and *disappointment*.

Katherine points out that we wouldn't get the Neapolitan cycle if Lenù were a better friend, one that kept her promises. "But can we really be upset about that **betrayal**? Without it, we'd have no Neapolitan cycle!" For Merve, it is a more cumulative reaction, acquired through hours of frantic reading: "By the time I finished, I was exhausted, sated, and yet, much to my own surprise, **disappointed** by where I—and where Lila and Lenù and Naples and the modern world as such—had ended up. Why was I **disappointed**?" (bold mine).

I feel disappointed, too. But in all these cases, the disappointment is with Lenù, the fictional character, not the books themselves. I am disappointed that she is a bad friend, or a bad feminist, sometimes a halfway Marxist or halfway radical. What does it mean, exactly, to be disappointed with a fictional character's choices at the end of a novel but not disappointed with the novel itself? It's not as though I wished Ferrante had made Lenù into some model feminist-radical-lover-mother propaganda. It's not as though I expect, from a novel, a formula for how to be a woman in the world.

The Story of the Lost Child is no manifesto. Who would want it to be? It is the story that an imposter might write, knowing herself to be one. An upstart's novel, of bad mothers and bad feminists, bad politicos, of the kind of self-regard necessary to close oneself off in a room of one's own and write away the day. Or better, it is a story of the trade-offs that went into the making of Elena Greco, the novelist. Maybe it is better to say that my disappointment lies with the realism of the novels that is so like this world, where there is no purely good choice, no correct answer in choosing between mother, friend, feminist, radical, writer, lover.

What does it say, finally, that I have been fretting this last week or so, after finishing the Neapolitan cycle, that maybe I have become too personally attached to these books, too subjective, sentimental, uncritical? I've caught some sort of flu from my students and am sitting here amidst all the Kleenex, in a Dayquil haze, worried that this last post, on disappointment and endings, is really bad writing, maybe even dipping into bad feminism, or bad radicalism, in favor of literary congratulation. It's not funny-ha-ha, but it's something: The thing I keep coming back to is that terrible interview question, the one that can only be side-stepped, "Do you think this anxiety of yours has something to do with being a woman?"

Love,
Jill

Princeton, NJ
Sarah, September 25

For the last time—dear Jill, Katherine, Merve—

Once upon a time, we wondered: What are the stakes of Ferrante's realism? What does the real contain for her? By what means, in what strange forms, does she enclose it? Looking at the first book, we talked about the occult tendencies of Ferrante's style, markedly *not* magical realism but sometimes lurking somewhere nearby. Now that we've reached the end, I wonder if it's time to revisit these questions via a related genre: the fairy tale.

After all, from the beginning, but especially in the last two books, the Neapolitan cycle invokes a number of modern fairy tales. Both the title of this last book, of course, and its cover (an ad for EuroDisney Naples?) point directly at this relationship.

So what are the fairy stories that Lenù and Lila grow up with? First of all, Ferrante's equivalent of the thinking reader's twentieth-century princess fantasy: the autonomous and respected female intellectual. Second, the familiar story of class ascension and bourgeois ambition. Third, in perpetual tension with the second, the revolutionary struggle. We've all felt the pull of these potentially transformative narratives throughout the books, and we have all expressed it in different moments over the course of the summer. We *wanted* so much for Lenù and Lila! For many brief, shining moments scattered throughout the books, we longed desperately for them to stay friends, to foment revolution, to make art, to be good mothers, to save the world; or if not the world, then at least the neighborhood; if not the neighborhood, then at least each other.

But as Jill notes, Lenù could never be "some model feminist-radical-lover-mother" (I'd add to that "writer"). After all, Ferranteland isn't fairyland. In fact, the issue here isn't even the dream of magically having it all. The real question here, as Jill also highlights, seems to be more grim (ha!): Can Lenù, or any woman, occupy even *one* of those roles without consequences for the others? Or is that seemingly simple desire as futile, in the bleak and limited modern world—*our* bleak and limited modern world—as wishing on a star?

The structures and tropes of the fairy tale also emerge as the fourth book wends, somewhat wearily, to its conclusion. I can't help but think about the punctual reappearances of Nino Sarratore as a kind of incrementally repetitive warning that our failed heroine Lenù consistently disregards, as he devolves from Marxist Pixie Dream Boy[18] to Reactionary Seedy Bluebeard. But Lenù doesn't heed the warnings until too late, as Nino moves blithely from Lenù to Lila to Lenù again, carelessly tossing the ruined lives of other women and their assorted lovechildren in his cabinet of banal, philandering conquests along the way.

Nino's personal unfaithfulness emerges nastily alongside his political unfaithfulness. Notably, the couple's final break is forced not only by his sordid tryst with the nanny but by his condescending dismissal of the magic—fairy tale—idea of revolution: One time he was lecturing Dede . . . and to soften his pragmatism, I said:

"The people, Dede, always have the possibility of turning everything upside down." Good-humoredly he replied, "Mamma likes to make up stories, which is a great job. But she doesn't know much about how the world we live in functions, and so whenever there's something she doesn't lie she resorts to a magic word: let's turn everything upside down." (*SLC*, 229)

We long for a better, more radical, more rigorous Lenù to put him in his place, but of course, Ferrante is pointedly not Angela

Carter and *The Story of the Lost Child* is not "The Bloody Chamber." This is a story *about* the seventies; it is not written *from* the seventies. Instead of schooling him, Lenù accepts this condemnation and subsides meekly as "he started a lesson with Dede on the division of powers, which [Lenù] listened to in silence and agreed with from A to Z" (*SLC*, 229). Ultimately, there is no vindicating, violent second-wave feminist twist at the end of these fairy tales. Instead, the surprise comes in the bathetic letdown of their failures. By the time Lenù is totally free of Nino's spell, they're both old and sad, and her ultimate rejection of him is one marked with weariness and anxiety, not fierce vindication: "I found [Nino] large, bloated, a big, ruddy man with thinning hair who was constantly celebrating himself. Getting rid of him, after the funeral, was difficult. I didn't want to listen to him or even look at him. He gave me an impression of wasted time, of useless labor, that I feared would stay in my mind, extending into me, into everything" (SLC, 470).

Looking back, "Bluebeard" isn't the only fairy tale I see woven into the personal and political fabric of the Neapolitan novels. We wondered about the significance of Lila's passion for designing shoes way back when—notably, just after her authorship of the mythical "Blue Fairy" story—and in retrospect, it seems to me that it was another almost-magic source of thwarted possibility, another tantalizing but doomed gesture towards a happy ending. After all, remember the Grimm tale, "The Elves and the Cobbler": A poor, honest shoemaker has only enough scraps of leather to make one pair of shoes. In the morning, he discovers that it has been miraculously marvelously crafted in the night. He sells them and has enough money to make two pairs; multiply that several times, and he's all of a sudden back on his feet, as it were. One night, he and his wife stay up to see who their strange nocturnal craftsmen are, and find two tiny, naked elves, working away like mad. To show their gratitude, the cobbler and his wife sew tiny clothes and shoes for the elves and lay them out the next night. The elves, delighted, don their new attire and dance away, never to be seen again. The now-successful shoemaker and his wife live happily ever after.

Lila, miraculous creator that she is, is the prodigious elf—but as we know, neither she nor her shoemaker father and brother live happily ever after, an early indication in book 1 of the other thwarted fairy tales we're yet to encounter.

Now—follow me on this weird intertextual journey—put that alongside that the curious history of revolutionary shoemakers that Eric Hobsbawm and Joan Wallach Scott depict in "Political Shoemakers":

> To say that shoemakers, or any other trade, have a reputation for radicalism may, of course, mean one or more of three things: a reputation for militant action in movements of social protest, whether confined to the trade in question or not; a reputation for sympathy or association with, or activity in, movements of the political left; and a reputation as what might be called ideologists of the common people. . . . Shoemakers as a trade had, in the nineteenth century, a reputation for radicalism in all three senses.[19]

As Hobsbawm and Scott later state, "There can be little doubt . . . that as worker-intellectuals and ideologists shoemakers were exceptional," and furthermore, they were frequently prolific readers and writers: "Who says cobbler surprisingly often says journalist and versifier, preacher and lecturer, writer and editor."[20] Sound familiar? As a worker-intellectual, Lila is, as both the student radicals and her compatriots at the Soccavo factory realize, "exceptional."

On a neat textual level, tale and essay dovetail nicely. They both address anxieties about speed of modern manufacture and fair compensation for skilled labor (though those elves should definitely unionize). For our Ferrante-centric purposes, though, let me just highlight the idea that Lila is, through the bifocal lens of these folkloric and historical texts, both elf *and* shoemaker— a doubly mythologized figure. Again, though, we see that neither of these folkloric roles fully function in the world of Ferrante's Naples, perhaps another reason that Lila, the vessel of so much transformative potential, *has to* disappear.

On that over-determined symbolic note, I also keep thinking about another author for whom fairy tale/folkloric tropes offer structure and a way of framing the political, Bertolt Brecht. Every time I encounter the dramatis personae that open each novel, I cannot help but think of Brecht's characters in parable plays like *The Caucasian Chalk Circle*. The cross-cutting of realist(ic), individual characters like Lenù and Lila with impersonal, folkoric epithets like "The Porter's Family" and "The Shoemaker's Family" recall Brecht's similarly interspersed cast of characters, made up of both named characters (Grusha, Michael, Simon), stock figures ("First Architect," "Fat Prince"), and one who moves between modes (The Singer). There's something in Ferrante's theatrical framing device that evokes a Brechtian alienation from these characters, even as the body of the text itself—"such drama!"—invites us to identify, or at least to *try* to identify, with Lila and Lenù as real people. Unlike Brecht's epic theatre, though, there is no clear didactic, political message at the end of this cycle of dramas; they do not necessarily raise us to consciousness or rouse in us an urgency of action.

Yet this alienation effect still functions as a means to critical reading, even if not in a directly Brechtian fashion. By the end, I wonder how much we're meant to see these characters as real and how much as figures in a parable. I mean, obviously they're both. But in the light of the personal connection we form with the novels' characters and world—that which breeds the sense of disappointment and betrayal that we've all commented on in the ending—is it possible that it is this very disappointment that gives the last book a certain kind of critical heft? Is our by-now-complete alienation from Lenù actually necessary for a clear-sighted examination of the crises of female existence, or radicalism, or authorship that Ferrante depicts?

Finally, in the finale's return to the scene of childhood, Ferrante ends with a weary critique of the very idea that we grow up believing in the recuperative nature of tale-telling. "Epilogue: Restitution" recalls, in some ways, the epilogue to yet another modern fairy tale, Ian McEwan's *Atonement*. Lenù, like McEwan's manipulative author Briony, never quite relinquishes the very childish idea that rewriting a story can somehow remake it. But of course, writing a story the way you wish it could end does nothing at all, despite Briony's famous claim that "the attempt was all." Ultimately, none of these fairy tales come to their clear, much-longed for, written and rewritten ends, for—to quote Merve quoting Lenù—"Unlike stories, real life, when it has passed, inclines toward obscurity, not clarity." Obscurity and irresolution, uncertainly ever after.

As ever,
Sarah

II

ESSAYS (2018)

UNFORM

SARAH CHIHAYA

1.

It's taken me the last ten months to completely reread all of Elena Ferrante's books to date: her three shorter novels, the Neapolitan Quartet, the amusingly hellish children's book *The Beach at Night*, and *Frantumaglia*. It's hard to say exactly why it took so long. I am a fast reader and have traditionally been a very fast reader of Ferrante in particular. Even in the midst of "The Slow Burn," a self-declared experiment in slow-form criticism, I couldn't help but speed through each volume of the quartet the first time, even if it was in the ultimate service of processing slowly. Those initial readings were rowdy and impassioned and even a little brutish, as first readings usually are, and the letters I wrote in response to them are—I think—animated by at least some of that breathless energy. The effect of this long rereading process, however, has been the opposite: rather than panting hotly through the books, I've found myself turning the pages slowly, sighing achy sighs.

Rereading Ferrante is hard. It is an exercise in self-inflicted surgery, wherein you painstakingly extract the heart she forcibly ripped from your chest the first time around—all the while knowing full well that, over the course of the book, you're going to put it back and take it out again (and again and *again*). But different things hurt this time around too, and different things amaze, confuse, confound, delight, repel. This rereading, at once knowing and unknowing, is weirdly exciting. So, this slowness clearly was not because I was bored, or tired, or unwilling—in fact, the opposite was true. I'd look forward to reading twenty or thirty pages of Ferrante every day, but I found myself somehow unable to continue beyond that, to sustain long readings of a hundred, two hundred, or even three hundred pages the way I had the first time. The Neapolitans actually lend themselves to this kind of staggering, foot-dragging read; their inconsistent numbered sections accumulate uncertainly while maintaining the metronomic illusion of a steady tempo. The few sections I'd read every night were somehow too much and too little at once, a bizarre oscillation that left me in a fretful state of half-resistance, half-immersion—a strange and, I have to admit, oddly titillating friction of discomfort and delight. Those irrepressible exhalations of this go-round were in equal parts ones of pleasure and something that is not pleasure but also neither ennui nor pain.

Rereading like this—feeling both impelled to continue and compelled to stop—made me wonder about something that has been on my mind since I first picked up *My Brilliant Friend*: what do we actually *enjoy* about reading Ferrante? Is *enjoy* even the right verb for the visceral responses provoked by these texts? Legions of her critics and fans attest to the manifold pleasures of the Neapolitan novels, but they don't often clarify what exactly they are. Yes, Ferrante gives her readers pleasure, but we cannot always say what that pleasure is or, more esoterically, *how* that pleasure acts on or in us. There are some obvious surface-level answers. Pleasure might have to do with the seeming plottiness of the novels (though plot as we know it becomes less and less important or even compelling), it might have to do with the textured world of the neighborhood (though in itself, the neighborhood remains a densely unknowable space), it might have to do with identification with one or the other or both of our two brilliant friends (though simple identification is always framed as a problem, an impulse both desired and not to be trusted). These are the obvious ways to "enjoy" Ferrante, to find her immediately "captivating" as James Wood's somewhat out-of-context cover blurb suggests.

But I don't think that these superficial delights, redolent though they are of the standard practices and conventions of what some critics might brush off as mere pleasure reading, are at all the things that generate the most intense pleasure in reading Ferrante—at least, not for me. No, the strange, disturbing, confusing, magnetic, compulsive, and often horribly ecstatic pleasure of reading Ferrante's fiction is in fact situated in the ungraspable nature of its perturbations. The clearly defined aspects of structural convergences, descriptive writing, character work—these small formal satisfactions drift limply atop the vast, seething unknowability of the *real* real that strains to break through these artificial constraints, the irrepressible and irresistible disorder that Ferrante calls *frantumaglia* that churns under the shaky scaffolding of the knowable or sayable. To me, it becomes increasingly clear that the dangerous height of my pleasure in reading Ferrante is the feeling that she, and we with her, are on the cusp of disintegration of the safely contained forms of fiction and of life. To give yourself over to the Neapolitan novels is to feel at once like you are wholly enclosed within the world of the books (both within their surprising unities of place, action, and time, and within their luxuriant, multivolume bulk) and like that entire, encompassing world is always on the brink of utter rupture and dissolution.

Perversely, this incipient destruction of form is itself a distinctly formal pleasure, ripe for exegesis—Ferrante is one of those writers you look at and say, "How does she do this? How can this work?"

But I also think we need to conceive of it equally as formal pleasure's uncanny other: a matter of *un*form and *un*pleasure.

2.

The last Ferrante book I read was *Frantumaglia: A Writer's Journey.* I'd been resistant to it, peevishly upset by the idea of it. I am that kind of Ferrante reader who does not want to know more. I dutifully preordered my copy of Goldstein's translation, and when it arrived, I added it to the unstable archipelago of books-I-should-read-but-probably-won't that extends across a treacherous strait of my office floor. Yet when I unwillingly excavated it for the purposes of this essay, it instantly gave shape to the shapeless conceptual matter I'd been slowly composing in my readings of the novels. About a hundred pages in, I texted a friend:[1]

> *I am reading frantumaglia rn and it is so good it makes me want to curl up and DIE*

It slays me because in its jumble of self-described tesserae (mosaic tiles) that frequently feel out the same concepts, turning them over and over, I saw many iterations of the very thing to which I'd been trying to give shape in my own thinking. Ferrante invokes the dialect word *frantumaglia* incessantly, and each usage speaks more closely to the thing I'd been feeling out tentatively as unform:

> *Frantumaglia*: Bits and pieces whose origin is difficult to pinpoint, and which make a noise in your head, sometimes causing discomfort.[2]

The frantumaglia is the part of us that escapes any reduction to words or other shapes, and that in moments of crisis dissolves the entire order within which it seemed to us we were stably inserted. Every interior state is, ultimately, a magma that clashes with self-control, and it's that magma we have to try to describe, if we want the page to have energy. (*FR*, 312–13)

Our entire body, like it or not, enacts a stunning resurrection of the dead just as we advance toward our own death. We are . . . interconnected. And we should teach ourselves to look deeply at this interconnection—I call it a tangle, or, rather, *frantumaglia*—to give ourselves adequate tools to describe it. (*FR*, 366)

Tangle, magma, "bits and pieces"—these object-images are not sufficient to get at the sensational texture of the frantumaglia, which contains, in the way Ferrante describes it, both matter and time. It is at once both the jumbled and confused, mobile *stuff* of the inner and outer worlds that we cannot contain or control, and the *moment* of breakdown, when we stop the desperate shape-work of form-making, and dissolve back into that terrifying mass.

3.

From the very beginning of *My Brilliant Friend*, we enter into a world that is made of unpredictable stuff: people and things are revoltingly compounded of malleable living matter, imbued with odd powers and poisons. As a child, Lenù imagines the very water and air swarming with foul, creaturely life:

Tiny, almost invisible animals that arrived in the neighborhood at night, they came from the ponds, from the abandoned train cars beyond the embankment, from the stinking grasses called *fetienti*, from the frogs, the salamanders, the flies, the rocks, the dust, and entered the water and the food and the air, making our mothers, our grandmothers as angry as starving dogs.[3]

The world is a pestilent and arbitrary place, in which even language is frighteningly vivified, "full of words that killed: croup, tetanus, typhus, gas, war, lathe, rubble, work, bombardment, bomb, tuberculosis, infection." This compendium of nouns, at once abstract and concrete to young Lenù, pairs with a succession of "things that seemed normal" (*MBF*, 33) that, invested with the dark magic of childhood myth, could also kill you, like drinking water that's too cold, or swallowing gum or cherry pits, or being hit on the temple. Seen through this dirty scrim of fear and confusion, the whole neighborhood is as dangerously murky and undefined as Don Achille's dark cellar, full of "things not identifiable, dark masses, sharp or square or rounded" (55) where—horror of horrors—Don Achille himself "slithered, he shuffled among the indistinct shape of things" (56). The cellar episode leads to an extended period of "tactile dysfunction" that, Lenù tells us with a disarming nonchalance, "was an enduring malaise, lasting perhaps years, beyond early adolescence" (57). This intense sensory malady renders the texture of the most ordinary objects horribly fantastical and suffused with a grossly physiological vivacity; "solid surfaces turned soft under [her] fingers or swelled up, leaving empty spaces between their internal mass and the surface skin" (57).

In these childhood years, well before her first episode of the phantasmagoric state she eventually calls dissolving margins or boundaries, Lila experiences a similar material confusion. In a moment of intense violence, as she is thrown from a window by her enraged father, she "felt absolutely certain, as she was flying toward the asphalt, that small, very friendly reddish animals were dissolving the composition of the street, transforming it into a smooth, soft material" (*MBF*, 91). The very stuff of the neighborhood is seething with a quality we might not exactly call recognizable life but rather an uncanny, cellular *liveliness*. This quality is by turns frightening, like the vile swarms of miniscule vermin or swelling membranes in Lenù's visions, or strangely reassuring, as in the near-whimsical, muppety alchemy of Lila's. So too are the people who live in it: at this time, Lenù endures the revolting sense that "[her] own body, if you touched it, was distended . . . [she] was sure that [she] had cheeks like balloons, hands stuffed with sawdust, earlobes like ripe berries, feet in the shape of loaves of bread" (57). The monstrous Don Achille is rendered even more monstrous by the vision that Lenù has of his body, composed of and intermingled with the things he illicitly deals in: "For years I imagined the pliers, the saw, the tongs, the hammer, the vise, and thousands and thousands of nails sucked up like a swarm of metal into the matter that made up Don Achille. For years I saw his body—a coarse body, heavy with a mixture of materials—emitting in a swarm salami, provolone, mortadella, lard, and prosciutto" (36). All of these early visions and sensory experiences are, of course, only precursors to the real exposure of the disorder seething just below the skin of the world, revealed gradually in Lila's episodes of dissolving margins.

Nothing in this world can be relied upon; the conventional forms of childhood experience (family, education, friends, neighborhood) are like gelatin molds into which this unpredictable and grotesque matter is poured but never completely sets. In order to truly appreciate the genuine weirdness of Ferrante's vision, we might briefly think of this alongside what Jane Bennett calls vital materiality or vibrant matter. Like Ferrante's lively materials, these are concepts that seek to undo the distinction between "dull matter (it, things) and vibrant life (us, beings)."[4] Bennett's account, in the context of the various new materialisms currently being debated, seeks to undo this distinction in order to develop a political ecology, or an ecological politics, that asks humans to imaginatively "cultivat[e] the experience of our *selves* as vibrant matter."[5] Ferrante, however, is not demonstrably interested in this kind of environmentally-minded renegotiation of how things and people interact. Instead of suggesting, as Bennett does, a Latourian network of relations between the human and nonhuman matter, Ferrante's fantastical, grotesque descriptions suggest a terrifying *sameness*: everything, including Lila and Lenù, the *stradone*, the buildings, the swarming air and water, everything might be made up of the same teeming *stuff*—what she describes in *Frantumaglia* as "a fluid matter that drags everything along in its wake" (FR, 367). The most terrifying and most real moments in the books are the ones when it seems that the true nature of this vilely vivid material might break out, and, as Lila raves during the earthquake, "the waters would break through, a flood would rise, carrying everything off in clots of menstrual blood, in cancerous polyps, in bits of yellowish fiber."[6]

The only possible way to stay safe in this magmatic and seething world is to vigilantly keep at the acts of forming and being formed: we must always think of *form* in Ferrante as a verb more than a noun. *Form*, as it is so frequently discussed in literary study (and particularly in contemporary debates about our newest formalisms) is often regarded as a thing, a thing we all define differently, but a thing or set of things nonetheless. In the Neapolitan novels, however, form or forms cannot stay static or stable for too long; people, places, and things seem always to be in the process of forming, unforming, being formed, becoming unformed. *To form* is action, or being acted on, a dynamic process to which everyone and everything is subject. Similarly, in her protean lecture-story-essay "On Form," Ali Smith writes that, "form is a matter of clear rules and unspoken understandings. . . . It's a matter of need and expectation. It's also a matter of breaking rules, of dialogue, crossover between forms. Through such dialogue and argument, form, the shaper and moulder, acts like the other thing called mould, endlessly breeding forms from forms."[7]

Form, forming; mold, molding, moldering. These processes are both natural and unnatural, as is writing itself. At the heart of Smith's reading of that troublesome single word, *form*, are both controlled buildup (the cultivation of rules) and uncontrollable breakdown ("breaking rules . . . dialogue . . . crossover"). This dialogic process—form in perpetual fluxing motion—leads to the mold-like, thrillingly grotesque proliferation, "endlessly breeding forms from forms." There's something neurotic about this compulsive artistic impulse to create new forms out of old ones, and in so doing, to break them down, to do what "the other thing called mould" does—which is to say, to decompose them, to mulch them, to breed them together in new and stranger lives.

This vital moldiness or mold*ing*ness is visible throughout the four volumes of *L'amica geniale*, as they are singularly titled in Italy. Ferrante's sharp invocation and abrupt dismissal of specific narrative and novelistic forms (the fairy tale, the children's book, the love story, the Bildungsroman, the *Künstlerroman*, and many more) does not impose any one of them as *the* predominant form of *L'amica geniale*; there is no such thing. As they enter and exit the text (and circle back, and slide out again), each of the forms invoked suffer various breakdowns and are demonstrated to be insufficient to the task of shaping Lila and Lenù's lives at any length. But in their different ways, each of them *form* the text, as they move in and out of the book's thousands of pages, and interestingly, each of them are themselves somehow *unformed* by contact with the text itself. We must reexamine and renegotiate the expected parameters of forms we think we know, like the fairy tale or the Bildungsroman, as the frantumaglia of Ferrante's Naples batters and tumbles against their constraints.

Ferrante, it seems, is an inveterate lover of genres but a philandering manipulator of them. As she writes in *Frantumaglia*, "I can't respect the rules of genres—the reader who reads me convinced that I will give him a thriller or a love story or a Bildungsroman will surely be disappointed. Only the weave of events interests me and so I avoid cages with fixed rules" (FR, 279). The rich "weave of events" that comprises *L'amica geniale* is tinted and illuminated by the different tropes of discourse and motifs of character or plot type that given genres introduce, but the book as a whole refuses to conform to the conventions of a single one. Indeed, the book refuses to conform to the conventions of the writing of narrative— most importantly, our desire to trust it—as we expect them in a realist novel full stop:

> Maybe capturing the fluidity of existences on the page means avoiding stories that are too rigidly defined. We're all subject to continuous modification, but, to escape the anguish of impermanence, we camouflage it, until old age, with countless impressions of stability, the most important of which emanate precisely from narratives, especially when someone tells us: that's how it happened. I don't particularly like that kind of book; I prefer books in which not even the narrator knows what happened. . . . In the Neapolitan Quartet, I wanted everything to take shape and then lose its shape. (FR, 368)

The pleasure one finds in the supposed perfection of novelistic form, in the precise and proportional lineaments of a world made by, say, Henry James, is the very opposite of the visceral pleasure-unpleasure I find in Ferrante's writing, where "everything take[s] shape and then loses its shape." Like the relationships and the disorderly city it depicts, the Neapolitan Quartet is caught up in an endless struggle between the desire to inhabit a singular, stable form and the impartially cruel impossibility of that desire—the undeniable multidirectional tide of the frantumaglia, the hectic but irresistible activity of unforming and being unformed that undoes any progress that the busy work of form might accomplish.

4.

If *unform* is a strange or uncomfortable idea to consider, perhaps it is because *un-* is a strange and uncomfortable prefix. What does it mean to *un-* a word? To un-do, un-ravel, un-make, be un-dead? In *Frantumaglia*, Ferrante mulls over a Spanish word, *desamor*, that Ann Goldstein translates as "unlove," contemplating what exactly it means for love to be un-ed:

> I'm more hesitant about *"desamor"* [unlove], I have to think about it. How does the word sound in Spanish? My characters are not at all without love, not in the sense that we give the word. The love that Delia, Olga, and Leda have experienced in different forms has, in their confrontation with life, certainly been disfigured, as after a disaster, but it preserves a powerful energy, so it's love put to the test, eviscerated, and yet alive. (FR, 176)

Ferrante here is uncertain about the packaging of her three early novels in a single volume for her Spanish publisher, under the title *Las Crónicas del desamor* (which the press itself translates with sad conventionality as *Chronicles of Heartbreak* and which appears in Italian as *Cronache del mal d'amore*, lovesickness). *Desamor* seems to Ferrante not exactly right. She points out that a distorted or disfigured love continues to be love all the same, not its absence. Regardless of her reading of *desamor*, though, I am attracted to Goldstein's strong, odd English *un*-word, *unlove*. We cannot say, as

Ferrante does of *desamor*, that unlove is "*without* love." We might instead read the un- in *unlove* as undoing, unravelling, unmaking—a processual and active thing that *does* "preserv[e] a powerful energy," and is in fact more *alive* and vital than the malingering, after-the-fact quality of "heartbreak" or "lovesickness."[8] Her description of the love her characters experience inflects the way I have been thinking about both form and pleasure in the Neapolitans: "put to the test, eviscerated, and yet alive."

So: *unform, unpleasure*. We might say something is *unpleasurable*, but that adjective doesn't really tell us much, just suggests a kind of sour-faced discontent. *Unpleasure*, another word that doesn't fall trippingly from the tongue but perhaps should, is a bit weirder, a bit foggier, and is not as clearly *bad* as displeasure. In psychoanalytic terms it is a kind of libidinal disruption; Freud rather ambiguously defines unpleasure (*Unlust*) in *Beyond the Pleasure Principle* in intimate relation to pleasure, saying that unpleasure is an increase in a kind of mental excitation, while pleasure is its diminution. In the familiar terms of the *fort-da* game, unpleasure is the lamentation of disappearance as the child throws away his toy ("*Fort!*") and pleasure the pert satisfaction of return as he pulls it back ("*Da!*"). Similarly, as Freud goes on to remind us, "the artistic play and artistic imitation carried out by adults . . . do not spare the spectators (for instance, in tragedy) the most painful experiences and yet can be felt by them as highly enjoyable," or, summed up concisely, art can provoke "unpleasure for one system and simultaneously satisfaction for the other."[9] Seen in this light, the Neapolitan novels operate in a similar tension, with regards to both (un)form and (un)pleasure. We might ultimately derive something like conventional readerly pleasure from Ferrante's inventive transfiguration of the familiar elements of novelness—for example, genre, character, plotting, temporality—that *L'amica geniale* engages. Yet along the way, this pleasure is disrupted (and ultimately heightened) by the various moments in which those basic elements of novelistic form begin to break down and seem at risk of disintegration. The reader's experience is thus one of oscillating pleasure and unpleasure, and that oscillation provides its own unique, often unsettling thrill. Likewise, what we might view as the formal innovations of Ferrante's prose and structure are actually generated by the irruption of that underlying force of disorder that is marvelous in a terrible sense, and, to use one of Ferrante's favorite images, like magma—form and unform in perpetual tension.

A pithy enactment of this tension within the frame of the book itself can be found in Lila's creation through destruction of her wedding portrait in The Story of a New Name. The photograph is one of the few things of beauty that we see widely acknowledged and celebrated as such, not only by the characters we know but also by passersby, shoppers, wandering movie stars. It is a beautiful thing in the comprehensible shape of a beautiful thing: a beautifully composed picture of a beautiful woman, in a beautiful dress and shoes, with beautiful flowers in her hair. This perfectly articulated form may superficially resemble Lila, but it is not her. In Lenù's eyes, and in ours, Lila emerges instead in the artful disarticulation of her own image, revealing her understanding of herself both in conversation and in the physical action of making-by-unmaking. The process of making the collage panel, and the thing itself when complete, seem to stir up a constant back-and-forth between what is known and unknown, seen and unseen, made and unmade. In its creation, Lila is at once brutally erased and brilliantly revealed, in both the act of reinventing the image and in the abstract provocation that remains—an obliterated face and "a very vivid eye, encircled by midnight blue and red."[10] Do we see into that eye, or does it see into us? Is its shocking aureole a bruise or war paint?

The result of this making-by-unmaking is a piece of work whose meaning far surpasses the conventionally beautiful form of the original photograph: the picture is transfigured from a thing that demurely accepts praise to a thing that contemptuously rejects it, and in so doing demands greater consideration. Similarly, it is only in the *fort-da* game of form (gone, then back again) that we completely inhabit the amplitude of readerly experience offered by the books. We can only perceive the fullness of time as the years and decades pass through their curious and unpredictable distention; we only truly sense the shapes of Lila's and Lenù's characters through the various moments when they are disfigured, lost to themselves and each other; we only ever know the neighborhood through its dark, phantasmagoric unknowability.

This back and forth of pleasure and unpleasure, form and unform, is a good start, but doesn't fully get at the lively and weird excitation that I'd like us to read into the *un-* of *unlove*. Ferrante emphasizes that the thing she wants to preserve at all costs is the disfigured yet still-living quality of love in the stories of Delia, Olga, and Leda, or in this case, of Lila and Lenù. I want to do the same for pleasure and form in her work, and argue that the *un-* of *unpleasure* or *unform* is not simply the absence of pleasure or form that alternate terms like *displeasure* or *formlessness* would suggest. Rather, I read the *un-* of these terms as active and alive, rendering them vividly uncanny versions of themselves. *Un-* is a potent invocation, a spell that doesn't make something silently disappear but instead wildly transfigures it, working a dark alchemy to make something entirely new. *Un-* is the sign and cipher of woman's creation and revolt. When Lady Macbeth calls out to the spirits to "unsex me here," she does not simply ask to be made a man; she instead invites a gloriously grotesque transformation into something that it not simply the opposite of woman but rather a new and thrilling monstrosity ("make thick my blood. . . . Come to my woman's breasts and take my milk for gall"). When Penelope unweaves what she has made each night, she does not simply buy time, she makes anew

the invisible fabric of the days that have gone and are yet to come;
the secret labor of unweaving is a strange and magical operation
whose workaday cost cannot be calculated. Paula and Keith Cohen
translate Hélène Cixous' *dé-penser* in "The Laugh of the Medusa" as
the mysterious yet imperative and powerful "to *unthink*":[11] "Woman
un-thinks the unifying, regulating history that homogenizes and
channels forces, herding contradictions into a single battlefield."[12]
Susan Winnett, taking a fair and savvy crack at Henry James's com-
plaint about the lack of tension in the thread of plot "on which to
string the pearls of detail" in writing by women, challenges us "to
start again, to see what comes of unstringing the Masterplot that
wants to have told us in advance where it is that we should take our
pleasures and what must inevitably come of them."[13] All of these
un-s wildly and thrillingly unwrite Pound's unidirectional dictum:
*Un*make it new.

In this tiny prefix there is, I think, at once a dark reinvention
and vibrant revivification at work. To go back to Ferrante: we see
in these novels both form and *un*form, working against and within
each other, seething together in their tension. "Put to the test, eviscerated, yet alive" describes perfectly the novel form, the many
other literary forms invoked, the forms of the characters themselves, the form of the city around which all of this is constructed,
all roiling with a disfiguring and unquenchable vitality: *unform*. The
experience of wholly inhabiting this tumultuous space is at once
both hideously and deliciously stimulating: *unpleasure*.

5.

In retrospect, I wonder if my last almost-year of microdosing
Ferrante has been spent in a slightly altered state of consciousness,
the way people talk about microdosing acid or MDMA, in which I've

developed my own version of Lenù's tactile dysfunction. (I regret not making the parameters of this experiment more scientific.) Part of my difficulty in writing this essay stems from the fact that my thoughts about Ferrante and the buildup of tension between form and unform are clearest to me—like the depiction of intoxication so frequently seen in movies—as a sequence of visual metaphors that fill me with the most intense and paradoxical sensation of exquisite unpleasure. Thinking about the unformed/unforming argument I'm trying to construct here, I project a series of film clips, abstract images that are fittingly suggestive rather than deductive: stained wallpaper bulging with water from a leak upstairs, about to burst; the scrabbling dance of scree down a slope that portends a massive rockslide; a grotesquely beautiful, brilliantly colored transparent membrane stretching and about to break.

But the mental technology accidentally developed in the course of writing this essay is more science fictional than the old-fashioned film clip. Some of these clips are not just visual but haptic, a Ferrante immersive VR experience made up of a wild array of unrelated sensory stimuli both laughably trivial and frighteningly intense. My argument *feels* to me like my heart has swollen to such size that my ribs about to split open, crude and violent as a spatchcocked bird. It feels like that forced collaboration of surface tension and willpower when I strain to keep tears standing in the eye from falling. It feels like turning my ankle on a broken pavement and not knowing if I will tumble into traffic. Like the warm pluck in the gut that says a late period might be about to start, after days of deepening heaviness and thickening anxiety. Like the urgent, tiny drama of whisking custard on the stovetop and not knowing if it will break. Like the horribly delicious instant in a fight when I know I am about to say something that cannot ever be taken back. Like the vertiginous rush of jolting back from a falling dream and not knowing if I am alive—and if alive, then awake—and if awake, then still who I think I am.

Trying to put all of this in words I am, and probably will always be, hung up on the moment in *Frantumaglia* when Ferrante says that, "when I write, it's as if I were butchering eels. I pay little attention to the unpleasantness of the operation and use the plot, the characters, as a tight net to pull up from the depths of my experience everything that is alive and writhing, including what I myself have driven away as far as possible because it seemed unbearable" (*FR*, 226). I similarly *feel* this sentence even as I cannot truly think it: feel that wonderful-horrible, muscular writhing of writing, that violent liveliness that twists and jerks in the hands and makes you wonder, fearfully, who or what is being channeled into the words on the page and in what unknown shape they will emerge. It is the feeling of being made and unmade, the worst feeling and also the best. It is the inmost and least knowable pleasure I have, a pleasure that penetrates so deep that it comes out on the other side of easy gratification as its terrible, marvelous other.

6.

I strongly suspect that I am not alone this histrionic, synesthetic sensitivity to Ferrante's prose. Dwelling, even temporarily, in the world she makes can make us feel unmoored and unformed in our own worlds, a powerful sensation that may or may not go away after the last page of the book. Life as she reveals it is a constant struggle between form and unform, where everything is always at risk of being reduced to a contingent fluid mass, moved by strange and arbitrary forces. If that is the case, then how can people possibly be expected to survive it? The struggle for individual personhood here is a struggle to keep oneself on form, *in* form—which is, as we've seen already, an unrelenting and often futile activity. As a result, the people we meet, especially the women, are in constant states of formal disruption, at risk of falling apart entirely, either mentally (in the case of the madwoman Melina) or physically. Consider Gigliola's unrecognizable corpse in *Those Who Leave and Those Who Stay*, a rough tumble of objects strewn about the public garden, impossible to synthesize as the silly, mercurial, living girl Lenù (and we) once knew:

> Her beautiful face was ruined, and her ankles had become enormous. Her hair, once brown, was now fiery red, and long, the way she'd had it as a girl, but thin, and spread out on the loose dirt. One foot was shod in a worn, low-heeled shoe; the other was encased in a gray wool stocking, with a hole at the big toe, and the shoe was a few feet beyond, as if she had lost it kicking against some pain or fear.[14]

The holey stocking receives as much attention as the ruined face; the garishly dyed hair scattered over the dirt is as flatly sad as the lost shoe. This assemblage is no longer Gigliola. But what *was* Gigliola, or any of the other girls of the neighborhood in the first place, but assemblages of unsynthesized elements, unrealized or unrecognized desires struggling against each other inside insufficiently thick skins? As we watch characters, both minor and major, morph through the decades, we see that the body—again, especially the female one—proves just as mutable and irruptive as the world it inhabits. The characters themselves are constantly engaged in the frenzied activity of forming and reforming themselves, in futile attempts to reach some state of safe inertia. There's even a peculiar sense that the *will* to form can effect physical change, as we see through Alfonso's eerie transformation into Lila in *The Story of the Lost Child*: "My old desk mate, with his hair down, in the elegant dress, was a copy of Lila. His tendency to resemble her, which I had long noted, came abruptly into focus, and maybe at that moment he was even handsomer, more beautiful than she" (*SLC*, 164).

This particular example, infused with both envy and revulsion, is a good reminder that the emphasis on this frenzy of forms surely has to do with our focalization through Lenù. It is she who obsessively looks for clearly defined shapes and desires them always, she who submits herself so willingly to the forming hands of others (Lila's, the Airotas', Nino's) and who so endlessly seeks the right form for her writing. Early on, when she reveals that Lila has turned beautiful, she instead says that Lila "had become shapely" (*MBF*, 142). It is Lenù who is neurotically preoccupied with her own formlessness (the "cheeks like balloons, hands stuffed with sawdust, earlobes like ripe berries" (57) of that childhood vision) and with the much-desired clarity of form achieved at times by others—most often, in both prose and in body, by Lila. Lenù seemingly works harder than anyone else at rigorous self-formation, seeking to mold herself into literary, social, and physical forms that are stable, perceptible, and hopefully compelling to herself and, more importantly, to others, yet is never content with the ones she adopts. Through these discontented eyes, Lila's apparent mastery of form—of transformative self-formation—is a source of wonder and envy. Lila is a shapeshifter, who slides through ages, names, appearances with what looks like an incredible facility. She appears, in Lenù's eyes, in a higher resolution than anyone else, and even in the moment of greatest chaos, the earthquake, Lila is clear-cut as ever: "She didn't respond, she seemed solid, the only one of all the shapes impervious to jolts, tremors" (*SLC*, 171).

Yet just as the role of "brilliant friend" shifts from Lila to Lenù at the end of the first book, a stunning reversal occurs in this moment. In the earthquake—the moment in which the frantumaglia gushes through the boundary between internal and external, undoing formal control in the mind and in the very real world—Lila reveals the secret of her multiplicity. It lies, of course, in her perpetual proximity to the unformed chaos that undergirds everything. Here, finally, as the external world dissolves into itself, we see most clearly what Lila means by *dissolving margins, dissolving boundaries*. As she desperately explains to Lenù, "the outlines of things and people were delicate, that they broke like cotton thread. She whispered that for her it had always been that way, an object lost its edges and poured into another, into a solution of heterogeneous materials, a merging and mixing" (*SLC*, 176). Lila's shapeshifting (from precocious child, to shoemaking prodigy, to wife, to tragic lover, to worker, to boss, to mother, to former mother, to nothing) is a defense mechanism, a constant invocation of the process of formation against the forces of unform, as she struggles to escape the cruel cycle of "redo, cover, uncover, reinforce, and then suddenly undo, break" (177). In the face of these revelations, Lenù realizes that, for all her fears of unwanted transformation and uncontrollable growth, she is in fact the one who makes order: she is the one who forms and is clearly formed. She takes the magma of the frantumaglia and cools it into "orderly sentences, in harmonious images . . . a pavement of black stones like the streets of Naples, a pavement where [Lenù] was always and no matter what the center" (179).

Lila's and Lenù's obsessive relations to both physical order and to specifically *writerly* order make better sense when considering the original language that Ferrante uses to describe Lila's experience. What translator Ann Goldstein describes so evocatively as "dissolving margins" or "dissolving boundaries" is *smarginare* (verb) or *la smarginatura* (noun), a peculiarly untranslatable and double-edged typographical term. *Smarginare*, oddly, indicates both excess (as when an image bleeds across its boundary, or the margin of the page), and boundedness (as in the cropping or cutting of the image to size), both the breakdown and strict maintenance of margins. It is at once extremely curious and exactly perfect that Lila should use this typographical jargon to describe her experience—seemingly an uncommon word outside the trade, one whose specificity Lenù (and Ferrante) insist upon: "Usò propria *smarginare*. Fu in quell'occasione che ricorse per la prima volta a quell verbo, si affanò a esplicitarne il senso, voleva che capissi bene cos'era la smarginatura e quanto l'atterriva."[15] This conflation of Lila herself with the printed page invites us explicitly to see the female self (the malleable body, the changeable mind) as the impossible and unstable text: Lenù is always trying to find her critical voice and her personal identity; Lila is always switching genres, plotlines, character tropes. To that end, one might think again of a text I briefly turned to earlier, Hélène Cixous's "Rire de la méduse," in which she famously rallies women to write freely and wildly, to create an *écriture feminine* that "burst[s] with forms."[16] In a sense, Lila and Lenù's story is just that— in Smith's words, Ferrante's long novel "endlessly breed[s] forms from forms." Yet the two edges of smarginatura suggest both joyfully endless production and violent limitation. Paradoxically, the page spreads beyond its limits and comes into tight shape at once. Unlike the orgiastic proliferation of forms that Cixous advocates, what we see here are the generatively tense processes of unforming and forming, always ongoing. It is almost too perfect that the typographical words we use in English for the antithetical meanings of smarginare are "cut" and "bleed": how odd and right it is that we use these dangerous words for the printed page—that thing that we, with vulnerable hope, believe can at once contain and express us better than our stupid, insufficient bodies.

8.

I had a drink with my friend Rebecca last night, one of the veteran Lila-Lenùs of my life. I am, I think, very prone to this kind of deep-cut friendship; deep-cut because it seems to go right to your core (painfully, wonderfully), and deep-cut because that kind of friend knows the words to all of your B-sides and ephemeral singles, all of those moments and memories that aren't on any top-ten list. My relationship with her has been, as they say, formative.

Last night we talked about one of the funny things about our relationship—how differently we remember things. I like to call her my memory palace because she stockpiles and catalogues moments and events in a way that I do not, cannot. I don't clearly remember any of the formative events you're supposed to remember in the traditional, plot-driven version of *Bildung*; I don't remember my first major lie or first kiss or the first time I had sex or the last time I saw a friend before he died too young. She, on the other hand, remembers word-for-word things that people said to her that became personal laws or prohibitions, granular feelings that solidified into actions and habits, moments that were definitive and shaping, events like building blocks that make her what she is today. When challenged to describe the same moment dredged up from years ago, we do it completely differently—yet these opposing memories come together and make something fuller and more true ("She was trying to understand, we were both trying to understand, and understanding was something that we loved to do" [*MBF*, 170]). We cleave to and from each other in both senses of that weirdly doubled word: we crave closeness, to form and be formed by the other, and yet we each also form ourselves *against* the other, sometimes in simple opposition but also in amorphous resistance or inexplicably violent rejection. The insufficient "covering," to use Lila's word, that we use to loosely contain these often nonsensical and lawless practices, is friendship.

A formative friendship. A formative text. Both of these things are important here because at their best, they demand critical consideration of the work of self-forming, being formed, and unforming, which—hopefully—leads towards a clearer understanding of the shape of the individual. The Neapolitan Quartet's slow enactment of a near-lifelong friendship demonstrates this work of internal tension and critique through its characters, and in a weird way, also through their readers. In *Frantumaglia*, Ferrante writes that, "We are heterogeneous fragments that, thanks to impressions of unity—elegant figures, beautiful form—stay together despite their arbitrary and contradictory nature" (*FR*, 368). The truly marvelous unpleasure of reading Ferrante has to do with the fact that she forcibly reveals those fragments that always hide under the mask of beautiful form in a text (or in a person) whether we want to see them or not. In so doing, we might look inwards and see our own rough, unfinished seams, not completely stitched together, perhaps already in the midst of falling apart. Through reading the stories of Lila and Lenù and how they read each other over the years, I am given a strange and agonizing lesson in how to read myself—not in the way that one might initially read a formative text (as a kind of knitting pattern, a design for the garment of personality) but as its opposite, a text that demands that you brutally rip away the garment of beautiful form and reveal the raw-edged fragments beneath. Not in the manner of Roland Barthes's coy textual striptease (*texte de plaisir*) or in his evocative but rather bloodless "cut" or "gape" (*texte de jouissance*), but rather, with a bodily urgency and violence. Reading Ferrante fills me with a dangerous abandon and wild disregard for disciplined self-containment. More than anything, she makes me want to write as she writes—viscerally, bloodily, "like butchering eels"—and in so doing to somehow know, like Lila reworking the portrait, that ecstasy and clarity of vision that comes with making-by-unmaking one's *own* form, to be both Orpheus and the frenzied Maenads.

In a way, thinking and feeling through Ferrante make me wonder if the whole project of literary criticism, for some of us, might be one of *un*-pleasure reading. To me, the joy of writing about a text is the twisting, rupturing, pleasurable unpleasure of unforming and *being* unformed as I work to shape an argument. To read a book to its core, to get under its skin and let it get under yours, is to engage with it in a mutual process of transformation and sometimes-ecstatic contortion. This is, some might say, highly *un*-professional (whatever this profession is), definitely *un*-objective, possibly even *un*-ethical. But for me, to write a piece of living interpretation, to share in gutsy, real conversation with a piece of art, is always to invoke *form* as a verb, not just to submit to the noun of its existence—a forming that is process-oriented but not simply procedural—and to somehow animate that constant movement in words. In my life as a critic, as in Ferrante, this is an impossible yet irresistible desire: the little stories I've told you along the way here, my shape-making narrative impulses, are the legible coverings that skim over the roiling blurriness of ongoing forming-unforming beneath, the frantumaglia of reading and being read (shades of Calvino here, too). This is the last thing I'd call *pleasure*—and yet . . .

If this risks getting too wildly abstract, consider a somewhat more sedate literary example: the first formative text we encounter in *My Brilliant Friend*, Louisa May Alcott's *Little Women*. It is an eminently lovable and hateable book, one with and against which many millions of readers have formed themselves. The reader cleaves *to* writerly Jo (or to kind, beautiful Meg, or possibly arty cool girl Amy, but—let's be honest—probably not to dull, doomed Beth), and yet the famous dissatisfactions of the ending drive her to cleave away *from* her model and from the novel. It is that dance of identification and disappointment that can make *Little Women* a powerful work of critical self-formation. We ask ourselves why we might be angry about Jo's marriage to mansplaining Professor Bhaer, or Meg's widowing, or the nagging suspicion that Amy is ultimately just Laurie's consolation prize, and in so doing, wonder what we actually want for them (ditto Lenù and Lila)—or more interestingly, what we want *via* them. To have an adult relationship with a text, or a friend, we have to first work within their constraints and then eventually work against them. It's in that pushback, the move away from the formative thing, we actually learn the most about ourselves.

This brings to mind a moment that feels like a potential point of departure and growth from *Those Who Leave and Those Who Stay*. Lenù realizes that all her form-making efforts have been molded somehow around Lila's unknowable, unpindownable, and multiplied self:

> *Become*. It was a verb that had always obsessed me, but I realized it for the first time only in that situation. *I wanted to become*, even though I had never known what. And I had *become*, that was certain, but without an object, without a real passion, without a determined ambition. I had wanted to become something—here was the point—only because I was afraid that Lila would become someone and I would stay behind. *My becoming was a becoming in her wake*. I had to start again to *become*, but for myself, as an adult, outside of her. (*TWL*, 346–47)

This is one of the moments where we see Lenù, now in her thirties, start to realize that the formative as a mode is not sustainable: to form yourself around or after someone else is only halfway to becoming. In this moment, and the months that follow, Lenù struggles to become in her own model; she and Lila do not speak, she tries to cultivate other relationships, to *unform* the habits that her relationship with Lila has created. It is, we sense, an important time for Lenù, as it leads her to her next book project about the male creation of female automatons through history. Even that most seemingly independent act of writing, however, comes out of her lasting desire to cleave to Lila, not from her; in considering this new theoretical idea, she has an unrealizable fantasy of what life would have been like if she and Lila had kept going to school together, "elbow to elbow, a perfect couple, the sum of intellectual energies, of the pleasures of understanding and the imagination. We would have written together, we would have been authors together, we would have drawn power from each other. . . . But the opportunity was gone, lost decades ago" (*TWL*, 354).

Just admitting that loss and impossibility feels sad and important but also, in its way, liberating. Yet the strongest formations have an inexorable pull back, and a few years later, in *The Story of the Lost Child*, Lenù finds herself drawn back into the old pattern she and Lila molded around each other, reconjoined by their pregnancies. In this unity, they are defined most clearly through their opposition and tension, which somehow makes them more perfectly part of the same whole: "We liked sitting next to each other, I fair, she dark, I calm, she anxious, I likable, she malicious, the two of us opposite and united, and separate from the other pregnant women, whom we observed ironically" (*SLC*, 157).

As we know from the very first page of the very first book, though, this renewed solidarity cannot last; Lila and Lenù's tale begins and ends with their final breakup, the ultimate unforming (but not erasure) of their lifelong intertwinement. It is that unforming that forms the long and winding narrative we receive in these four books. It's an intriguing thought experiment to consider the difference between this long work, *L'amica geniale*, and the short novel that Lenù produces at the end of volume 4, simply titled *Un'amicizia* ("A Friendship"). That book, whose publication revives Lenù's literary celebrity, proves the end of Lila and Lenù's relationship. Lenù speculates about what makes Lila turn away from her when it comes out, but none of her guesses seem to strike at the implicit truth, visible to Ferrante's readers if not her narrator. It is perhaps the novella's static precision and taut shapeliness, so unlike *L'amica geniale*'s long, ungainly battle between form and unform—between, in Lila's paraphrased words, "telling things just as they happened, in teeming chaos" and "work[ing] from imagination, inventing a thread"—that makes it such a dishonest and inauthentic betrayal of the truth of their lives, both together and apart (*SLC*, 464).

To keep forming ourselves as writers or people, then, means to break with the things that have formed us and to incorporate that breakage into the work we make. Maybe not forever but with some regularity and with some necessary, hopefully generative violence, like cutting a plant back to force new growth. Every time we do it though, it is freighted with danger—there is always the risk that every break might be the last. Sometimes that ur-thing, the formative object, can be pushed too far: friends that stay together through decades but no longer really know each other, texts that we've read or taught too many times and have lost their magic. Or worse, friends whose love curdles to resentment and then to silence (or total disappearance), books we come to hate because we once loved them too much. These are the risks. But breakage, Ferrante suggests, makes things new and strange; breakage—unmaking, unforming—makes *life*. We are most whole and alive ("put to the test, eviscerated, yet alive") through our splitting apart, that unformal unpleasure of imminent destruction—and creation. There's something almost religious about it, though *sacrifice* is too grim a word for this sensation. I can only describe it obliquely through citation, in this moment from A.S. Byatt, characteristically invoking just the right amount of wry but miraculously uncondescending religiosity at the happy-sad, beautiful end of *Possession* (1990): "In the morning, the whole world had a strange new smell. It was the smell of the aftermath, a green smell, a smell of shredded leaves and oozing resin, of crushed wood and splashed sap, a tart smell, which bore some relation to the smell of bitten apples. It was the smell of death and destruction and it smelled fresh and lively and hopeful."[17]

9.

I finished my rereading of *The Story of the Lost Child* at that strange moment that is no longer night and not yet dawn, the morning equivalent of twilight. In Spanish, it's *la madrugada*—I don't think we don't have a word for it in English, or as far as my limited knowledge goes, in Italian either. It's not *l'alba*, dawn; nothing so clearly marked as that. It is the loneliest time, the most liminal, the most wonderfully frightening. In Swedish it is *vargtimmen*, "wolf time," the hours between night and dawn that are always tundric and raw, even when you're bundled under heavy blankets. It's the time that most fills me with both pleasure and unpleasure. I especially love finishing a book in the wolf time, especially if it's a real wrecker— that kind of book that ends and makes you feel like everything outside the warm circle of your reading light has been utterly obliterated, eroded and carried off on the inexorable tide of the real-unreal thing I now want to call frantumaglia.

Arriving for a second time at the anger-making epilogue, with its uncharacteristically sanctimonious title ("Restitution"), I was glad I'd come to it in this darkest, strangest moment of the night. The first time I finished the book—in a hot September noontime, in a frenzy to write my last "Slow Burn" letter, late as always—I remember feeling an irate sense of betrayal. It felt like a cheat; the sudden return of form, via what Merve called in her last letter of the summer "too transparent an example of A Literary Device." To return to the novels' facile point of origin, the day of the dolls, seemed too tidy a resolution, almost classical in its allusion towards the dramatic unities of time, place, and action. In my own final letter, I tried, a little desperately and stretchily, to work through my frustration by returning to my initial fixation on Ferrante's peculiar brand of realism, constructed as it is with the disassembled pieces of other genres, like fairy tale and Brechtian epic theatre.

However, try though I might to theorize my way through those initial feelings of dissatisfaction, I couldn't, and the end remained an exasperating anomaly.

Looking at it this time, though, it felt right. My former irritation dissolved into an unpleasureable pleasure that actually resides *in* this seeming betrayal. By the time we arrive at this unlikely, too-neat ending, the entire project of *L'amica geniale* has taught us how to read for the real: how to recognize that the perfections of balanced structure and symmetry in fiction are paltry coverings that only do the work of camouflage. Like Lila's shapeshifting, they can never truly settle, but always "redo, cover, uncover, reinforce and then undo, break" (*SLC*, 177). This final act of forcible formation, the tight cap of the epilogue, cannot contain the seething matter of the world we've dwelled in for the last many hundreds of pages; it spills out and mingles with the chaotic matter of our own worlds. Reading the ending this time around, I was struck by the clear fact of its insufficiency, not as a flaw, but as Ferrante's final signal to her readers that we must always be on the lookout for the forces that both form and unform our experiences, inside or outside of the text. Lenù, form-loving manipulator that she is, may try to give the story a dramatic ending, one that looks like The End. Her readers, however, know by now that there is no such thing as beginnings or endings, just the obscure, unknowable categories of what the child Lila simply called "Before," and that interminable, disorganized thing that we can only vaguely refer to as "After."

THE STORY OF A FICTION

KATHERINE HILL

1.

This happened and it did not happen.

My friend called me one Saturday, out of the blue, to tell me she needed to talk. Her tone was secretive, but I could sense it had something to do with her and not with me—a relief that allowed me to respond in the supportive, easy-going manner I'm always striving for with friends. I told her I could stop by in the afternoon, and she said thank you, two o'clock is good. But when I arrived promptly at two, she greeted me as though I had come too soon. There was no evidence in her space of any activity interrupted, and yet it was clear from her manner—distracted, evasive, her eyes seeming to seek something invisible in the room—that I had shown up at an inconvenient time.

She made us coffee and we sat in her little kitchen with the blinds raised to let in the dimming light.

I have been writing, she told me at last.

I almost laughed. That was it? She'd confessed as one might to a murder or a pathetic affair. And yet something in her bearing, the absolute seriousness with which she was holding her cup in her hands on the table, suggested I shouldn't tease her.

Apparently this had been going on for years. She'd been writing in secret, in little corners here and there, mostly at home when everyone else was out. Now she had completed a novel. And she had given it to our mutual friend, who was also my editor. This mutual friend thought it was a very good novel and was now trying to convince her to publish it.

No one can know about this, my friend insisted. I am telling you because I know you won't tell anyone.

I told her I thought it was wonderful that our friend admired the novel. I asked her why she gave it to her if she didn't want to publish it, and she laughed and said, because I'm an idiot, and continued to look resolute and grave.

It was her privacy that most concerned her. She had worked hard on the novel, she knew it was good, and as she said this, a sly smile crept onto her face, and for the first time that afternoon I saw that my friend was proud of what she had done. She had enjoyed the labor fully, she told me. When she was writing well, she felt free and weightless, charged with a life force normally absent or in retreat. It was the best feeling she'd ever had, better even than being pregnant or on the beach, smelling salt, feeling all at once in invisible flecks the movements of water, air, and earth. How could she surrender this feeling now that she'd found it? How could she kill herself by becoming a book?

She told me she had made up her mind, and there was no changing it. She would publish the novel with our friend, but only with her, and she would never put her name to it or to any other book she might one day write. She seemed very determined on this point and also determined that I try to talk her out of it—I, who had written a book and was not dead. It was a game, I realized, and she needed to play it with me to make sure her thinking was sound.

Why would it kill you to put your name on a book? I asked, dutifully. If the book is as wonderful as our friend says, wouldn't you want to take credit for it?

She grimaced, then looked me right in the eye in an accusing manner, as though I had been the one to introduce the subject, with no regard for her sensitive feelings. She explained again about her privacy, insisting that she was shy, which might've been true in certain contexts, but never, in our long friendship, with me. In any case, what she called shyness, I understood in this instance to be fear—and of what? I asked her. Was she really so afraid that one little novel would make her famous? Wasn't that a little paranoid and, to be honest, a little grandiose? No one had read my book, remember.

She grimaced again and said that to her even the smallest amount of personal recognition amounted to the same thing as fame. It was about having to be someone for other people. It was about the expectations of any public at all, however miniscule. The only expectations my writing can bear are my own and my imagined readers', she said, and those are already quite a lot. If I publish the book, she told me, I will have already performed the fullest, freest gesture of authorship. I will have handed the work over to real readers, to discover or to ignore. If they love it, wonderful. If they hate it, wonderful. Either way, it should have nothing to do with me personally, and as long as I remain unknown, it won't.

I had worked very hard to promote my book, and she knew it, and so she probably knew I would not like her position. It had never occurred to me that attaching my face and name to a book I had actually written could be anything other than honest and transparent and maybe even brave; qualities worth cultivating, not disparaging. The idea that she should write a wonderful novel and not claim it as her own was offensive. A man would claim it if she didn't. She would be abused no matter what—for hiding, for lying. And women everywhere would have one less source of inspiration, a resource still in short supply. How can the world ever change if talented women won't even allow themselves the slightest recognition—to be known as the person who wrote a book? Isn't anonymous publication a counterproductive choice? A gesture not of advancement but of defeat?

I told her this, as she surely wanted me to, and the more I talked, the more resolute she became. That is it exactly, she said. We can never prove ourselves by exposing ourselves. We can only work to expose the truth. That's what good writing does. And it also happens to give me great pleasure. Why shouldn't I defend that pleasure, which is also one of the few remaining sources of truth? The truth will still reach the reader and, all right, if it's important to provide female inspiration, maybe it will even reach the reader under a woman's name. But not my name. That, I am keeping for myself. Only that.

I left her apartment infuriated. The wind had picked up in advance of an evening rainstorm, and all along my block, it was shaking hard little acorns from their trees. They pelted the street, landing on cars with cracks as loud as small explosions, and as I ducked uselessly—if an acorn was going to hit me, it would hit me— I could not help feeling assaulted by her special exemption, her absolute refusal to be wounded on the thoroughfare with the rest of us.

I came home and took my book off the shelf. It is not the best novel that has ever been written, but it is a solid effort. Certainly it seeks inconvenient truths. Was I holding back ethically or aesthetically, either then, as I was writing it, or now, writing my next book, because I couldn't separate this paper object from myself? I didn't think I was. I looked at myself in the mirror and in photos as much as the next person, but I had no sense of that shell when I wrote. When I wrote, I wrote. The words and ideas came, my fingers did their bidding, and the personal self who possesses those fingers for the most part kept out of the way. Surely I didn't need to erase that self to write. Did I?

For many days I thought about this, and in that time I talked to my friend only sporadically.

2.

Elena Ferrante is a fictional character, one of my favorites: a disembodied person in my head, a mind inside my mind. She occupies a large, elastic space in there, in the same neighborhood with a lot of my real friends and mentors, all the Sarah–Merve–Jills, and everyone else with whom I have ever seriously corresponded, even though she's never written anything that's strictly just for me. She's one of my Lilas: a sometimes-close, sometimes-distant friend and rival, who keeps winning by being smarter.

It's easy for me, as a reader of Ferrante and as a writer and friend to writers myself, to imagine the woman who wrote Ferrante's books confiding her secret in me. The novels are already a confidence shared intimately with every reader, no two exchanges alike. It's also easy because this author has shielded her name, body, and biography from public knowledge, but not her persona, which coheres across the letters and interviews collected in *Frantumaglia* and in her weekly column for *The Guardian*. The persona is visible even in the novels themselves, which share so many features and preoccupations.

Though the human writer remains invisible—"I believe that books, once they have been written, have no need of their authors,"[1] she told her publisher Sandra Ozzola in 1991—Ferrante does seem to want to be known in this other way, as the implied author or authorial persona who has something to teach us about reading narrative. The Neapolitan novels, after all, invite us to think a great deal about authorship, as well as fiction writing and its relationship to life, within the figure of their narrator, the writer Elena Greco. In one of the quartet's many reflexive scenes, near the beginning of *Those Who Leave and Those Who Stay*, Gigliola tells a newly-published Lenù:

> "I read your book, it's wonderful, how brave you were to write those things."
> I stiffened.
> "What things?"
> "The things you do on the beach."
> "I don't do them, the character does."
> "Yes, but you wrote them really well, Lenù, just the way it happens, with the same filthiness. They are secrets that you know only if you're a woman."[2]

Gigliola here stands in for many contemporary readers who have no trouble with the paradox of most referential fiction: this happened and it did not happen. She knows Lenù's novel is fiction, just like Ferrante fans know the Neapolitan novels are fiction, but she also knows it derives at least some of its power from its relationship to real-world truth. Lenù generally depicts Gigliola, the wife of Michele Solara, as coarse and materialistic, not someone whose aesthetic opinion she'd much respect—and in fact, Gigliola's comment is typical of the naïve readers novelists love to complain about, the kind who, however admiringly, conflate verisimilitude with reality. But Gigliola is also right: Lenù *did* do the things her fictional character does on the beach.

Reading this, it's hard not to feel that Ferrante is toying with us. Is she hinting at the truth of her own fictions, "the secrets you only know if you're a woman"—and an author? Is she making an ironic joke about the author-reader relationship in general? Or, wait, is she merely invoking the *idea* of authorial secrets to create a plausible fiction, since everyone knows writers draw from life and have all sorts of feelings about that process and its consequences? I have to admit this uncertainty is part of my pleasure, or *un*pleasure, as Sarah would say. The ambiguity such moments generate—and the impossibility of ever learning Ferrante's secrets—keeps these novels open to multiple readings, not to mention rereadings, which invariably involve my own particular construction of Elena Ferrante, a someone and a no one at once.

Though all of Ferrante's novels have been published under her pseudonym, and all are narrated by educated, Neapolitan-born women telling personal, apparently unmediated stories, the Neapolitan Quartet, more than any previous work, seems to invite the reader's invention of an author. It is her longest work, the only one I would call a life narrative, and, most significantly, the only one to be narrated by an Elena, a name Ferrante long ago gave herself and still claims as "the name that I feel is most mine" (*FR*, 239). This Elena, moreover, is not just any educated, Neapolitan woman. She is the novelist-theorist Elena Greco, who gets entangled in all sorts of writerly problems over the course of her life and whose writing *is* the novels, as well as an active agent in their intricate plots.

Surely this is autofiction, not as Serge Doubrovsky first defined it, "fiction of strictly real events or facts,"[3] but as Gerard Genette understands it: an "intentionally contradictory pact" in which an author, through a fictionalized version herself, *seems* to tell a true story, but doesn't.[4] Most autofiction trades on the understanding that the author is just playing, or just theorizing, and not really revealing herself, but Ferrante's work invites the opposite reading. In giving us two author characters, one inside the text and one outside, who share a given name and birthplace, she tempts us to understand her as an author who fictionalizes her own life story, not by aggrandizing but by hiding. This, combined with the confessional narration of experiences many readers recognize as "just the way it happens," suggests that crucial, dangerous aspects of this story existed in life before they found their way into fiction. Even readers versed in Barthes—"*who speaks* (in the narrative) is not *who writes* (in real life) and *who writes* is not *who is*"[5]—can easily imagine a translation from the real Ferrante to the fictional Greco, a writer who has a private life to protect but who cannot seem to write about anything but herself and the people she knows.

Ferrante lends some support to this theory in *Frantumaglia*, where she describes her desire for "absolute creative freedom" (FR, 62) and to be "sincere to the point where it's unbearable," while simultaneously acknowledging the challenges these desires pose, both personally and artistically: "It seems to me that making a clear separation between what we are in life and what we are when we write helps keep self-censorship at bay" (80). In other words, she has to invent a self, free from personal bonds, if she's going to write anything good. Yet, in her quest for sincerity, she is also careful to distinguish between literary truth and biographical truth: "Writing that is inadequate can falsify the most honest biographical truths. Literary truth isn't founded on any autobiographical or journalistic or legal agreement. . . . Literary truth is the truth released exclusively by words used well, and it is realized entirely in the words that formulate it" (260). But biographical truth requires qualification, too. When asked by Paolo di Stefano for *Corriere della Sera*, "how autobiographical is the story of Elena [Greco]?" Ferrante replies, in her characteristically direct yet elusive manner, "If by autobiography you mean drawing on one's own experience to feed an invented story, almost entirely. If instead you're asking whether I'm telling my own personal story, not at all" (235). In another interview, with Deborah Orr for *The Gentlewoman* (UK), she argues for a yet more flexible understanding of autobiography, which she frames in terms of process rather than results. She adopts an autobiographical persona, she says, not to tell her own personal story but because it offers surer footing on the path to *literary* truth: "Using the name Elena helped only to reinforce the truth of the story I was telling. . . . The fictional treatment of biographical material—a treatment that for me is essential—is full of traps. Saying 'Elena' has helped to tie myself down to the truth" (360).

If we take her at her word here, Ferrante's autofiction harkens back to older understandings of the autobiographical novel—works like *David Copperfield*, *A Portrait of the Artist as a Young Man*, and *À la recherche du temps perdu*—that are nominally fictional but draw heavily upon their authors' lives and lived experiences. The difference, of course, is the pseudonym. Dickens, Joyce, and Proust all published under their personal names, as do most autofictionists, from Doubrovsky to Sheila Heti. Ferrante refuses to do this, and the choice produces all kinds of ripple effects in her work, inviting us to consider the moral and technical limits of autobiographical writing and especially of autofiction, a genre drenched in cynicism but founded on claims to sincerity.

The choice also protects her. She gets to live entirely in her readers' minds on the page and entirely in her own life off of it. How, I wonder enviously, was the woman who writes as Elena Ferrante so much smarter than me about this? For me, it's already too late. There is already a novel out there, written by my legal name, with my picture on the back as a certificate of authenticity and a face to blame if the book disappoints. I could start over as a pseudonym—every day I'm tempted—but I can't ignore the nagging sense that it's harder to erase an existing presence than it is to be invisible from the start.

I'm sometimes annoyed that the writer of Elena Ferrante's novels figured out how to avoid this trap, and I didn't. But mostly

I'm just grateful that she did. In creating Elena Ferrante "entirely in the words that formulate" her, she has helped me, as no other writer or theorist has, to recognize the fantasy of the author that the reader develops in the reading of a book. And this author, in my fantasy, sets traps for narrator and reader alike as a way of identifying and avoiding them herself.

3.

In *The Situation and the Story: The Art of Personal Narrative*, memoirist Vivian Gornick promotes the figure of "the truth speaker—the narrator that a writer pulls out of his or her own agitated and boring self to organize a piece of experience."[6] This, Gornick argues, is the writer's on-the-page "persona . . . this other one telling the story that I alone—in my everyday person—would not have been able to tell."[7] The process sounds an awful lot like Ferrante's vis-à-vis her pseudonym. But even more interesting than what Gornick might suggest about Ferrante is what she illuminates about Greco. Though both Elenas are autobiographically inflected fictional entities, Greco is the only one who claims to be writing a personal story—the first of Ferrante's many careful traps.

At the start of *My Brilliant Friend*, Lenù candidly asserts that she's writing in a competitive rage. Her childhood friend, Lila Cerullo, has disappeared, leaving no trace of the life she'd lived, and this autobiography of their friendship is Lenù's best revenge: "I was really angry. 'We'll see who wins this time,' I said to myself. I turned on the computer and began to write—all the details of our story, everything that still remained in my memory."[8] Never make any big decisions when you're angry, right? This is our first hint that memoir might be a trap for Lenù—and for us. "Autobiographical nonfiction," Phillip Lopate contends in *To Show and to Tell: The Craft of*

Literary Nonfiction, "has traditionally encouraged readers to regard the narrator, whatever else his flaws, as reliable, sincerely attempting to level with us"[9] To a certain extent, Lenù is leveling, admitting she is writing out of anger. But she's also refusing to level, which requires some engagement with balance or counterweight. Hers is a commitment to emotion over reason and to unreliability over its opposite, which is part of what makes the Neapolitan novels so *unpleasurable*. It's also part of their claim to be read as novels rather than a thinly veiled autobiography of a writer who refuses to show her face.

Yet the novels do tempt us with this reading, in part because the narrator who emerges from Lenù's anger meets so many of Gornick and Lopate's other requirements for autobiographers. She narrates a life from memory, giving it shape with "all the details of our story" (Lopate, 79). In her narration, she turns herself into a character, emphasizing physical traits, gestures, and patterns of action and language that set her apart from others, especially Lila. She develops a "double perspective that will allow the reader to participate vicariously in the experience as it was lived . . . while benefiting from the sophisticated wisdom of the author's adult self" (26). And she demonstrates in the piling clauses of her distended syntax "a supple mind at work" navigating "the twists and turns of a thought process working itself out" (6). It is probably because so many of these contemporary nonfiction elements are at work in the Neapolitan cycle that it takes some strength to resist the suggestion they cumulatively make in the reader's mind: that all of this stuff actually *happened*. But to arrive at this conclusion and to think no further is to ignore the very technique that has led us there—to fall into Ferrante's memoir trap ourselves.

Since the eighteenth century, when fiction emerged as what Catherine Gallagher calls the "conceptual category" of "believable stories that did not solicit belief,"[10] the genre has imitated and borrowed from a range of nonfiction forms: the diary, the letter, the history, the biography. The Neapolitan novels are no exception. Here, Elena Greco's nonfiction craft serves Elena Ferrante's pursuit of *fictional* verisimilitude, a literary effect most contemporary readers crave and, if coaxed, will eagerly pursue in collaboration with the writer. While contemporary verisimilitude privileges plausible action and sensory language—the images and details that supposedly help readers see the scene—Ferrante pursues a lifelikeness of another kind. "Verisimilitude is the real that has long since found a reassuring symbolism," she tells the Turkish journalist Yasemin Congar in the online journal *T24*. "The writer, on the other hand, has the job of describing what escapes the story, what escapes the narrative order. We have to get as far away as possible from verisimilitude and instead shrink the distance to the true heart of our experience" (*FR*, 312). Perhaps to this end, Lenù's narration tends to be highly emotional but visually flat: "There was something unbearable in the things, in the people, in the buildings, in the streets that, only if you reinvented it all, as in a game, became acceptable" (*MBF*, 106–107). Whether this rings true depends on literary fashion and individual taste but, in the current dominion of realism, the general effect is that of a nonfiction story told by the person to whom it happened and unmediated by artifice of any kind. The writer, we imagine, is so intimate with and so affected by her subject that hurried outlines of things, people, buildings, and streets are enough to do the job. She knows what everything looks like; to lavish them with detail would render them false. It's the reader, who wasn't there, who has the imaginative job of fleshing out.

But intimacy doesn't equal omniscience—not in honest nonfiction writing—so from the very beginning of the quartet, Lenù also qualifies her personal narration with various appeals to its limits. She frequently acknowledges the fallibility of memory: "What happened right afterward I don't remember, I remember only the dark bundle of the teacher's motionless body, and Lila staring at her with a serious expression" (*MBF*, 32). She also acknowledges the ways in which time and the act of writing have required her to revise her interpretations: "Only now, as I write, do I realize that Fernando at that time couldn't have been more than forty-five, Nunzia was certainly a few years younger" (314). In the reader's compact with a nonfiction writer, these kinds of qualifications buy trust. They help us to feel that the author is doing her best to relate the whole story while dutifully reminding us, by calling attention to her limited perspective, that the whole story can never be known. The fictional narrator who proceeds in the same way thus feels, paradoxically, less fictional, and more true—more like the author herself.

This illusion gains strength and complexity because the narrator of *My Brilliant Friend* doesn't shy from assertion when she feels confident in her facts. "It was like that," she insists, when emphasizing the violence of her childhood (*MBF*, 51). We believe her because she was there to witness it; her experience is her expertise. But sometimes, in the Neapolitan novels, she *wasn't* there, and we tend to believe her then, too. Early on in *My Brilliant Friend*, she shows us a dinner at the Cerullo home. Rino is demanding a salary for the work he does in his father's shoe shop, and the argument quickly devolves into a fight, in quoted dialogue, over Lila's education, which Rino supports and Fernando does not (*MBF*, 68–70). The moment gives us pause—where's Lenù to record this, we wonder?— but we quickly assimilate it. Lila must have told her, we reason; they are intimately connected, lifelong friends. We make similar excuses for the richly detailed scene of Don Achille's murder, which no one witnessed. It is a story Lila tells Lenù repeatedly "with great seriousness, always adding new details . . . as if she had been present" (84) and which Lenù recounts for us in the same spirit: "He had on worn blue pajamas, and on his feet only socks of a yellowish color, blackened at the heels. As soon as he opened the window a gust of rain struck his face and someone plunged a knife into the right side of his neck, halfway between the jaw and the clavicle" (83). Though they've only imagined this novelistic scene, we accept its necessity in Lenù's memoir, so formative is the figure of Don Achille to the life/story of both girls.

Lenù continues to showcase her nonfiction technique in *The Story of a New Name*, but for the first time we also glimpse some distance between narrator and author. In the first chapter, we learn that a twenty-two-year-old Lenù read, even studied, and in some places memorized, Lila's box of personal writings before pitching it in to the Arno in Pisa. Ah-ha, we think, still fooled, *this* is how she knows Lila's story: she's a good researcher; she's read the original documents. But, look again, she also destroyed them, an ethical red flag. "Behind their naturalness, was surely some artifice, but I couldn't discover what it was," Lenù says of Lila's writings.[11] So might the reader say of Ferrante's.

The Story of a New Name goes out of its way to introduce many such primary sources, including first-hand accounts from Lila and other trusted witnesses, and gossip, both of which shape what anthropologist Elinor Ochs and psychologist Lisa Capps call "living narrative" in a neighborhood like Lenù's.[12] Together, these sources seem to support Lenù's method of composition. Specific, dramatized moments fill the page when Lenù's memory or witness testimony is strong, while sketches or outlines of events appear when it becomes necessary to fill in gaps. Again, we are left with the impression that our narrator is telling a true story, even as her narrative grows increasingly novelistic, regularly entering the subjectivity of others.

Reinforcing this impression is Lenù's reminder, at the beginning of each volume, that she is the author of these books and that she is writing them on her computer in Turin, even as we read. "For weeks now I've been writing at a good pace, without wasting time rereading," she tells us in *Those Who Leave and Those Who Stay*, just after relating a moment when Lila ordered her never to write about her (29). Likewise in *The Story of the Lost Child*: "This morning I keep weariness at bay and sit down again at the desk. Now that I'm close to the most painful part of our story, I want to seek a balance between her and me that in life I couldn't find even between myself and me."[13] Altogether, Lenù seems to be telling us: I am a novelist writing this story of myself and my friend, and it is true but partial and imperfect, and also something of a betrayal, so I am trying to counteract those limits by telling you everything I can, by giving you all the events the way I would in a novel, even the ones that didn't directly concern me, by being honest about my emotions, and by trying hard, as I write, to see things not just from my point of view but from Lila's point of view as well, even though she wouldn't want me to. She conveys all of this to us in those characteristically mounting sentences, with dependent clause after dependent clause, each one relevant and exerting pressure on her meaning, sentences like this one I'm currently writing and like the one that came before it, too, sentences I can't resist composing in imitation and admiration every time I sit down to try to understand Ferrante. I must, in some way, associate that syntax with sincerity—the literary truth Ferrante and Greco both claim to pursue in these books.

4.

I've mentioned that Lenù, the character, is a novelist and theorist. But we don't know this at the beginning of *My Brilliant Friend*; we know only that the adult narrator sits down to write, which any literate person could do. To read this long, tangled series of novels, experiencing Sarah's dialectic of form and *unform*, is to watch Lenù become an autobiographical fiction writer—first as the narrator of her own life story, and then in her career. This is Ferrante's greatest trap for Lenù, set with such skill—an important word in this quartet—as to belie its own artifice.

While Lenù the novelist doesn't fully emerge until volume two, *My Brilliant Friend* prepares us subtly, recounting the friends' youthful obsession with *Little Women* and Lila's authorship of *The Blue Fairy*, which Lenù greatly admires. For the girls, writing becomes linked to upward mobility: "We thought that if we studied hard we would be able to write books and that the books would make us rich" (*MBF*, 70). Lila soon abandons the book-writing dream, and in time Lenù appears to follow suit, even though she's still drawn to literature and thinks of her life as "the novel I felt myself immersed in" (325).

We're further prepared for Lenù's fictional turn by her frequent acknowledgments of her lies. She usually lies to protect her sexual desires and personal ambitions—from Lila, from her family, from the neighborhood, and even from herself. Lila lies, too, for the same reasons but also for the benefit of others. Her lies look bad because they are aggressive and often vulgar, and always disruptive to established powers and norms, whereas Lenù's are so mannered—typically taking the form of feminine denials rather than masculine performances—that she continues to look good. The people in her life are fooled by her outward adherence to social convention, and because we are on the inside with Lenù, this is something most readers can see. What readers might not see is the way in which *we* are being fooled by an analogous adherence to narrative convention. Her memoir of individual progress via established channels doesn't just win our meritocratic hearts and minds, it also covers her deceptive leaps into fiction—but only because we've forgotten the suspicious emotion with which her narrative begins.

From a technical perspective, those leaps are necessitated by the divergence of Lenù and Lila's lives, both socially and geographically.

After the fateful summer in Ischia, in which the married Lila embarks on a dangerous affair with Lenù's beloved Nino, Lenù recommits herself to school, ultimately heading to Pisa to study. Lila, meanwhile, remains in Naples. A memoirist might tell us that Lenù can no longer narrate Lila's life from first-hand experience, so she's permitted to speculate a bit, and speculate she does. Though she never stops telling us who her sources are—Lila's notebooks, Antonio, Carmen, Pinuccia—she takes greater and greater liberties with her material. Among her many invented moments is a dialogue between Lila and Maestra Oliviero in the gardens of the neighborhood church, where Lila has been reading *Ulysses* while her infant son Gennaro naps in his carriage. That dialogue soon gives way to a richly imagined representation of Lila's thoughts:

> She is discovering that I am stupid, she said to herself, her heart pounding harder, she is discovering that my whole family is stupid, that my forebears were stupid and my descendants will be stupid, that Gennaro will be stupid. She became upset, she put the book in her bag, she grabbed the handle of the carriage, she said nervously that she had to go. Crazy old lady, she still believed she could rap me on the knuckles. She left the teacher in the gardens, small, clutching her cane, consumed by an illness that she would not give in to. (*SNN*, 382)

In her characteristic run-on sentences, the future novelist is already at work here, turning real people into characters who speak in extended, quoted dialogue, whose thoughts and feelings she claims to know. Lila, after all, is only Lila in Lenù's novels; to everyone else, she's Lina, even to herself.

Lenù doesn't just fictionalize Lila in this period; she takes liberties with everyone back home. When her crippled, critical mother turns up at her dormitory to nurse her back to health from the flu,

Lenù is so overcome by the gesture that she imagines, in a knowing, free indirect style, her mother's solo journey home:

> She would never spend the money for a bus, she was careful not to waste even five lire. But she would make it: she would buy the right ticket and take the right train, traveling overnight on the uncomfortable seats, or even standing, all the way to Naples. There, after another long walk, she would arrive in the neighborhood, and start polishing and cooking, she would cut up the eel, and prepare the insalata di rinforzo, and the chicken broth, and the struffoli, and without resting for a moment, filled with rage, but consoling herself by saying, in some part of her brain, "Lenuccia is better than Gigliola, than Carmen, than Ada, than Lina, than all of them." (*SNN*, 414)

For a long stretch in the middle of the quartet, the farther Lenù gets from Naples, first to Pisa for university, then to Florence with Pietro, the more novel-like her books become. Is Ferrante suggesting an ambitious girl like Elena Greco has to leave her backward community to become a novelist? And that leaving Naples, the great, tangled city of her real life and inspiration, is also what frees her to imagine and invent?

It certainly seems so in Chapter 113, near the end of *The Story of a New Name*. By this point in the narrative, Lenù has destroyed Lila's notebooks and is no longer in communication with her friend. For a strict memoirist such a break might require a gap in, or even an end to, Lila's story. But not for Lenù, who continues on, undeterred. Back in Naples, the business entanglements and romantic affairs of the neighborhood have come to a head, leaving Lila alone in her bedroom, contemplating how to protect herself and her child: "Just thinking of her son saps her strength. What ended up in Rinuccio's head: images, words. She worries about the voices that reach him, unmonitored. I wonder if he heard mine, while I carried him in my womb" (*SNN*, 428). With this present-tense narration, switching abruptly, yet seamlessly, from third person to first, Lila is entirely Lenù's character. The situation persists into Chapter 114, in which Enzo arrives to rescue her from her bad marriage, a sequence of thought, action, and dialogue delivered entirely in scene, as though Lenù were there to record it. Though we later learn that Ada has given Lenù some of this story, the narrator offers no immediate evidence for her knowledge. At last, it seems, she is free to invent, to have her way with Lila's life.

Meanwhile, back in Pisa, the character Lenù is becoming a fiction writer as well. In the very next chapter, she writes a private draft of what will become, by the accident of good connections, her first novel, a third-person bildungsroman centering on her sexual encounter with Donato Sarratore—a scene we've already read. Her perspective has changed—the sex, then experienced a mix of pleasure and disgust, is now understood as pure degradation—and though she isn't proud of the pages, the process of writing them calms her, "as if the shame had passed from me to the notebook" (*SNN*, 433). Again, we might feel permitted to forgive Lenù's novelizing: fictionalizing Lila helps her understand her friend while fictionalizing a complicated sexual experience helps her overcome its trauma. All hail the redemptive power of fiction! The second volume ends with Lila's destruction of her promising juvenilia, *The Blue Fairy*—if only Lila appreciated fiction's power— and Lenù's sudden arrival as a new literary voice, making her debut at a book signing in Milan.

But remember, reader: it's a trap. If the first two volumes track the development of the autobiographical novelist, highlighting her method of making sympathetic and therapeutic fiction from life, the next two volumes dramatize the often-devastating personal consequences of such work. In an early moment in *Those Who Leave and Those Who Stay*, Lenù speaks, for the first time, as an author back home in Naples:

> Whenever I saw the book in a window, among other novels that had just come out, I felt inside a mixture of pride and fear, a dart of pleasure that ended in anguish . . . it never occurred to me, while I was writing, that I was making something of value. But the effort of finding a form had absorbed me. And the absorption had become *that* book, an object that contained me. Now, *I* was there, *exposed*, and seeing myself caused a violent pounding in my chest. I felt that not only in my book but in novels in general there was something that truly agitated me, a bare and throbbing heart (*TWL*, 53).

The image is doubly reflexive: Elena Greco, our Neapolitan author, sees her book as "an object that contain[s]" her, describes it, in fact, as though she is looking into a mirror ("seeing myself"). I have tried again and again to retain a critical detachment reading this passage, but every time I find it impossible not to imagine my Elena Ferrante, who our book flap tells us was born in Naples, who is contained entirely in *our* book, whose existence *is* her writing.

But this is autofiction, setting its traps. The reader has to stay flexible throughout *Those Who Leave and Those Who Stay*, as Elena Greco narrates her development as an author, encountering various emotional, practical, and formal challenges—the feeling of exposure that attends publication, finding the time to write amid family life, what to do about a second novel no one likes, the turn to criticism when fiction gets frustrating, and so on. Here's where I have to admit that I stiffen, because the parallel to my own experience is spooky—more so because I couldn't have predicted any of those challenges when I chose writing, not just as a practice but as a career. To paraphrase Gigliola, these are secrets every author knows.

Who else can I hear in that "bare and throbbing heart" but a real-life author, who is smarter than Lenù and me about the dangers of writing, who wisely won't show her face?

In the quartet's final volume, *The Story of the Lost Child*, Lenù continues to worry about authorship. Book 4 is full of commentary on the literary life, concentrated in particular on two publication events. The first is Lenù's second novel, a political thriller about the neighborhood, and the second is her last novel, an eighty-page narrative called *A Friendship*, about Lila and her missing daughter, Tina. Lenù writes the thriller in book 3, in Florence, during her marriage to the well-bred classical scholar Pietro Airota, but after Lila and Pietro's mother Adele dismiss it as bad, Lenù puts it away in shame. Only later, in Naples, after her marriage and long-awaited affair with Nino are both over, does Lenù submit the old manuscript to her editor. She is under contract for a novel she hasn't been able to produce, and this is her last, desperate attempt to make good on that agreement. To her great surprise, the editor loves it, mistakenly attributing its origin and power to Lenù's return to Naples. She doesn't correct him, allowing instead for the literary world to grant her this major step forward: "My name, the name of a nobody, was definitely becoming the name of a somebody" (*SLC*, 291). *A Friendship*, meanwhile, is a radically condensed version of the book we are reading: the Neapolitan novels in toto and *The Story of the Lost Child* in particular. It's the book Lila demanded that Lenù never write, but that we know, if not from our narrator's initial anger, then certainly from her subsequent novelizing, that she will—that, in fact, she already has. She can't avoid the trap.

For the Lenù who is writing the Neapolitan novels has become, in book 4, a significant literary figure, whose picture appears in the paper whenever she publishes an important new book. At times, *The Story of the Lost Child* reads like a celebrity memoir, full of the kinds of sensational material we've come to expect of the genre—the torrid affair with the future socialist politician Nino Sarratore, the murder of the notorious Camorrist Solara brothers, the irrevocable loss of Lila's daughter. The effect is helped by Ferrante's decision to send Lenù back to Naples to write, allowing her to return to her original, memoiristic mode of narration. Living in the apartment above Lila, our narrator is once again a first-hand witness to her own life as well as the life of her brilliant friend's.

But celebrity memoir also tends toward self-mythology, and that rhetoric is largely absent in Lenù's narration. If anything, the final volume reads more like self-critique, an apology for writing insincerely. In a scene near the end that parallels the early-career moment in the bookstore, Lenù's grown daughter Elsa teases her, reading her mother's work aloud at a family Christmas gathering: "Her voice skillfully highlighted flaws, excesses, tones that were too exclamatory, the aged ideologies that I had supported as indisputable truths." Though the teasing is affectionate, "something inside [Lenù] changed." Afterwards, she surveys her life's work: "Occasionally I took down one of my volumes, read a few pages, felt its fragility" (SLC, 458). In contrast to the likely genius of the book she believes Lila to be writing, Lenù feels her own insufficiency, the nagging sense that she's fallen into literary production's greatest trap: "My entire life would be reduced merely to a petty battle to change my social class" (459). Three years later, still coping with the emotional aftermath of this realization, she writes A Friendship, and she loses Lila for good.

Ferrante sets this final trap for Lenù, not to mock or torment her, or to suggest that she is somehow less ethical than other writers, but to draw our attention to the traps that await every writer, especially those who draw from life. To this end, Ferrante structures Lenù's narrative quite carefully. To experience the danger of Lenù's fiction we have to first find her memoir reliable. We have to think we understand the life she is betraying when she writes those books. The irony of course is that no part of the Neapolitan novels is actually Lenù's life; it's all just writing, and fiction writing at that. It's tempting to attribute this approach to "reality hunger," David Shields's term for his impatience with the aesthetics of conventional fiction. Ferrante certainly appears to be with him, in her writing's "emotional urgency and intensity," in its invitation to "reader/viewer participation," and in its "blurring (to the point of invisibility) of any distinction between fiction and nonfiction: the lure and blur of the real."[14] But despite the pall the Neapolitan novels seem to cast over fiction, we shouldn't forget that it is their fictionality as much as their reality that engages the reader's participation—right down to the artful figure of Elena Ferrante. In the end, her autofictional effects appropriate the excitement and reality of autobiography for a linear character- and plot-driven novel, narrated by an unreliable narrator, and situated within a classic storytelling frame. It's a move characteristic of the reality-hungry that's nonetheless a reversal of their aims. Far from promoting a new breed of nonfiction, Ferrante reminds us, again, what fiction is.

5.

This happened and it did not happen.

My friend wrote to me a few days ago, while I was trying, attempting, to work on this essay about her, and because my attempt was, for the moment, failing, demanding fresh revisions to accommodate my most recent rereadings, I allowed myself to open her message. Reading it, first, through the filter of my admiration for every feature of her writing, and second, through the filter of my insecurity about my own, I found myself experiencing this note, not as a gesture of connection but as a hostile and uninvited visit.

She was working on a new book, and it was not going well. She had found that she could talk to me about these things because I was also a writer, which meant I understood the stakes. Because this one was not going well, she told me, she had decided to destroy it. No reader would ever see it.

By this time, she had published many books. As one of the few who knew she was their author, I was sworn to secrecy, which I of course maintained, admiring the work when it came up in conversation and professing no interest in knowing who she was. Of course it was a woman, I insisted, when a man suggested otherwise, as I had assured my friend would happen. I wish, I said, when someone asked if I were the author, an admission that's wholly true.

At any rate, she was going to destroy her newest book, and this annoyed me. It annoyed me because I never thought I had any such right. Once I'd started a book, I saw it as my obligation to see it through, salvage what I could of it. I never dared to start anything big without committing to it completely, and there was nothing I'd ever written that was so precious it couldn't be rewritten. At the same time, the idea of the book itself *was* precious to me. You could rewrite every single word, but you should never give up on the idea of the book—the book you were chasing, that didn't yet exist, but that would, one day, if you persisted.

Instead of writing this essay, I wrote her back something to this effect, and she must have been sitting there waiting for my reply because hardly ten minutes passed before the line containing our correspondence popped to life again, in bold.

One doesn't have to finish a book to honor the idea of it, she explained, like a voice inside my head. Even a finished book finds a new shape in every reader, each of whom reads in that book a story by no one, a story that is her own private book. If anything, it's a betrayal of the idea of the book to publish something that falls short, that feels forced, that isn't alive to this flexible necessity.

Again, she seemed to be avoiding the acorns, which have turned, this winter, to slick brown leaves, and cold, ashy snow that accretes on every block, but especially, it seems, on mine. She seemed to be avoiding traps by pointing out the ones that keep ensnaring me. She doesn't have to finish her book. She can't be contained by its finished form. She is no one. The book is everyone's. She can disappear without a personal trace, leaving behind only words.

I tried not to get angry, because I'm too defensive when I'm angry and therefore not very honest or smart. I tried instead to remember my own qualities, the ones I'm proud of. I am an earthly creature, I began to tell her, I value criticism—the engagement with another interested mind, the private work held to public account—and it is perhaps for this reason that, after standing up and sitting down several times, and shuffling my books around, and heading to the kitchen to make some useless noise with cups and dishes in the sink, I actually found myself cottoning to her argument, slowly working my way around.

Of course.

In being no one, she has declared, as so few petty writers seem to have the courage to declare, that her work is open to multiple readings, not just a single, authoritative critic's, not even just her own. It is this belief in multiplicity that keeps it alive, that insists that no single person, however violent, angry, rational, or foolish, can own it, harm it, or kill it.

This belief invites me, in fact, to create her, to see and hear her when she's not in the room. There she is, in the lusting voices of all her narrating first persons and in all the confounding alter egos—the friends and mothers and daughters and neighbors—that these first-person narrators discuss. There she is in Ann Goldstein's English words *dissolving margins* and in the original Italian *smarginatura*, a word borrowed from the language of printing. *Frantumaglia* is also her, rigid and uncompromising in the decisions she makes for her writing and herself.

I know her, not because I know how she was raised or how many children she has, but because she has created openings for me in her writing. "I'm Nobody!" she cries with Dickinson. "Who are you?" All narrating "I's" implicitly address a reading "you," and Elena Ferrante's "I's," whether Greco or Ferrante, always seem to address that you in a manner that invites a response. The approach, I realize, is really not so different from the way my coauthors and I have addressed each other here, trading ideas in pursuit of truths that avoid the traps of any one, fixed form. Unlike us, though, Elena Ferrante has kept her own life separate from the life that suffuses her writing. She has insisted upon it, and this, too, is an invitation to us. Because she is nobody, her characters, her readers, and the author herself all have the freedom to be somebody. All those bold, suggestive outlines in the Neapolitan novels—the things, people, buildings, streets, and author of Lenù's real life—are there for us, with our own ideas about narrative and Italy and history and politics, and our own tangled biographical material, to fill in.

THE QUEER COUNTERFACTUAL

JILL RICHARDS

Lenù and Lila are not lovers, but let's say they were. This is not a story we can find in the Neapolitan cycle. But it is the story I wanted to find. For a long time, I thought that this desire said more about me than the novels themselves. I was embarrassed about it, really, as a kind of naïve lesbian wistfulness overtaking my years of critical training. When I'm teaching a literature course, I tell my students that their ideas about how a novel should have ended are not the interpretive responses I want to see in their papers. Conversations about what might have been are interesting, I say, but this is a topic for a creative writing project, like fan fiction or counterfactual history. Literary criticism works with what is already there. It does not confuse fictional characters with real people in the world.

But the Neapolitan cycle is all about this confusion. The novels provoke a counterfactual imagination, in part because they so consistently dramatize the scene of reading and writing over someone else's story. Lenù throws Lila's notebooks in the river, but then she obsessively chronicles the texts that were destroyed, this time using her own words. "The pages were full of descriptions: the branch of a tree, the ponds, a stone, a leaf with its white veinings."[1] How faithful is Lenù to the originals? Is this a scene of interpretation or a more active rewriting? The descriptions of the notebooks take up a listy vein, sentences piling into run-ons and fragments, full of more and more precise details. "Isolated words appeared in dialect and Italian, sometimes circled, without comment. And Latin and Greek translation exercises. And entire passages in English on the neighborhood shops and their wares, on the cart loaded with fruit and vegetables that Enzo Scanno took through the streets every day "(SNN, 16)." Sometimes Lenù steals directly from Lila, approximating the form in question, the sentences twined together with commas. "Everything then became breathless, the sentences took on an overexcited rhythm, the punctuation disappeared."

Lila's writing itself rarely appears verbatim, in quotations. It's as though this particular style, Lila's style, could only be conveyed through someone else in a paraphrase that is also like ingestion. Sentences become too lively, almost animated, rather than a neutral container of information. They cannibalize the character who does the narrating until she is not quite herself saying the words of another but some more strange, more alien and desirous amalgamation. Not a recap, not a telephone game, or even passing of notes—this style requires a different language of bodily mediation. As in, I want to put your words in my mouth and chew. Sometimes it is more precisely anatomical. Words and their owners get confused. As in, I want to open my chest and embrace you with my rib cage. Get some viscera on your face.

This is a translation effect, but it is not among the ones we are used to. Lenù translates the feeling of reading Lila's writing, so that we can only know the original notebooks by proxy. One wonders if the text itself, the original text, Lila's missing notebooks laid out in whole, would only disappoint. There is an absence here—the notebooks we never see and, in my perpetually overeager mind, the queer love plot that might have been in them. These absences connect to

elena

Ferrante

Le nouveau
nom

roman

du
monde
entier

Gallimard

Cover of a French edition of *Story of a New Name* (Gallimard, 2018).

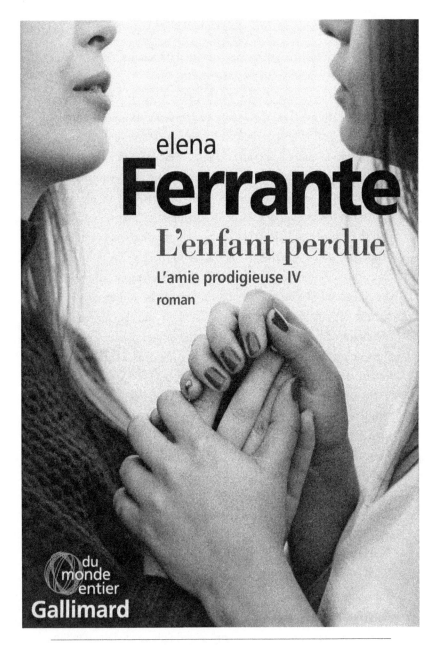

Cover of a French edition of *Story of the Lost Child* (Gallimard, 2018).

one another. They are not so much missing fragments. They expand and colonize, more like an invasive species.

The missing notebooks are a detail about plot. But this missing thing, the thing that then cannibalizes everything around it, resonates with the experience of reading the Neapolitan cycle in translation more generally. When I first started reading the English translations, at a brisk pace that summer, I assumed that the translator, Ann Goldstein, had chosen not to convey passages written in Neapolitan dialect in an Anglophone patois. I assumed that the loss of the dialect was a loss of translation. Only in Italian, I thought, would a reader be able to note these shifts in diction, from the subjunctive and baroque clauses of school Italian to the dialect of the neighborhood. However, the Italian originals do not contain dialect either. Occasionally, maybe once every two hundred pages, there is an isolated word of dialect in italics, but the language across the novels remains consistently Tuscan Italian, the national standard.

Here is Lila, after Marcello rips the bracelet off Lenù's wrist. "She said calmly, in dialect, 'Touch her again and I'll show you what happens.'"[2] In Italian, the language in quotation is not, in fact, Neapolitan dialect, but standard Italian. Goldstein speculates that this decision, to add *she said in dialect* (*disse en dialetto*), but not the dialect itself, might be because Ferrante feared Italian readers would not understand the Neapolitan, which is quite distinct from standard Italian.[3]

Neapolitan dialect is a central feature of the novels' plot, but we don't get the words themselves. A number of commenters consider this uniformity of style among the reasons Ferrante's works are so popular internationally in translation. "In Italy, Ferrante novels are sold at airport book stores," my friend Filippo explained when I asked him about the comparatively less enthusiastic reception of Ferrante's work among readers in his home country. So then

I wondered if Elena Ferrante was like an Italian version of Edgar Allen Poe. Some critics consider Baudelaire's French translations of Poe's stories superior to the English editions, as if Baudelaire's writing had not only conveyed the original text but improved upon it.[4] For T. S. Eliot, this translation effect necessitates a somewhat condescending account of Poe's work:

> It is certainly possible, in reading something in a language imperfectly understood, for the reader to find what is not there; and when the reader is himself a man of genius, the foreign poem read may, by happy accident, elicit something important from the depths of his own mind, which he attributes to what he reads. And it is true that in translating Poe's prose into French, Baudelaire effected a striking improvement: he transformed what is often a slipshod and shoddy English prose into admirable French.[5]

Let's bracket the suggestion that the reader need be a man of genius. Suspend the value judgment that the original text is something that requires improvement. I am not interested in making an argument about quality. It's not that the novels in translation are better, but that the experience of reading them in translation is importantly distinct: "It is certainly possible, in reading something in a language imperfectly understood, for the reader to find what is not there." This is true about reading in translation as well, to somewhat different effect. The reader understands that she is losing something. She imagines that, were she to get to the original text, things would only become better, more precise, more finely grained.

However, when we compare the Italian and English editions of Ferrante, this model does not work. In the English translation, here is Rino: "He tried to respond but he did so in an awkward, muddled, way, half in dialect, half in Italian. He said he was sure that his mother was wandering around Naples as usual" (*MBF*, 19). Reading in English, I assumed the reported speech, *He said he was sure that his mother was wandering around Napes as usual*, is free indirect style. That is to say, I assumed that this sentence borrows from Rino's spoken language, taking up the awkward muddling of Neapolitan dialect and standard Italian. But Ferrante does no such thing. The sentence is all standard Italian, from the Tuscan dialect, "Ha detto che s'era convinto che la madre fosse in giro per Napoli come al solito."[6] In any language, the reader has only Lenù's paraphrase of the way Rino speaks, the "awkward muddled way, half in dialect, half in Italian" but not the awkward, muddled words themselves. Finally, it is important, here on the first page of the first book, that the half-dialect half-Italian sentence we are left to imagine is a description of Lila, who has mysteriously disappeared. *He said he was sure that his mother was wandering around Naples as usual.*

In either language, the sentences paraphrase what was said rather than quoting directly. They set up the expectation of a borrowed language, noting the presence of dialect, but then offer a more distant summary. In the rest of this essay, I want to take up this kind of absence through a series of linked effects: the phantom notebooks, the missing dialect, the queer counterfactual, and finally, the pseudonymous mystery of Elena Ferrante herself. It is a life of the author particularly relevant, in this case, in that her pseudonymous form shares a name and potential biography with the novel's protagonist, Elena.

The kind of reading I am describing does not unearth what is hidden or repressed in the text. There is no there there at all, as Gertrude Stein would say—nothing to hold on to. This is a focus on what is *not* there, but maybe imagined, midway through the series. In the following pages, I turn to fan fiction and its associated paraphernalia—advertising copy, theatrical adaptations, and our own collaborative speculations—to locate a kind of reading somewhat more promiscuous than we are used to, one that can account for a more flexible relation between text and the world outside of it.

In the academic book I am writing alongside this one, on radical feminist and queer social movements, I think about approaching texts this way as reading from the middle, without knowing what the ending might be. This is a moment when the future conditional is still active. Consider, for instance, the first-time reader at the midpoint of the Neapolitan cycle. At this moment, younger Lila and Lenù might still run away together. Older Lila might be found. Ferrante's identity might be revealed. As a way of thinking about historical pasts, this kind of reading posits a moment when the revolution might not fail, this time around, for us. It is an attempt to think about a historical period from hat it might have looked like then, for the persons on the ground. Of course, this pose is always a fiction, because I know, we know, already, how things turned out. To think about a story from its midpoint does not mean we are just choosing to ignore the brutality of historical fact. It means suspending these facts for a moment, to imagine how things might have looked from the middle of the action.

This kind of counterfactual speculation is written into the structure of the Neapolitan cycle, through the symmetry between Elena the author and Elena the character. The possibility of revelation is in the books but also outside of them. From the beginning, journalists and critics have been asking: What if Elena Ferrante is a man? What if Ferrante isn't even Italian? What if she is a lesbian? What if she is an aristocrat? What if these novels are, in fact, all autobiography? It seems Ferrante the author has been identified, but that is not the story I am interested in. Rather, the effect I want to describe emerges through our sustained uncertainty about Ferrante's identity, leaving a gap in reference—no there there, no real Ferrante. The mystery of the author's identity, outside the text, creates counterfactual versions of how we might understand the novels themselves.

Ultimately, there are another set of questions that most people don't ask, but that I think are related. These are questions that take, as their object, Italy's Years of Lead, or the social unrest of the 1960s–1980s, to wonder what it would have been like, then, there, in the classrooms and the kitchens and the streets. This counterfactual narrative takes up the matter of being in the middle, not knowing how a story is going to end, and lingering in the possibilities you most desire, anyways. It is a particular structure of feeling that involves holding out an entirely impossible desire and wanting it anyways, if anything more fervently, for all the contradictions. In this case, that desire involves a historical imagination of what it would have been like in those years, in Italy, in the midst of Creeping May and Hot Autumn, to not know that that revolution would fail, too.

* * *

Any novel might be fodder for a counterfactual imagination—our readerly sense of what might have happened, but didn't. But the Neapolitan cycle seems to plant seeds for a queer counterfactual all the way through, for the ways that it foregrounds Lenù as an interpreter of Lila. Lenù is always writing over and through Lila, so that this interpretive pose, of writing over someone else's story, over the fact of what actually happened, begins to seem pretty commonplace. These scenes of interpretation are sometimes explicitly homoerotic. The covers of the French editions play up this tendency to the full effect, so that the unknowing reader might find herself disappointed that what lies therein is not, in fact, soft-core lesbian erotica. However, what I mean by the queer counterfactual does not refer to overtly homoerotic content. This mode instead registers the strange grammars of attachment that accompany these eroticized scenes of interpretation and rewriting.

Consider, for instance, the moment after Lila marries Stefano, at the end of the first book and the beginning of the second, when Marcello walks into the reception wearing the Cerullo shoes. The first book ends with description, all declarative. There is a lead up. We look at Lila looking, then get the article in question as the novel's last sentence. "It was the pair she had made with Rino, making and unmaking them for months, ruining her hands" (*MBF*, 331).

Usually a wedding at the end of a novel is a kind of ending, in the marriage or death vein. But this is a cliff-hanger, in part materialized through the shoes themselves, as another kind of pair made and unmade. It's a kind of making that ruins the hands, Ferrante reminds us. Hard, here at the end of the book, to not think of Lila's hands still somehow under and inside of those shoes as Marcello—stalker, rapist, fascist, infatuate—walks across the room and sits down.

Book 2 picks up here, at the wedding reception, but this time the narration is all from Lenù's perspective. At this moment, Lenù narrates what Lila could do, what she is capable of doing, then what she would have done. There's uncertainty here, in the beginning. "What was happening, what would happen?" (*SNN*, 10). It's a pile-up from there on, somewhat bloody, as though alternatives to heterosexual union could only be imagined on the other side of an orgy of destruction. What Lenù describes is a kind of knowing, a being inside someone else's head.

> My friend tugged her husband's arm with both hands. She used all her strength, and I who knew her thoroughly felt that if she could she would have wrenched it from his body, crossed the room holding it high above her head, blood dripping in her train, and she would have used it as a club or a donkey's

jawbone to crush Marcello's face with a solid blow. Ah yes, she would have done it, and at the idea my heart pounded furiously, my throat became dry. Then she would have dug out the eyes of both men, she would have torn the flesh from the bones of their faces, she would have bitten them. Yes, yes, I felt that I wanted that, I wanted it to happen. An end of love and of that intolerable celebration, no embraces in a bed in Amalfi. Immediately shatter everything and every person in the neighborhood, tear them to pieces, Lila and I, go and live far away, lightheartedly descending together all the steps of humiliation, alone, in unknown cities. (*SNN*, 19)

The person I want to track here is not Lenù, nor Lila, but the composite pair, *Lila and I*. Note that this phrase, *Lila and I*, sits at a verbal intersection, amidst a series of commands, to shatter everything and everyone, then "go and live far away." Something strange is happening here, more violent than sympathy or identification. Lenù imagines Lila's feelings inside of her, Lenù: "Her rage expanded in my breast, a force that was mine and not mine" (*SNN*, 19).

There is an entire branch of narrative theory devoted to this effect, the feeling of someone else's feelings as if they were our own. It is often called *identification*, a term grammatically oriented around *with* or *as*. The reader says to herself, in the midst of the action, I identify with this fictional person's experience. Or, more fervently, more fantastically, I identify as this fictional person-I feel as she feels.

Ferrante does something different. It's as though the machinery of identification, of feeling with or as, suddenly became literal, almost anatomical or parasitic, so that *with* or *as* are no longer adequate as grammatical markers. "Her rage expanded in my breast, a force that was mine and not mine." A page later, at the reception, "To be inside Lila's head was, as usual, difficult: I didn't hear her shouting, I didn't hear her threatening" (SNN, 20). Is this Lenù the character, speaking of an imaginative act? Or is this the description of a much more mundane narrative effect called free indirect style, when the narrator enters into the mind of a character to speak through her, as it were?

Literary critics sometimes describe free indirect style as a matter of overidentification on the part of the narrator. The narrator talks *through* a character, appropriating the precise inflections and diction of her speech, without the distancing effect of quotation marks. D. A. Miller describes this effect, free indirect style, as a "*third term* between character and narration."[7] In *Jane Austen or the Secret of Style*, Miller links this narrative effect with its seeming inverse, the reception of the text by the literary critic. In Miller's account, the relationship of the literary critic to the text is fraught by a similarly impossible identification: "For the practice of close reading has always been radically cloven: my ambition to master a text, to write *over* its language and refashion it to the cut of my argument, to which it is utterly indifferent; there, on the other, my longing to write *in* this language, to identify and combine with it."[8]

Miller's account of overidentification is particularly germane to our case because it develops through close attention to Jane Austen, often pegged as Ferrante's more genteel predecessor. The American edition of *The Story of a New Name* includes the following directive on the back cover: "Imagine if Jane Austen got angry and you'll have some idea how explosive these works are." Both Austen and Ferrante are traditionally considered women's writers. In each case, true devotion signals a specific brand of femininity. "The butch number swaggering into a bar in a leather get-up opens his mouth and sounds like a pansy, takes you home, where the first thing you notice is the complete works of Jane Austen, gets you into bed, and—well, you know the rest."[9] That's Leo Bersani, who appears in

Miller's book as well. Miller uses Bersani's ventriloquized insult as evidence of a wider cultural expecation, that the boyhood love of Jane Austen is indicative of a future homosexuality. In Miller's auto-biographical sleight of hand, Austenophilia "wound up giving their puerile reader, still at an age of sexual inexperience and vagueness, as much credit for an inclination to sex perversion as if they had been the wrong kind of pornography."[10]

I turn to Bersani and Miller, side by side, as a conversation about queer reading practices. This is about excess—not liking Jane Austen in general, as an important novelist of the eighteenth century, but liking her *too much*, unduly or disproportionately, in a manner that begins to confuse the fictional and the real. For women readers, extreme Jane Austen fandom is culturally intelligible as the lot of dissatisfied spinsters, unlucky in love. For the male reader, whether butches or prepubescent boys, Austen fandom signals something altogether different, a perverse form of the feminine, the swishy or fey, associated with queerness. Through this turn to Austen, both Bersani and Miller confirm Eve Sedgewick's early theoretical intervention, the claim that the hetero/homo distinction is not a liminal matter, relevant only to overtly queer persons, but centrally important to our understanding of Western culture as a whole.[11]

In the following pages, I take up this matter of overattachment, of liking a book too much, excessively or unduly. However, rather than focus on the singular reader of Ferrante's Neapolitan cycle, I want to consider the transnational fan cultures of the books' reception. More pointedly, I want to document a subgenre in the wider arc of fan fiction called slash.[12] Slash fiction offers a counterfactual narrative in a particularly queer vein. It is an interpretation that writes over the text, in the language of the text, sometimes translating and mistranslating it, to depict the romantic configurations that might have been or could be. The nomenclature *slash* comes from the shorthand notation for the imaginative recoupling of same-sex characters as a singular pair, like Starsky/Hutch, more often abbreviated to S/H or, in our case, Lenù/Lila, as L/L.

* * *

Fan fiction is not *about* fiction. It is fiction written through another text, in response to it, that takes up already established characters to change a story or continue it past the original ending. It is a genre mostly closely associated with popular culture and derided with similar archness. The critique goes like this: The problem with the fan of popular culture is that she does not possess critical distance. She favors proximity. She is overidentified, overinvested in a story, and therefore confuses what is real and what is a representation.[13] Fan fiction only ratchets up these risks. What presumption indeed, to appropriate wholescale someone else's fictional world as though your own imagined ending could replace the real one.

Beginning in the 1970s, fans of the *Star Trek* franchise began writing in what would become a subgenre of the wider fan-fiction universe. This writing imagined the romantic, often sexually explicit coupling of the series' male protagonists Kirk and Spock.[14] This writing spawned further subgenres of homoerotic romance, from soft core to the sexually explicit, now widely available online. Slash fiction isn't always pornographic, but as Abigail De Kosnik has noted, "it is easier to find erotic fiction in fic archives than it is on the shelves of most bookstores.[15] For Kosnik, the proliferation of internet databases devoted to slash fiction make up what she calls a "female public sex culture" organized around all manner of practices beyond the electronic publishing of sexual content, including the formation of fan communities, websites, chat groups, trivia archives, video games, artwork, and performance.[16]

What kind of female public sex cultures emerged around the Neapolitan cycle? Posted on the fan fiction database Wattpad, Zoe Dinovi's *My Brilliant Threesome* rewrites the summer at Ishchia to include a sexual entanglement between Nino, Lenù and Lila.[17] On *An Archive of Our Own*, the story "L'amica crudele" returns to the moment before Lila's wedding, when Lenù bathes and dresses the future bride.[18] The story is a time-loop, so we return to this scene again and again. Each return grows more sexually explicit. There is a kiss. Bathtub sex. Bed sex. Each version of the wedding day goes differently, but in the end nothing changes. Lila still marries Stefano. The comment thread is full of enthusiasm for the time loop effect. "God, I love the bathing scene, in the book and in the TV show now also, and it's crying out for exactly this sort of eroticism between them. Bless you for this <3."

As a female public sex culture, Ferrante fan fiction creates a space where anonymized fans connect through their shared desire to produce and consume queer alternatives to the Neapolitan cycle. However, there are other narrative trajectories in this fan fic universe. One story is tagged "getting revenge on Nino because he wasted all of our time."[19] Another considers Ferrante's novels as a reference point for a particular mode of fan fiction: "The thought had come into her head when first starting to go Ferrante-style on the book. Change everyone's names, change slight details, and give herself a pseudonym."[20] To go "Ferrante-style" on a book here becomes an act of rewriting the truth into a thinly veiled fiction, one that toys with its own liminal status, perpetually highlighting the instability between fictional character and real person.

Much of the speculative writing about the author Elena Ferrante could be classified as fan fic, though the journalists involved might see this as an insult. But what else is it, exactly, to persistently reconsider how a novel might be read differently, to hold it up to the light and peer at it through different angles, according to the hypothetical biography of the author? Ferrante fever, sometimes derided as a bio craze over the infinite worlds of possible authors that might be Elena Ferrante, depends upon a reader's capacity to absorb alternative possibilities of authorhood and then expand on the cycle into a perpetually receding future.

Live performance only complicates this temporal suspension, as we all discovered through a version of slash fiction much closer to home. This is the play *Contemporaries*, written by Erica Wachs, directed by Aparna Nair-Kanneganti, and produced by Jocelyn Wexler in 2018. The play is an adaption and rewriting of the online posts from "The Slow Burn." It opens with fictional versions of the four of us, played by Phoebe Cardenas, Agnes Enkhtamir, Emily Harburg, and Stella Shannon. We/they are in a group chat, fretting over whether or not to commit to the extended Ferrante collaboration, given the ways nonacademic writing is virtually ignored by the various committees that will decide our tenure. The conversations launch into snippets from the posts themselves. Then our fictional selves morph into Ferrante's characters, so that I become Lila and Merve Stefano, while we are cooking together with a copper pot. Fictional Sarah then becomes Lenù to my Lila, over the phone. Katherine turns into Nino, the impossible object of my and Lila's love.

The transformation from one character to the next is aided by props. Sarah puts on glasses, as Lenù saying to Lila, "What you do I do."[21] Our fictional selves develop rivalries and talk each other down on the couch. It's a maze of misperceptions: "You ended up attributing to her capacities that are only yours," says Katherine/Nino to Sarah/Lenù. Fictional me develops an unrequited crush on fictional Katherine who is, in the play and real life, a married and heterosexual person. This is an infatuation mediated by our Ferrante counterparts, through Lila's love for Nino. Both of these selves begin to take over their host bodies in a way that fictional me finds entirely distressing: "To not be in control of yourself like that, to be moving as one body but thinking as another." Unable to solidify these dissolving boundaries, fictional me has a nervous breakdown and my fictional long-distance girlfriend jumps ship, which is both real and not real. Or that happened and didn't happen, as Katherine would say.

It is hard to describe the mixture of flattery and mortification involved in watching a fictional representation of your life written and performed by unflaggingly earnest undergraduate Ferrante fans. Their feminist enthusiasm and overall smarts were a life-affirming force during year two of the Trump administration. But it was also like listening to a recording of your own voice, in that all number of potentially self-annihilating questions emerged, as though a whole new world of interpersonal awkwardness had suddenly come into view. I wondered; Do I actually sound like that? Do other people think I have always sounded like that? Should I change my entire way of being so that I do not ever sound like that? As Merve noted, our undergraduate avatars were all much younger, hotter, and more glamorous than real us. Their fictive interactions were sometimes disturbingly apt and often hilariously mistaken, usually in the service of generating a plot with forward momentum.

However, beyond the case of the dissolving margins, I turn to the play because it offers a specifically theatrical version of the fan fiction subgenre called slash. The play rewrites Ferrante's love plots as heterosexual and queer at the same time. Katherine turns into Nino, but this is a purely imaginative transformation, so that the sexual tension between Nino and Lila, say, is simultaneously the sexual tension between the two female actresses appearing on stage. Consider this exchange, between Sarah (as Lenù) and Katherine (as Nino), "Tell me you won't forget me, tell me you won't leave me, tell me you love me."

It's a line from Ferrante, recast through fictional Sarah and fictional Katherine. This isn't quite slash fiction in the normative sense. The performance allows for the simultaneous existence of alternative versions in conflict—Ferrante's novels, our letters, the theatrical adaptation. In the present tense of the play's performance, the love plots between Nino/Lenù and Sarah/Katherine happen at the same time, refracted through one another.

Amidst these refractions, I began to rethink some of my earlier claims about female friendship and attachment more generally. In one of my first posts, I argued that Ferrante's work is unusual for the ways that female friendship gets the kind of complex and extended attention usually devoted to romantic love. I still think this is true. But there needs to be a caveat, because it can be easy to generalize about female friendship as a heterosexual form of attachment that does away with the messier complications of sexual desire. In this account, sex is the negative category of a positive formulation: on one hand, platonic female friendship; on the other hand, sex and romantic love. This bracketing insists upon the heterosexual couple as the presumed norm, so that female friendship and romantic love are mutually exclusive domains.

Queer female friendships open up more varied possibilities of attachment, including the open possibility of future sex and the now-friends who are past lovers. Within this arc there are so many minute variations, for which I don't have discrete terms. Instead I think of what Lauren Berlant has named as one of the motivating projects for queer theory more generally, to account for "patterns of attachment we hadn't even yet known to notice, patterns in which sexuality and intimacy are enacted in a broad field of social relations that anchor us to life." These attachments extend beyond the dyad of platonic friendship and romantic love: "Being a friend, a regular, a neighbor, a part-time lover, an ex-lover, an intimate; being gender dysphoric, or just plain gay or straight—all of it is seen as an effect of many causes and a complex, intimate practice of world-building."[22]

Fan fictions like *Contemporaries* offer an "intimate practice of world-building" but might also be considered a queer theory on their own terms, for the ways that these fictions pivot between received plotlines about romantic attachment and imagined alternatives, so our final version involves a combinatory understanding of both. Here it is useful to turn to Carolyn Dinshaw, who is an object of my own fan-girl attachments, in part because she has written so perceptively on the alignment between queerness and the figure of the amateur. "The concepts that typically characterize amateurism—immaturity, belatedness or underdevelopment, inadequate separation from objects of love, improper attachment inappropriate loving—sound just like what a developmental psychologist trained within the paradigm of a normative life course might say about the sexual 'deviant,'" Dinshaw contends.[23] Fan fiction is an amateur practice, usually unpaid and understood through this language of stunted, even perverse development. But we might also note that the sort of writing we are doing through the letters here, in a collaborative, too-personal mode, has something of the amateur about it, because it happens outside of the channels of writing and research that are rewarded by our respective institutions.

A number of people within these institutions have made this clear to me in the well-intentioned and entirely unmalicious suggestion that I devote more of my time to the writerly labors that will ensure future job security. It has also been suggested to me that my academic writing is too personal, as though the journalistic endeavors had contaminated the more scholarly ones. Finally, it has been suggested to me that I might like Ferrante's work because I think I'm her—or really, that I think the novels are about me, a middle-class lady academic. To this I have three responses, ranging from the petty to the somewhat existential. Response one goes: no one says this about the critics of Knausgaard or Roth or Pynchon or McCarthy or Lerner. Though all of these authors have created multivolume author/protagonist metafictions, these fictions center white male heterosexuality, so they go unmarked, as neutral or universally sympathetic. Response two: I am no more like an exceptionally upwardly mobile Italian superstar novelist-academic in her sixties than I am like any other metafictional author/protagonist I encounter.

But my third response, more forceful, less irritable, can only be posed as a series of questions; Isn't reading always about these confusions, or the suspended belief necessary for the identification with a fictional personality that is not you? Does writing through Ferrante, even over her, appear to others as though I had momentarily lost my wits and forgotten this basic fact, that I am not her? Even worse, is my fixation on latent sexual tension, on the queer counterfactual love plot of Lenù and Lila, a naïve or perverse fantasy, silly even, in that it shunts aside the real ending, the real novels, in favor of my own improper attachments? Finally, why can't all of these things be true?

Rather than turn to a more distanced, properly academic mode, I want to linger with the problem attributed to myself and fan writers: that the female spectator, the amateur, is confused. She mistakes herself for a character. She is improperly attached, too close really, to assess her object as something distinct from herself. Or, for the writer of slash fiction: she forgets the real story, the true story, in favor of her own projected fantasy.

Instead of the language of mistaken, unknowing fixation, I want consider the status of the amateur, the fan writer, and the female spectator as a composite category within the wider arc of the counterfactual. To insist upon a counterfactual involves sustaining two versions of events that can't both be true. As a structure of feeling, this isn't quite confusion, nor dilettantism, but extreme dissonance. It involves a particular mental acrobatics: holding two incompatible propositions in your head at the same time and insisting, with equal strength, on both, anyways.

* * *

This structure of feeling, the one that insists upon two incompatible truths, is better known in its Freudian incarnations as the structure of the fetish. In the 1927 essay, "Fetishism," Freud begins with a story about heterosexual development.[24] The young boy notices that his mother lacks a penis and is struck with horror. He fears that he, too, will be castrated. To overcome this trauma, the boy must find a substitute for the missing penis, which then becomes the fetish object. But the boy doesn't really forget. Instead, the fetish is a contradictory substitute, one that disavows the mother's lack while also affirming it. The fetish thus allows for "two incompatible assertions," usefully glossed by analyst Octave Mannoni as "I know very well, but all the same."[25]

What I never liked about this story is its basis on heterosexual masculinity. The fetish, for Freud, "saves the fetishist from becoming a homosexual, by endowing women with the characteristic that makes them tolerable as sexual objects."[26] What I like about this story is the way that it allows for negativity. Freud makes it clear that inhabiting "two incompatible assertions" is not a comfortable place to be. To rethink the counterfactual as a fetishistic structure is useful because it allows the *it might have happened otherwise* to be steeped in both longing and horror.

So far, I have considered a number of counterfactuals directly related to Ferrante's narrative as absences that the reader imaginatively reconstructs in a conditional tense: Lila's writing in the destroyed notebooks; the Italian dialect lost in translation; and the queer love plot that might have been. But here at the end I want to think about counterfactual endings to the historical moment of the Neapolitan cycle.[27] This final case is slightly different.

Persons that insist on the *It might have been otherwise* in their accounts of the historical past are rarely understood as confused or inappropriately attached fan-girls. Instead, they might be seen, usually sympathetically, as utopian or, less sympathetically, as naïve. This assessment forgets the second half of the sentence: that history might have been otherwise, *but it wasn't.*

To hold these two facts in your head and insist equally upon them is not a comfortable place to be. Or to rephrase someone else, history hurts, but so do its counterfactual alternatives. For this structure of feeling, the Freudian allegory is not particularly helpful, in part because it is so deeply based on heterosexual object choice as the unmarked norm. Instead, I want to consider a different narrative structure for disavowal and affirmation twined together, or *I know, but all the same.* Fittingly enough, this narrative is a historical cousin to Freud's, in that it also emerges in the 1920s during a period of prolonged scientific experimentation.

The story starts with Pavlov's dogs. The history that most people know is about positive reinforcement. The dogs drool as soon as they see the technicians that will feed them. Then they start drooling according to a metronome associated with feeding, then according to specific tempos on the metronome. Pavlov called this salivating a conditioned response, because it could occur apart from its object, the food. The part that I am interested in is something different.

Late into Pavlov's career, seven years after the October Revolution, there was a massive flood in Leningrad.[28] This was September 1924. The river Neva rose five feet by the afternoon. By 3 p.m. the canals and rivers were overflowing. That evening there were four assistants left at the Academy of Sciences on the Petrograd side of the river. The assistants realized too late that the waters would have flooded the building where the dogs were kenneled, a quarter mile away. When they got to the building, the cages had filled with water and the dogs were all paddling at the surface, trapped inside. The assistants took each dog by the collar and forced it underwater, through the door of the cage, then led the dogs to a second lab on higher ground. They did this in three groups. By the time the assistants got to the last group, they had to swim too, against the current and alongside the dogs, to the buildings a quarter mile away.

After the trauma of the flood, the dogs' conditioned responses stopped working. The dogs would hear the metronome but not associate it with food. They would not leave their cages or even get up to eat. Pavlov concluded that the flood had temporarily short-circuited these learned behaviors. When the waters were rising, the dogs remained trapped in their cages, creating a traumatic collision between opposing instinctual reactions for survival. The short-circuit happened at an extreme moment of incompatible tensions set against one another, between excitation and inhibition, or more colloquially, between fight and flight.

The story about the Neva flood offers a different kind of structural narrative for the coexistence of two opposing impulses, or *I know very well, but all the same*. But this time the narrative is not based on the heterosexual family romance. It rests on an identification much more pointedly fantastic, all projection. That is to say, for this story to work, you have to think about what the laboratory dogs would have felt like, trapped in their kennels, while the waters were rising. The flood would not be like anything that had ever happened to them before. All the habits that had organized a recognizable world could not be used to make sense of this particular event. The footholds that used to work would no longer provide their expected purchase, no matter how long you ran through the trail of associations, of this thing that leads to the other, so that, so that. Then you reach out for something familiar, only to hold it up in your hand and realize that that, that thing, was not your hand at all, not you.

It's amidst this narrative confusion, right down to the level of grammar and pronouns and species, that I want to place the short circuit of competing impulses that is the historical counterfactual *I know but all the same.* Not deluded or naïve, but something that hurts. I think about this structure of feeling as a single moment of contradiction that then bleeds into everything else, screwing up the learned behavior that Pavlov called a conditioned response. It is a structure of feeling caught between instincts equally rapt: between excitation and inhibition, fight or flight. In this version of instinctual short-circuit, our identification is marked as a projection across species. It will always be a bit wobbly, in part because you are inserting yourself into a narrative just as narrative begins break down as a recognizable method for arranging time. Narratives usually align cause and effect, like metronomes and then food. But the story of the Neva flood is also a story about the way trauma can totally gut narrative as a sense-making form. It's an admixture of fact and what we can't possibly know: that the dogs woke up and were lying in water, then standing in it, then swimming noses tilted right up to the ceiling of the world. That there was the day before and every other day before that, waking up on solid ground, what you were always touching but not really noticing as an unmarked foundation for everything else. That what had been the ground beneath your feet on all the other days was now only water, and freezing cold.

* * *

These were unstable times, arcing in waves. Many of us feared a return to the flat calm and stayed on the crest, holding on to extreme formulations and looking down with fear and rage. When we learned that the security force of Lotta Continua had attacked a separatist women's demonstration, we grew bitter to the point where, if one of the more rigid participants discovered that Mariarosa had a man in the house—which she didn't declare but didn't hide, either—the discussion became fierce, the ruptures dramatic.[29]

This is late into *Those Who Leave and Those Who Stay*. It is still a kind of middle. The passage describes being on the crest of a wave that threatens to roll backwards. The threat of backtracking provokes a kind of heightening, as if more rage, more fear, more bitterness, amongst whoever is closest at hand, might somehow create a combustion that could feed the times themselves, prolonging the wave's arc. Here antagonism loses its wider social dimensions so that this sense of *against* becomes redirected, moving away from the state and towards competing left tendencies.

In the first half of the novel, there is a sense that anything might happen. Mariarosa urges Lenù to become part of what she calls "*the unstoppable flow of events*" (*TWL*, 62–63). At this moment, Lenù is mostly a spectator to the actions of men: "The young heroes who faced the violence of the reactions at their own peril were called Rudi Dutschke, Daniel Cohn-Bendit, and, as in war films where there were only men, it was hard to feel part of it; you could only love them, adapt their thoughts to your brain, feel pity for their fate" (63). But Lenù briefly steps into another political formation, apart from the men, through the feminist collective that gathers to plan and read and think together in Mariarosa's apartment. "Her apartment was a sort of gathering place, she welcomed everyone, intellectuals, middleclass women, working-class women fleeing abusive companions, runaway girls," Lenù explains, before adding, "so that she had little time for me, and anyways she was too much a friend to all for me to feel sure of our bond. Any yet in her house the desire to study was rekindled, and even to write" (351).

I want the novel to end there, with the women in Mariarosa's apartment and the open horizon of Lenù's rekindled desire. It doesn't. Over the past two years, I've spent a long time looking at the actual end of the novel. It is pockmarked with sticky notes. I know what I would say about it if I were writing an article for an academic journal. I would say that the historical energies of Hot Autumn, this sense that anything could happen, disrupting the old ways of doing and thinking, moves from a collective tendency to something more isolated. Amidst the fracture of political possibility, these energies are relocated to the romantic couple. In those last pages, as Lenù leaves her husband and children for Nino, she is still using the language of revolution. "I thought: Something great is happening that will dissolve the old way of living entirely and I'm part of that dissolution" (*TWL*, 418). Notice that "I thought." It conditions the claim, which is no longer about the world per se, but about Lènu's affair with Nino. This romance seems revolutionary to Lènu because it upends her entire life, breaking up her marriage and separating her from her children. The last sentence of the novel literalizes this effect from the air during Lenù's first plane trip: "At times I had the impression that the floor under my feet—the only surface I could count on—was trembling" (418).

This moment at the end of the novel is profoundly sad, because we know Lenù is wrong. It is difficult to think of a less promising suitor to break up the old ways of living. Nino is the absent father of Lila's child and Silvia's child. In her cannier moments, Lenù knows this: "He had loved many women, he went from one bed to the next, he sowed children carelessly, he considered marriage a necessary convention but one that couldn't keep desires in a cage" (*TWL*, 390). In my first reading of the novels, I had no time for Lenù's infatuation with Nino. He's terrible and she *knows*, but all the same. He's in love with someone else, and she knows, *but*. No one can talk her out of it, because reason is not the point. That last *but* is beyond reasoning entirely.

Here too, I should say, is where my properly academic reading breaks off, because I don't know how to get at this problem of ending without talking about what I like and don't like. What if my relationship to this book is the relation of a fan, rather than a critic? What if this attachment is characterized by a sense of ownership, a kind of protective glaze, that also entails a more fungible relation to the plot, in terms of what happened and what might happen?

So then I think about Pavlov's dogs, as a scenario of knowing and not-knowing, that could also be a story about the counterfactual. There is the historical world that is Italy in the 1970s—a story with an ending that we already know. There is the novel that Elena Ferrante wrote that constructs a fictional world against this historical backdrop. It is possible that this fictional world is actually an autobiography, not make believe. These are the things that I can work with, as a literary critic. But more than anything else I want to stake out a position midway through *Those Who Leave and Those Who Stay*, just at that moment in Mariarosa's apartment, and stay there, crouched. I want to pull the rest of the pages around me like a blanket and hide.

In this particular imagination, other narratives get reanimated as distinct possibilities. Consider, for instance, this scene: after the first student meeting, after watching Silvia nurse her child while arguing with the others, and then amidst the debate that continues into Mariarosa's apartment, Lenù is struck. She realizes that Lila will never be a part of this political momentum. "A pity, I felt guilty," she responds, predictably. Then, fantastically, "I should have carried her off, kidnapped her, made her travel with me. Or at least reinforced her presence in my body, mixed her voice with mine" (*TWL*, 75). Where is this second, more fantastic story? How might we consider it as something real, in that the *I should have* continues to haunt the text as a queer counterfactual?

So here I am, on page 75, staring at a statement made in the past conditional tense. *I should have carried her off, kidnapped her, made her travel with me.* It is and isn't true. It happened and didn't happen, as Katherine would say. This is the reanimation of that pairing, *Lila and I:* her body in another body, her voice with mine. It is a story that plays out at different moments, out of order. Lenù hears Lila talking, in her head. "It was a confusion of space and time, of distant moods" (*TWL*, 75). In this reading, the one where we linger in the middle of the book, pockets of the counterfactual possess a gravitational force. Or I am overly attached to them, so that this liking tips the balance, rendering the counterfactual somehow too weighty, as though the mixing, "her voice with mine," could infect other moments, other plotlines, real and not, even though we know, I know, that it didn't happen, but all the same.

To imagine this structure of feeling, I think of Pavlov's dogs, treading water where there used to be ground. I think of Lenù in the air, on the plane to France with Nino, imagining the revolution that will not happen. I think of the ways that so much of this narrative, across the series, involves writing through and over someone else. That doesn't mean forgetting what did happen; it insists on both incompatible narratives at the same time, anyways.

What would it look like if the queer counterfactual drives of fan fiction and academic literary criticism were to inch a little closer to one another? It might be a conversation between two women or a more collaborative back and forth in an epistolary mode. It might involve the reanimation of childhood pacts and the tying of loose threads, so that all number of things could remain true and not true, as a different way of ending. Indeed, any sort of story might be revived in the conditional future tense, not to take over, but as a more haphazard stumbling around, to wreak havoc in its zombie-like iterations. "Immediately shatter everything and every person in the neighborhood, tear them to pieces, Lila and I, go and live far away, lightheartedly descending together all the steps of humiliation, alone, in unknown cities" (*SNN*, 19). I think of a confusion of space and time, some words borrowed from the original, then given over in paraphrase, the dialect missing. This is a stubborn habitation, indeed. It is unreasonable, without half-measures. Promiscuous, too personal, an amateur practice, identifications wobbly and improperly attached, but all the same. It's as though the floor under your feet—the only surface you can count on— was trembling.

THE CAGE OF AUTHORSHIP

MERVE EMRE

Saverio Costanzo, the forty-three-year old director of the HBO limited series *My Brilliant Friend*, is a haunted man. For over a decade, he has corresponded with a woman whose face he cannot see, whose voice he cannot hear, whose existence is confirmed only by the many thousands of words she has written dissecting his artistic choices. When he speaks of her, his black eyes turn upward, as if seeking a trace of her in the cracks of the ceiling or in some metaphysical plane high above the penthouse suite of the Beverly Hilton Hotel, where Costanzo and the cast of *My Brilliant Friend* have arrived for HBO's summer press tour. "Sometimes she was so strong," he says gruffly. "I don't know. I'm still trying to put everything together. It's very hard. It was like working with a ghost."[1]

Costanzo's ghost has a name: Elena Ferrante, the pseudonymous author of the four beloved Neapolitan novels, of which *My Brilliant Friend* is the first to be adapted for television (it aired on HBO on November 18). She initially appeared to Costanzo in 2007, when he wrote to her Italian publishers, Sandro Fieri and Sandra Ozzoli Ferri at Edizioni E/O, to purchase the film rights to Ferrante's novella *The Lost Daughter*. He was drawn to Ferrante's "very small, very accurate, very dangerous" story about Leda, a middle-aged English professor seized by guilt and a sense of inadequacy over the one-time abandonment of her husband and children. While summering on the Ionian coast, Leda imposes on a young mother and her daughter, stealing the little girl's doll at the beach and watching as her mother tries, and fails, to contain the child's pain. Costanzo read *The Lost Daughter* as a tragedy: a tale of mythic, unrequited suffering designed to hurt its readers. He wanted to see if, as a filmmaker, he could create a visual idiom to match Ferrante's emotional brutality, her unparalleled ability to "hurt her readers."

Fieri and Ferri told him it was unlikely Ferrante would agree. She had been disappointed by the adaptations of her two previous novellas and, according to Costanzo, she wanted nothing more to do with what she called "the world of show business, with its many moving parts and conspicuous cash flow."[2] He had abandoned the idea when he received, through her publishers, an admiring message from Ferrante, issuing him a challenge. She was willing to cede him the rights to *The Lost Daughter* for six months, enough time for him to devise an adaptation that would please them both. For six months, Costanzo labored; for six months, *The Lost Daughter* resisted his intrusions, until finally, he told Ferrante he would renounce the rights. "I was thirty-years-old—just a kid," he recalls.

For nine years, Costanzo heard nothing from Ferrante. He grew up and became one of Italian cinema's youngest and most challenging auteurs. He directed a series of claustrophobic dramas not unlike Ferrante's novellas, featuring characters whose lonely and inscrutable acts of destruction—a teenager's self-mutilation in *The Solitude of Prime Numbers* (2010), a mother's slow starvation of her child in *Hungry Hearts* (2014)—poison the people around them. His characters, especially his female leads, inspired pity, fear, and revulsion before they inspired sympathy, and then only sparingly. Then, one day in 2016, he received a surprising phone call from

Edizioni E/O informing him that he was one of the two directors Ferrante had suggested for a television adaptation of My Brilliant Friend; then, some weeks later, they called again to tell him the producers had chosen him to direct.

Costanzo was reluctant. The last thing he wanted to do with his career was adapt a novel—and not just any novel but a novel that had surpassed ordinary best-seller status to emerge, instead, as an event, a sensation, a literary pathology: "Ferrante fever," as readers had taken to calling the frenzy that greeted the release of each Neapolitan novel—the midnight release parties; the grave discussions about the books' covers; the jostling reviews, with each critic claiming to know her art more intimately than the critic who came before. He did not want to deal with the expectations of Ferrante's readers, who were inclined to project onto her punishing tale of female friendship the faces of women they had once loved and hated in equal measure. But My Brilliant Friend was the rarest of opportunities: a second chance for him to create his own story with Elena Ferrate. "She was giving me her hands and saying, 'I did it. Why don't you do it?'" he tells me, reaching his hands into the empty space before him, as if she might appear to fold them into hers.

Now when Costanzo talks about Ferrante, it is with a deference one rarely sees directors exercise toward writers whose work they adapt. She has commented by email on drafts of all eight of his scripts. She has flagged moments when his dialogue verges on the melodramatic. ("She just says, 'This dialogue is ridiculous, the way she talks here is ridiculous.'") She has protected him from serious missteps, like when he thought to cut the loud, quarrelsome wedding banquet that ends My Brilliant Friend from the series because he was over budget and running behind schedule. ("She said, "Listen, the first moment I thought about My Brilliant Friend, the first image I had was a banquet, a very vulgar banquet of Neapolitan life. Please put the banquet back in.") "She is very strong," Costanzo repeated, permitting himself a sheepish little laugh. "I like that." When he recalls all the times he has risked disappointing her, he pouts, like a child who has failed, yet again, to live up to his mother's expectations.

* * *

The Neapolitan novels tell the story of a writer, also named Elena ("Lenù" for short), whose subject is the filth of the neighborhood in Naples where she grew up and her long acquaintance with Lila, the brilliant, disagreeable classmate she leaves behind and returns to intermittently over the next fifty years. When Lila disappears without warning at the age of sixty-six, leaving behind no clothes, shoes, letters, or photographs to testify to her existence, Lenù decides to write about their long and troublesome relationship: their shared love of reading, the education they defied their parents to pursue, the writing they collaborated on, the men they both loved, the children they raised together, all set against the backdrop of the Italian Republic's growing social and political turbulence. Spurred by anger and a desire for vengeance, Lenù sets out to counter Lila's self-erasure by preserving her life in the form a novel, making their history irrevocably present in her reader's imagination.

Though the novels are billed as tales of female friendship, friendship always skates on the edge of irony—intimacy is inseparable from violation. Lenù is the one making art out of Lila's life, but she suspects that Lila has driven her to do it, that the pleasure she derives from writing and reading is spiked by the pain of submitting to another's will. It is a fitting model for the relationship Ferrante's readers have with her novels, which are universally celebrated for their addictiveness. One is pulled, sometimes dragged, along by Ferrante's prose with an intensity that seems at once utterly

singular and reassuringly dispersed. To read her novels is to feel
that one is drawing on a reservoir of shared emotion—rage, disgust,
pity, indignation, tenderness—to which one has somehow, secretly,
contributed.

Ferrante's women are inscrutable, their minds deep and disor-
dered and disinclined to sentimentality, to easy morals. As a narrator, Lenù recalls her younger self tentatively, piecing together
hypotheses that tend to obscure rather than clarify her motivations.
Her choice phrases in examining her actions are *maybe*, *or*, and *who
knows*. "Maybe, I thought, I've given too much weight to the culti-
vated use of reason, to good reading, to well controlled language,
to political affiliation," she reflects on her education, the reason
she has escaped the neighborhood while Lila has stayed behind.
"Maybe in the face of abandonment we are all the same."[3] There is
consciousness here—the quickening of a mind eager to reflect on its
past—but no interiority: no private, orderly, honest *I* that maps the
depths and boundaries of the self.

Yet it is precisely because Ferrante's characters are so undefined
that they seem readily inhabited by others, both inside and outside
the novel. "I realized that she wasn't capable of thinking that she
was herself and I was myself," Lenù observes of Lila. It is a will to
identification she reciprocates, though it is hard for her to admit
it. "My model remained Lila, with her stubborn unreasonableness
that refused to accept half measures" she writes. "Although I was
now distance from her, I wanted to say and do what I imagined she
would say and do if she had my tools, if she had not confined herself
within the space of the neighborhood."[4] The *I* that Ferrate conjures
is restless, unbounded, permeable to the monstrous desires that
many women feel but few dare express. Her *I* is easy to mistake for
your own estranged *I*.

Though her characters' minds are indefinite and abstract, their
bodies are always present. The women in Ferrante's novels bleed

and break. They know the monotonous injuries inflicted on them by men seeking only their own satisfaction, as well as the frank, intense sexual pleasure that arrives when one least expects it. In an extraordinary scene toward the end of *My Brilliant Friend* when Lenù bathes Lila before her wedding and, many years later, remembers "the violent emotion that overwhelms you, so that it forces you to stay, to rest your gaze on the childish shoulders, on the breasts and stiffly cold nipples, on the narrow hips and the tense buttocks, on the black sex, on the long legs, on the tender knees, on the curved ankles, on the elegant feet."[5] Here there is no doubting *I*. There is only *you*—you, the reader—seduced into sharing the exquisite, confounding pleasure of desiring an imagined woman's body.

Lenù's agitated gaze mirrors the desires of readers who have sought, behind the name Elena Ferrante, the flesh-and-blood person who has inflamed their imaginations. Since the publication of *Troubling Love* in 1991, Ferrante has abstained from interviews, festivals, prize ceremonies. It is not clear when her abstention turned into anonymity, or when that anonymity acquired its peculiar aura, but it might have been in the mid-1990s, when she began to correspond with journalists, answering their questions about her life, always with the caveat that her answers might be lies. By 2000, there was an impressive shortlist of people rumored to be Elena Ferrante—men, women, couples, collectives. In 2006, mathematicians and physicists at the University of Rome used stylometric analysis to compare her novels to a corpus of over 150 Italian novels, and they concluded that she was Italian novelist Domenico Starnone. Ten years later, reporter Claudio Gatti used Edizioni E/O's leaked financial statements to name someone else, a woman, in the *New York Review of Books*. His disclosure was met with a public outcry that he had spoiled the fun.

What fun, exactly? The theorist Michel Foucault once observed that literary anonymity was nothing more than a puzzle to be solved.[6]

But literary anonymity, as Ferrante practices it, is not a puzzle—it is an expressive strategy. It has its styles and its goals, one of which is to multiply and muddle the distinct egos of the author: Elena as the writer of the Neapolitan novels; Elena as their first-person narrator; Elena as a commentator on the novels she has written. Sometimes the tension that holds these egos in check is precisely calibrated, thrilling to behold. "Elena Ferrante is the author of several novels," she wrote in an interview with *The Guardian*, weaving between the first and third person. "There is nothing mysterious about her, given how she manifests herself—perhaps even too much—in her own writing, the place where her creative life transpires in absolute fullness."[7] The final Neapolitan novel, *The Story of the Lost Child*, ends with Lenù writing a "remarkably successful story" about her and Lila called *A Friendship*, a double of the Neapolitan novels, which are full of urtexts written by Elena Greco. Armed with her anonymity, Ferrante has subsumed all traces of her life into an elaborate fiction and asked us, her readers, to help sustain its enchantment—to dissolve the boundaries between the Elenas until we can no longer disentangle fiction from reality or identify who among us is responsible for creating this enthralling state of affairs.

Ferrante often describes her novels as mysterious, inviolable creatures that have escaped her grasp and journeyed freely into the world. Their immortal life offers a supplement to her mortal one—and suggests that we can revive the historical moment prior to authorship, before writers owned the words they wrote, before the spines of books came bearing names. Yet, paradoxically, Ferrante's self-erasure has had the opposite effect from what she claims. It has resurrected a powerful, almost transcendent, myth of the author as removed from the realities of time and space, a creator whose novels spring from her head armored and fully formed, a theorist of her own conditions of existence. What other writer enjoys such power?

* * *

It is dangerous to draw too close to that power; it convinces you that you can share in it. When I first asked Ferrante's editor if I could interview her for this piece, she declined. Then she changed her mind for reasons unknown to me. It was impossible not to speculate about why she had capitulated. I was vain, imagining that the questions I had proposed to her editor about literary form and the politics of collaboration were smarter, more respectful, than the questions she was used to fielding about friendship or identity. I wanted to please, and I imagined that if I did, our exchange would vibrate with intellectual camararderie.

Yet over the course of a two-month correspondence, which was mediated by her editor, my editor, and her translator, Ann Goldstein, the distance between us seemed only to expand. She answered questions I had not asked and ignored the ones I had. She got irritated, apologized, misinterpreted my phrasing—willfully, I suspected. When I asked her what living authors she enjoyed reading, she wrote, "I would have to give a very complex answer, talking about various stages of my life. I'll answer you some other time."[8] When, I wondered, imagining that one day I might open my door and find a children's wagon full of moldy novels, with no address, no note, no glimpse of a telltale figure disappearing into the shadows.

An interview is a collaboration too, though like all collaborations with Ferrante, an imbalanced one. Often, she answered my questions in the same oblique style as her narrator. "Maybe in more than a few cases I was overly frank," she wrote when I ask her what instructions she gave Costanzo. "Maybe I intervened, with some presumptuousness, in irrelevant details." She told me she thinks collaborations between women are more difficult than collaborations between a woman and a man, whose authority a woman can either submit to or pretend to recognize while pursuing her own agenda. "It's more complicated to recognize the authority of another woman; tradition in that case is more fragile," she wrote. "It works if, in a relationship between the person in charge and the subordinate, the first wants the other to grow and free herself from her subordinate status, and the second gains her autonomy without feeling obliged to diminish the other."

As the subordinate, I could only strategize how to ask questions that would compel her to write useful answers for me. My initial strategy was to present myself as a new mother who found in Ferrante's fiction the emotional tumult of motherhood as I am living it. In the note that preceded my questions, I tell her that I have found myself returning to the third book in the Neapolitan Series, *Those Who Leave and Those Who Stay*, many times since having my two children. No other novel I have read captures the vicissitudes of motherhood with such precision: the power and vulnerability of caring for others, the intimacy and distance between mother and child. When I became a mother, it was painful to realize that my mother had a separate life, a different self, before she became my mother; painful too to think that my children might not realize this about me until it is too late.

She did not acknowledge my note.

I tried again with a question, only this time my tone was less sentimental, more acerbic. I observed that contemporary writing on motherhood has an irritating tendency to treat children as psychological impediments to creativity—as if a child must steal not only time and energy from his mother but also language and thought. But her novels are different: they entertain the possibility that motherhood might be an experience conducive to creativity, even when it is tiring or onerous. For a short time, Lila transforms motherhood into an act of grace, and though she finds her children burdensome, Lenù's greatest professional success comes after she

becomes a mother. What did she take to be the relationship between
time spent taking care of one's words and time spent take caring of
one's children?

She was more receptive this time, if a little scolding. "I very
much like the way you've formulated the question," she wrote.
"But I want to say that it's not right to speak of motherhood in
general. The troubles of the poor mother are different from those
of the well-off mother, who can pay another woman to help her.
But, whether the mother is rich or poor, if there is a real, powerful
creative urge, the care of children, however much it absorbs and
at times even consumes us, doesn't win out over the care of words:
one finds the time for both. Or at least that was my experience:
I found the time when I was a terrified mother, without any support,
and also when I was a well-off mother. So I will take the liberty
of asserting that women should in no case give up the power of
reproduction in the name of production."

There was something different about the style of this answer.
The *I* she wielded seemed more present, more forceful, the
defenseless voice of the writer behind the author. I ask her to say
more about being a terrified mother. What, I asked, was the nature
of that terror for her?

She retreated, adopting the impersonal tone and banal gener-
alities of the commentator once again. "I'm afraid of mothers who
sacrifice their lives to their children," she writes. "I'm afraid of
mothers who surrender themselves completely and live for their
children, who hide the difficulties of motherhood and pretend
even to themselves to be perfect mothers." It is tempting to rewrite
these statements to reclaim the immediacy of her *I*: "*I* was afraid
of sacrificing my life to my children; *I* was afraid of surrendering
myself completely." But nothing authorizes it. It may not even be
the right interpretation; she may really be talking about her fear of
other mothers. Why do I want to make it about her? To do so would

be to traffic in fiction. But the traffic in fiction is pleasurable. It prompts me to study her language carefully, to appreciate anew the words she has chosen, the phrases she repeats, how easily she moves between sentences. It prompts me rewrite her words to project fears I may or may not have onto the figure of the author— the character she and I are sustaining. It lets me speak without speaking for myself.

Last try. For the past two months, I told her, my two-year-old son has developed an obsession with her children's book *The Beach at Night*. The book involves a self-pitying doll that a little girl abandons on the beach at sunset, preferring to play with her new pet cat. At night, the doll is discovered by a Mean Beach Attendant, a man who pulls a thin golden hook from his lips and forces it into the doll's mouth, ripping from her a secret which she has guarded with great care: her name. It struck me as an unsubtle allegory for Ferrante's anonymity, and it was hard to shake the sense that children were not its target audience. But my son has two copies of the book: one he keeps in his schoolbag, one for his bedside table, and sometimes before he goes to bed, he stares for a very long time at the strange, sad pictures of the doll.

"I wrote *The Beach at Night* for a four-year-old friend of mine who, to her great disappointment, had just had a little sister," she writes. "I was very surprised that my little book was considered unsuitable for young children—my friend had liked it. I've always believed that stories for children should have the same energy, the same authenticity, as good books for adults. It's a mistake to think that childhood needs syrupy fables. The traditional fairy tales weren't made with cotton candy."

My son has also just had a little brother, I told her. He is also disappointed, and I use *disappointment* to mirror how I think she is using it: to minimize a child's sense of abandonment, making his despair more palatable to the mother responsible for upending his world. Maybe my son is more discerning than I have realized. Maybe he has taken the book as it is, innocent of authors and allegories, and found in it a trace of his experience: a story that begins with the injury of replacement and ends with partial restitution—the reunion of the little girl, her doll, and, begrudgingly, the new cat. In his innocence, my son may be a better reader than I am.

She did not respond.

* * *

Part of me wishes I had never pursued her. She eludes me, scolds me, ruins my pleasure in having written thoughtful questions. She has made me self-conscious, exasperated. The entire time I have been writing this piece, I have felt a prickling sense of guilt. Ferrante wrote at the outset of our correspondence that she does not like it when a text is taken as an opportunity for talking about something else—the author, her readers. "I prefer work that concentrates on the page," she writes. "A good critical work says to the reader: here's where the author started from, here's where he wanted to take me, here are the means he used, here are the goals he was aiming for, here are his debts to tradition, here's why I liked or hated it." I hear in this an implicit injunction, a command. I worry that I have behaved irredeemably.

But why should I let her drag me where she wants me to go? Submitting to another's will, staying faithful to their vision, may not do anyone any good—not the women who write essays, not the men who direct films. Over the course of two years, I learn, Ferrante and Costanzo have exchanged regular emails, with screenwriter Francesco Pioccolo describing her as "a kind of supervisor" of his work[9]. "There is nothing wrong with a man wanting to make a film from my books," she wrote in *The Guardian* shortly after our interview. "But . . . even if he had a strongly defined vision of his own, I would ask him to respect my view, to adhere to my world, to enter the cage of my story without trying to drag it into his."[10] How had Ferrante coaxed Costanzo and his actresses, who have all read the novels, into the cage of her story? What were her instructions to them for transforming the uncertain stuff of Lenù's consciousness into a definite series of images?

I tell Ferrante that the actresses have read her novels, and I wonder what it is she hopes her youngest readers might glean from her books. "I don't know how to answer you," she writes. I take this to be an expression of irritation—I have asked her to address something off the page—and not bewilderment, because she proceeds to answer me. "I'd like the youngest readers to take from them the necessity of being properly prepared: not in order to be co-opted into male hierarchies but in order to construct a world different from the one we know, and to govern it," she writes. "Reading good books, always studying, regardless of the work she intends to do, should be a part of every girl's plan for her life. The only way not to let what we've gained be taken away from us is to be smart and capable, to learn to design the world better than men have so far done."

More important than love or friendship is the liberatory promise of a literary education—this is the interpretation of *My Brilliant Friend* that the actresses, with Costanzo and Ferrante as their teachers, have embraced more assiduously than most of the novel's critics. Outside, the women of the neighborhood feud pointlessly over stupid men, but in the classroom, Lila and Lenù stake out a private battlefield, "challenging each other, without ever saying a word," Ferrante writes (*MBF*, 27). From competition springs the promise of literary collaboration. Reading together morphs into writing together, and their prose, like Ferrante's own, is mythic, spellbinding, a revelation of "the capacity that together—only together—we had to seize the mass of colors sounds, things, and people, and express it and give it power" (138). But when Lenù goes to middle school, and Lila does not, this simple divergence sets them on two different paths through life, though they come back together over the course of the four novels to think, to write, to care for each other's children, to care for each other.

When compared to HBO's other contemporary offerings (*Westworld*, *Game of Thrones*), it seems unduly modest to adapt a story whose dramatic tension and pathos emerges from how two ordinary girls are brought together by literature only to be driven apart by their unequal access to literary culture. There is no rational explanation for this inequality: not intelligence (Lila is the more naturally gifted of the two), not diligence (Lila has a more determined and passionate mind), not family support (both girls' parents are initially opposed to their education). There is something inexplicable, something extrinsic to the logic of the real world, that touches Lenù and sets her on her upward climb out of the neighborhood. Yet this is what makes *My Brilliant Friend* a modern epic instead of a bildungsroman: the novel begins with an act of chance that originates outside the character and, over time, shapes her psychology, her place in the world—traces the boundaries of herself.

Part of teaching the actresses and Costanzo how to read is teaching them how to map these invisible boundaries against the visible scenery of film. Though Ferrante pronounced the child Lila "perfect," and the child Lenù "effective" at setting up the narrator's "indecipherability," their excellent performances do not stop the episodes from feeling constrained. Costanzo outsources the communication of the narrator's emotions to a voiceover, which he worries Ferrante will find "cheesy."[11] Unlike the voiceover, which addresses the audience in formal Italian, the actresses speak in the 1950s Neapolitan dialect he and a team of linguists created for the series. The sets are realistic, but strenuously so, resembling the backdrops one often sees in heritage dramas, sufficiently dusty and poor but curiously underpopulated compared to the human density of Ferrante's neighborhood. In the novels, the violence of the neighborhood is conveyed through fantasy, through Lenu's imagination of the "tiny, almost invisible animals" that enter "the water and the food and the air, making our mothers, our grandmothers as angry as starving dogs" (*MBF*, 38). Costanzo treats her imagination bluntly: Lenù dreams that a sewer-grate vomits large, brown cockroaches that scutter down the streets and into the mouth of her sleeping mother.

Where Ferrante's guidance seems most apparent is in Costanzo's attempt to make the depth and disorder of a character's consciousness visible, a technique he and Ferrante both refer to as "acquiring density." Density works by cutting against psychological realism, casting off deterministic explanations for why characters do what they do: a girl defies her father because of her nascent feminist sensibilities; a father beats his child because he believes women must be kept in their place. These interpretations may be true, but they are too abstract, too neat—they have little to do with how a reader experiences a character's actions as real. "What decides the success of a character is often half a sentence, a noun, an adjective that jams the psychological machine like a wrench thrown into the works and produces an effect that is no longer that of a well-regulated device, but of flesh and blood, of genuine life, and therefore incoherent and unpredictable," Ferrante writes to me. "It's the moment when the psychological framework breaks and the character acquires density."

For Costanzo, density is key to a faithful adaptation, the hinge between word and image. "The thing she really told me was, 'I care about the density,'" he explains in our interview. "We worked on that word a lot with the kids, also with the girls." He illustrates the concept with a metaphor he has borrowed from Ferrante.

Imagine that the lines an actress reads are a river that runs calmly along the surface of the earth. Then imagine that the actresses are the earth, and that under the earth is another river, a wilder one whose current leaps in the opposite direction, whose roar is muted. Every time the actress speaks her lines, she must offer a glimpse of the river that runs beneath: the mysterious churn of her consciousness, the lawlessness of a person's doubts or desires.

Elsewhere Ferrante has referred to these hidden depths as *frantumaglia*, "an unstable landscape, an infinite aerial or aquatic mass of debris that appears to the I, brutally, as its true and unique inner self."[12] In the novels, Lila has brief spells of terror when she perceives the margins of the people around her dissolving, exposing their greed, their ferocity, their meanness; spells of chaos and destruction when—to borrow Ferrante's metaphor—the river rises and floods the earth with "excruciating anguish . . . a vortex like-fracturing of material living and dead."[13] "She had the impression that something absolutely material, which had been present around her and around everyone and everything forever, but imperceptible, was breaking down the outlines of persons and things and revealing itself," Ferrante writes in *My Brilliant Friend* (90). The senselessness of our inner lives, and the impossibility of representing that senselessness through language, is what density registers and conceals.

The show does not always convey that senselessness. Sometimes the glances or grimaces intended to convey disorder simply make the actresses look confused or vacant. But when they—Ferrante, Costanzo, the actresses—get it right, it is electrifying. There is a magnificent scene in the second episode of *My Brilliant Friend* just after Lenù has been beaten for skipping school, when she and Lila gaze at each other from opposite ends of the courtyard where they live. It is a shot familiar from Costanzo's recent films but intensified by Ferrante's feminist sensibilities: the space between the girls hangs heavy with pain, injustice, loneliness, but also the dawning of a collective consciousness. One can sense the confused stirrings of opposition which, over the course of the four novels, will swell into a will to defiance, a desire for retribution, the mutual yearning to fight alongside each other—a desire we, as viewers, can share, just as we, as readers, have shared Ferrante's *I*. It's an opening of Ferrante's cage, an invitation to join her in the shadows.

AFTERWORD

Lincoln College, Oxford
July 21, 2018

Dear Friends,

I address you as such, readers, because if you have come this far, we have finished a project together. The smaller we—the four of us—have read and talked and written through the last three years together. You, now, have done some of this with us. And we've all read Ferrante together, in our own ways, at our own paces: we may not actually be friends, but we have learned some good things and bad things together about what friendship is and what it isn't.

I'm writing this late at night, in my nearly-bare room in Oxford. The unscreened windows are all open and I'm enjoying the delicious liberty of night air without the threat of mosquitos, a pleasure unheard of in my regular New York life. Merve and her family have just moved here, and we're overlapping for the last couple of weeks of the summer class I'm teaching. I feel incredibly lucky to have this time together with them. Ferrante comes up on occasion, as Merve is preparing to interview her by email, but mostly we sit in the back garden with Christian and the kids, drink, make dumb jokes, gossip. In general, as we've wrapped up this project over the last few months, we've all been in touch more than usual. I text with Jill about our recent, deeply stupid breakups and the struggles we're having with our other books, how she's feeling weary of Brooklyn, and how I'm missing it. I write to Katherine about where and when she and Matt are traveling this month, and logistical questions about planning a fundraiser, and what we'll do when we're both back in the city. We have some book business to take care of, but we really don't talk about Ferrante so much anymore. These are perfectly normal conversations with friends, but as I put this manuscript together even the most trivial things, catching me off guard, are suddenly overloaded with feeling.

I know they're my real friends and will keep being my real friends after the final edits of this book are done, but still, every time I sit down and try to write about this project, I want to cry. To anyone who knows me in person, this revelation will be comically bathetic; mortifyingly, I've become a frequent public crier in the last few years, for a variety of reasons whose personal specificities I won't bore you with. Fill in the usual clichéd gamut of political anxieties, relationship anxieties, family anxieties, climate change anxieties, tenure anxieties, money anxieties, race anxieties, gender anxieties, age anxieties, health anxieties, nothing to see here!—and the constant, fluctuating vibration of fear and anger felt by everyone concerned about the interlocking, fragile futures of our cities, our countries, our planet. Suffice to say: I've cried a lot in the last few years, and I suspect a lot of you have, too.

But the tears that well up unexpectedly when I think about "The Slow Burn" come from somewhere else. They're not tears of fear or rage or of thrumming baseline anxiety. I cry when I think about this project and what it's come to mean to me because it has been a refuge from all those other fears and anxieties, even— or especially—when my writing in it has come out of them. As the olds say the kids say, it's been my safe space, one that has afforded a productive and unusual vulnerability that reminds me of why I read and write in the first place. Working with this collective of women I love and trust innately, as writers, thinkers, and people, has allowed me to let down my professional guard and remember what I really want creative work and thought to feel like: wild, a little dangerous, *magmatic*. It has also reminded me that sharing this feeling with others can be even more exhilarating. To think and talk and write together, to trust each other with half-formed thoughts and urge each other on—as Lenù says early on, to "play the game"—has been an addictive thrill, an inspiration, and an unforeseen comfort. This sensation of simultaneous danger and safety is incredibly liberating and generative; it reclaims the meaning of "work in progress" from the pressurized academic proceedings of the conference or work-shop. What began as a playful summer experiment ended up posing a joyful but serious ongoing challenge to what I thought about the enterprise of critical writing and publishing, and to my own writing, critical and otherwise. These incipient tears are not exactly tears of joy, in the style of that overwrought emoji, but something like tears of gratitude for the work we've done together and the fact that we all wanted to keep doing it, even when it seemed unwise or pointless to do so.

The end of this book is not the end of this project of collective criticism. It's something that all of us who read and write together already engage in, whether we think about it that way or not. "The Slow Burn" (Ferrante Edition) may be over, but I urge you all to find your true correspondents, to open your conversations to the world, to trust each other and your fellow readers and writers with some of the things you're afraid to share; to see what sparks may light, then draw in closer to the fire.

Yours,
Sarah

Appendix

GUEST LETTERS

Brooklyn, NY
Sara Marcus, August 6

Dear Jill, Katherine, Merve, and Sarah,

Thanks so much for inviting me into this conversation. Most of my friends who aren't subject to the strictures of school-year obligations started their Ferrante reading many months ago, so I'm very grateful to have a chance to crash this slow-reading book club. Untimeliness is always more fun with company.

And I'm charmed to hear about your inadvertent lunchtime field research, Merve! After finishing *The Story of a New Name*, I wondered to myself: Are there people who read this book as being primarily about Lila's romantic turmoil? I decided there were probably a lot—and there you were, eating lunch next to some of them.

As the very framing of my question makes clear, I'm not one of these readers. It's not that I'm fully insensitive to the charms of *Story of a New Name*'s (SNN) operatic, intertwining plots of love and betrayal—I mean, I do have a pulse. But what attracted me the most here was Lenù's persistent question about how class mobility does and doesn't work.

At the end of *My Brilliant Friend*, it looks to Lenù like Lila has won the class-mobility lottery, cracked the code: marry a man who not only has a job and money but is willing to pump capital into your family-of-origin's business concern and spotlight your own creative output; move to a sweet house with a telephone; get an open credit line at area shops and fill your closet with beautiful clothes. That's the way to get out of the neighborhood, to leave poverty behind forever. Apparently.

Lenù can't just copy Lila's successful strategy. She lacks Lila's boldness, her raw sex appeal. Yet she also has what Lila lacks: a potential alternate route out of the neighborhood, the route ostensibly offered by education. Lenù is still in the running for whatever meritocratic prize is available to a brainy daughter of the Neapolitan working class. But it's often unclear precisely what that prize is, and as *SNN* opens, Lenù is wavering, wondering whether she shouldn't just be satisfied with the variation on Lila's strategy that *is* accessible to her—leave school, marry Antonio, accede to the destiny her neighborhood and her gender have laid out for her. Once, the two girls were united in their determination to leave where they'd come from; once, Lila drew Lenù through a tunnel and out toward the sea. But without Lila for company, that journey seems far less desirable.

As soon as Lila and Stefano leave on their honeymoon, Lenù's misreading of the newlyweds swings wide. "She loved him," Lenù raves internally, deludedly, "she loved him like the girls in the photonovels"[1]—thus proving that women have never needed Instagram to misread their friends' lives as impossibly glamorous and full of love and to downgrade their own accordingly.[2] Shorn of Lila's companionship, Lenù feels useless, a bent and empty vessel:

> I, I thought, am not capable of loving anyone like that, not even Nino, all I know is how to get along with books. And for a fraction

of a second I saw myself identical to a dented bowl in which my sister Elisa used to feed a stray cat, until he disappeared, and the bowl stood empty, gathering dust on the landing. At that point, with a sharp sense of anguish, I felt sure that I had ventured too far. I must go back, I said to myself, I should be like Carmela, Ada, Gigliola, Lila herself. Accept the neighborhood, expel pride, punish presumption, stop humiliating the people who love me. (*SNN*, 22)

The bowl image is miserably piquant, a horror of an already obsolescent female sex as imagined by a hot-blooded teenage virgin. But who's the stray cat here, whose departure has rendered Lenù purposeless and pathetic? Her perennial crush-object Nino Sarratore? Lila? Antonio, the boyfriend she's been snubbing? Love itself? Since her "get[ting] along with books," that old familiar skill, is what spurs the image, perhaps it has to do with the collapse of her intellectual self-confidence. She had had value as long as she saw herself as intelligent, but now she can't even play the smart girl well enough to gain Nino's love or to get her essay published. This last interpretation feels compelling to me, but I acknowledge that it's not a great fit with the metaphor. None of my explanations fit particularly well, in fact: Lenù doesn't see Lila or Nino as comparable to a stray cat, and Antonio, yowly as he is, hasn't yet disappeared. The well-chosen metaphor was never Lenù's talent, anyhow.

Whatever the motivation for the dented and dusty bowl, Lenù is unable to bear this self-conception for even a full second. She flees it instantly, taking refuge in the answer that's stood ready and waiting her whole life: accept the neighborhood; emulate the other girls; placate the man who loves you. Simply returning to Antonio isn't enough; she also has to detox from all the schooling, because her education infuriates him. "He heard scarcely any dialect in my voice, he noted the long sentence, the subjunctives, and he lost his temper" (*SNN*, 22).

She used to think education was her ticket out. But Nino has just dangled, then yanked back, the possibility that she might be published, and the disappointment—intellectual and romantic rejection combined—is devastating:

> It seemed to me that, thanks to the humiliation of the unpublished article, I had thoroughly understood my inadequacy. Even though Nino was born and had grown up like Lila and me in that wretched outlying neighborhood, he was able to use school with intelligence, I was not. So stop deluding myself, stop striving. Accept your lot, as Carmela, Ada, Gigliola, and, in her way, Lila herself have long since done. (*SNN*, 46–47)

Again this musical litany of neighborhood girls, this siren chorus of names calling Lenù to join them. The sutures that tied her to the mast are weakening: if she doesn't have what it takes to succeed as an intellectual, if she can't win the smartest boy by being the smartest girl, she might as well quit now. She ditches school for two weeks after the wedding.

But the calculus changes, of course. She learns that Lila isn't in love or happy, that Stefano beats and rapes her. And Stefano's brother Alfonso tells Lenù he could never beat a woman, because he goes to school with *her*—which means, she realizes, that she doesn't have to settle for the violent, destructive way love and marriage play out in her neighborhood, even if the other girls do. She has the power to change a man's behavior—but only if she's seen as an intellectual equal. She returns to school.

Her vacillations go on for a good long while, though. Sometimes she's tempted by the prospect of marriage and family, the path of least resistance, but more often she's haunted by the possibility that all the school in the world won't do her any good. "There was no escape. No, neither Lila nor I would ever become like the girl who had waited for Nino after school. We both lacked something intangible but fundamental, which was obvious in her even if you simply saw her from a distance, and which one possessed or did not, because to have that thing it was not enough to learn Latin or Greek or philosophy, nor was the money from groceries or shoes of any use" (*SNN*, 84). This intangible something is class, and the particular versions of femininity that class makes possible. Lenù wants to get out of poverty, but she worries that education can only take you so far, especially when you're a woman.

Her resolve comes back, it seems to me, in two key scenes, both involving Professor Galiani, but in precisely opposite ways. At the party at the teacher's house, feeling appreciated and valued by all the cultured guests, and realizing that Lila is out of her element, Lenù has a breakthrough: "Suddenly I felt that the state of suspension that had begun the day of her wedding was over. I knew how to be with these people, I felt more at ease than I did with my friends in the neighborhood" (*SNN*, 157–58).The siren song fades— it was never that lovely in the first place.

In the second scene, Lenù has just aced her graduation exams, but Galiani greets her coolly. Because Lenù can't explain that Nino's unceremonious dumping of the teacher's daughter was Lila's fault, Galiani blames Lenù for the breakup, and Lenù realizes she has lost her champion. "I was used to being liked by everyone, to wrapping that liking around me like shining armor; I was disappointed, and I think that her indifference had an important role in the decision I then made. Without talking about it to anyone (who could I ask advice from, anyway, if not Professor Galiani?) I applied for admission to the Pisa Normale" (*SNN* 325).

Where Lenù's first epiphany came from affinity with a group of peers, her second epiphany comes from realizing that as long as she's based in Naples, caught up in Lila's life, she'll always be subject to Lila's actions, which are becoming at least as perilous as they are compelling. If the attention of other people—Lila, Nino, Galiani, the party guests—once helped Lenù believe she was smart enough to keep striving, the withdrawal of all that attention makes her realize that nobody else can take her out of the neighborhood, and that she can't bring anybody with her when she leaves. "I, Elena Greco, the daughter of the porter, at nineteen years old was about to pull myself out of the neighborhood" (I hear this line in my head with the reflexive pronoun emphasized: "was about to pull *myself* out"), "I was about to leave Naples. By myself" (*SNN*, 327).

Questions about the limits of class mobility stay with her throughout her time in Pisa: she's learned to put on a good show, to pride herself on "the mask worn so well that it was *almost* a face" (*SNN*, 327; I can't not think of Paul Laurence Dunbar's "We Wear the Mask" here), but she's haunted again by that *almost*. There's a stubborn distance between herself and her classmates who excel without visible effort, who possess wide-ranging cultural literacy "because of the families they came from or through an instinctive orientation" (*SNN*, 403)—so it's class but not *only* class, or, better, it's always class, but class in its most insidious form masquerades as something ineffable, something not so much inherited as merely inherent.

The Story of a New Name ends on an upswing, with Elena Greco taking unmixed pride in graduating, getting published. For the first time, she's known not by any of her neighborhood sobriquets, and not by the brusque surname-only address of grade school, but by her full, myth-infused name. And maybe whatever ineradicable trace of the old neighborhood persists in her might account, after all, for her own ineffable quality, the "something powerful whose origin [the publisher] can't figure out" (*SNN*, 452) and that makes the novel she writes so great. Elena is convinced that special something is Lila. But she's wrong about so much in *SNN*; how could she not be wrong about this too?

—Sara

Sara Marcus is a postdoctoral scholar at the University of Southern California's Society of Fellows in the Humanities. Marcus is the author of the riot grrrl history Girls to the Front, *and is currently writing a book about political disappointment in twentieth-century US culture.*

A plane from San Francisco to New York
Marissa Brostoff, August 10

Dear Katherine, Merve, Jill, Sarah C., and Sara M.,

I want to second Sara M.'s thanks for letting me crash the long-burning book club as a guest contributor. Like everyone else here, I've experienced the Neapolitan novels as an uncanny revelation. I read *My Brilliant Friend* lying on my couch in June with a bad summer cold. It was the first time in recent memory that I had read an entire book without a pencil in my hand. It felt wonderful. A few weeks later I started *The Story of a New Name*, and this time the compulsion to annotate returned but in a delirious way, without a particular project in mind, as though I had just invented literary criticism from whole cloth. When I discovered your *salone de Ferrante* it was, miraculously, exactly where I was: at the end of book 2, and bursting with the sense that these books must be talked about, not with a single critical take but in the digressive mode of the novels themselves.

So, as Merve did in a recent post, I'll start my digression with a childhood memory: I'm eight or nine, I can't get enough of Ann M. Martin's *Babysitter's Club* series, and I'm mad about Logan. Mad like *pissed.* To refresh your memory, Logan was prissy Mary Ann's quasi-boyfriend, and—more to the point—the herald of an era beyond the horizon of the series, when the utopic *BSC* sisterhood of baby butches, art geeks, and book nerds would give way to a *Sweet Valley High* of hetero romance. Jill talked earlier about her allergy to marriage plots, which I think is a grownup way of articulating the same thing. But since I was eight, it just felt like: *Why is he *here*?*

At many moments in *My Brilliant Friend* and *The Story of a New Name*, that would be a reasonable question to ask about Nino Sarratore. On the beach in Ischia, he's there; at Professor Galiani's

party, he's there. Yes, Lenù has been quietly stalking her intellectual emo boy since childhood, just as he has been secretly pining for
Lila, but his quality of serially *turning up*, despite a street and social
address far from our heroines', accords best with the overdeter-
mining logic of narrative—*he's at the beach because they have to meet
again.* The Neapolitan novels have the bulging shaggy-dog-story
shape of another long, unconventional bildungsroman, *In Search of
Lost Time.* Proust likewise presents a protagonist doggedly climb-
ing the social ladder of his milieu only to find childhood friends,
enemies, and crushes turning up over and over again, so that what
at first seemed like a linear ascent reveals itself to be more like the
Talking Heads's vision of heaven as an endless party: "Everyone is
there." *But why—my inner eight-year-old persists, wanting to get at the
logic behind the overdetermination—is he* there?

Technically speaking, Nino is not the first boy to break up Lila
and Lenù's party. Adolescent seed is spilt over Lila almost ritualisti-
cally from the second she hits puberty. If rivalries between suitors
in literature function, as Eve Kosofsky Sedgwick argues, as a means
of homosocial contact between men, then the entire male half of
the neighborhood is erotically bound by their greed to get in Lila's
pants. But precisely because their crush is collective, it takes power
away from every individual paramour and gives it all (in the short
term, anyway) to Lila. Indeed, Lila's gambit is precisely to show the
neighborhood that, as different as Stefano, the Solara brothers,
Enzo, and the rest may seem from one another according to the
subtle gradations of class status within their claustrophobic district,
they are all, from the perspective of the wider world, the same.

Nino is something else—he is the girls' intellectual equal, and
though he lacks their wit and imagination, he knows far more
about the world. What else can we say about him? Not much that
gets beneath the surface, it turns out. Lenù's enmeshment with Lila
runs so deep that grownup-writer-Elena's narration sometimes

bleeds from the first person into a limited omniscience that encompasses both brilliant friends. Lenù may not always be right or honest about Lila, but she makes claims about Lila's subjectivity just as she makes them about herself. Nino, though also brought to life by Lenù's desire, lacks this kind of interiority. The main thing we know about his inner life is that he hates his smarmy, hypocritical father. The rest, as far as Lenù can tell, he has exteriorized into a highly articulate but still hot-blooded passion for left politics. Eventually we will see this energy turn into a passion for Lila that effects the awful double betrayal that becomes the central twist of the novel. Then we will see that he can also be impetuous and single-minded in pursuit of a woman. But beyond this, he remains largely a blank, resistant canvas onto which Lenù can project her hungers.

Let me just come out and say it: I would have wanted Nino too. I probably have a hate-crush on him even now. The brooding Marxist boy can be a very attractive boy indeed. Zoom in on Nino jousting with (female) Professor Galiani's other protégés (all male) over "Gaullism, the O.A.S., social democracy, the opening to the left . . . Danilo Dolci, Bertrand Russell, the pied-noirs, the followers of Fanfani" as they smoke on the terrace of Galiani's beautiful apartment. (Interestingly, Nino tends to take slightly more moderate positions than his comrades. To a girl like Lenù, perhaps, there's ultimately nothing sexier than the reality principle.) Lenù, standing among these bloviators, reacts in a way that made me want to shake her, but that I could not disavow as the reaction I would have had at her age and in her place. First, she is struck with an acute flare-up of her chronic imposter syndrome, feeling that "the world of persons, events, ideas was endless, and the reading I did at night had not been sufficient, I would have to work even harder in order to be able to say to Nino, to Professor Galiani, to Carlo, to Armando: yes, I understand. I know." Then, listening to Nino carry on, she is "overwhelmed by emotion." She craves "to take care of him, to tend to him, to protect him, to sustain him in everything that he would do in the course of his life. It was the only moment of the evening when I felt envious of Nadia"—Professor Galiani's daughter and Nino's girlfriend— "who stood beside him like a minor but radiant divinity" (SNN, 158–159).

Gahhhhh! It's so awful and so familiar. And yet. While I couldn't agree more with Jill's description of the episode above as an "epic mansplaining incident," I depart somewhat from her assessment of it as the nadir of a "wincingly awful university party." Let me zoom out for a moment to try and defend my perhaps questionable position on this.

What first got me hooked on the Neapolitan novels, almost from the start of My Brilliant Friend, was the way in which the many things Lenù and Lila fervently desire—books, money, power, knowledge, experience, boys, sex, beautiful objects, political change, respect, escape, superiority, each other—refuse to arrange themselves into a fixed hierarchy. Any of these, in the girls' cosmology, may act in the service of any other at any given moment; all may be means and all may be ends. Which are which shift so frequently that the desires consistently catch the desirers themselves off guard.

I fell in love with something similar when I started reading Doris Lessing a couple of years ago; it was, in fact, a friend on whom I'd pushed Lessing, in longstanding feminist tradition, who pushed Ferrante on me. Lessing is a progenitor of what Sarah described as Ferrante's fever dream realism, and much of her work is similarly devoted to acidly representing the sexual politics of the postwar global Left. I had never read anyone else who better captured the vexed intersection of communism and boys until I read Ferrante or grasped why that obscure crossing is so terribly important to understand. From a contemporary vantage point, its significance is easiest to see if we work backward, recalling that radical feminism emerged in places including Lessing's adopted England, Ferrante's Italy, and the United States in the late 1960s in reaction to the pernicious sexism endemic within the era's left social movements. But Lessing's and Ferrante's young radical women aren't struggling with a feminist telos in mind; they have to figure out on their own what it means to be in thrall to a vision of justice and equality when the self-appointed agents of that vision are epic mansplainers and often much worse. And this was only the tip of the iceberg that feminism was yet to exhume. Even when sexual politics are buried deep, *how can we think the connections* between books, money, power, knowledge, experience, and so on? In the Neapolitan novels, how can we account for their absence in the lives that the neighborhood expects Lenù and Lila will lead?

Marxism conceived in Henri Lefebvre's terms as a critique of everyday life has ways of addressing those questions, but this conception has historically and sometimes violently been lost on the Left's mansplainers. After all, what does the drab texture of daily existence for a poor schoolgirl in Naples have on the theoretical prestige of Gaullism, the O.A.S., and the followers of Fanfani? Radical feminism, most spectacularly if not singularly among the new social movements of the sixties, changed the conversation by insisting on a revolution in everyday life as its core political demand. *The Story of a New Name*, like much of Lessing's work, takes place just before that shit hit the fan. And so Lessing's heroines hunt alone through the vagaries of sex and friendship, geopolitics and history, trying to make sense of how it all fits together and often going mad in the process. Her 1962 magnum opus *The Golden Notebook* is so-called for the color-coded notebooks that sometime novelist and activist Anna Wulf keeps in an attempt to compartmentalize this bewildering totality: black for memories of her youth in Rhodesia, red for her experience in the Communist Party, yellow for a fictionalized version of a doomed relationship, blue for dreams, and a golden notebook in which she tries to see the whole thing at once.

Is Lenù a young radical woman, though? Is she driven to try and get at the roots of things by seeing everything at once? Lila, after all, is the assiduous notebook-keeper of the two. For Lenù, in a fascinating twist, becoming conversant in left politics is largely continuous with her own individual social mobility. With a few exceptions, hers is a world of poor capitalists and rich communists. In the car on the way back from Galiani's party, Lila takes devastating note:

> They've read and studied in that house, fathers, grandfathers, great-grandfathers. For hundreds of years they've been, at the least, lawyers, doctors, professors. So they all talk just so, so they dress and eat and move just so. They do it because they were born there. But in their heads they don't have a thought that's their own, that they struggled to think. . . . You, too, want to be a puppet from the neighborhood who performs so you can be welcomed into the home of those people? You want to leave us alone in our own shit, cracking our skulls, while all of you go cocorico cocorico, hunger, war, working class, peace? (*SNN*, 163)

Arguably, political change is the weakest of Lenù's many yearnings or, more precisely, the one that is least an end unto itself. And that, oddly enough, is why a thrill of excitement accompanied my cringe in response to her experience at Professor Galiani's party. Because here's how the epic mansplaining incident ultimately plays out. Lenù reports:

> Then I heard myself utter sentences as if it were not I who had decided to do so, as if another person, more assured, more informed, had decided to speak through my mouth. I began without knowing what I would say, but, hearing the boys,

fragments of phrases read in Galiani's books and newspapers stirred in my mind, and the desire to speak, to make my presence felt, became stronger than timidity. I used the elevated Italian I had practiced in making translations from Greek and Latin. I was on Nino's side. I said I didn't want to live in a world at war. We mustn't repeat the mistakes of the generations that preceded us, I said. Today we should make war on the atomic arsenals, should make war on war itself. If we allow the use of those weapons, we will all become even guiltier than the Nazis. Ah, how moved I was, as I spoke: I felt tears coming to my eyes. I concluded by saying that the world urgently needed to be changed, that there were too many tyrants who kept peoples enslaved. But it should be changed by peaceful means. (*SNN*, 159–60)

With her own political rhetoric, she has moved herself to tears.
Sometimes the way we get turned on to politics is to get turned on. From Plato's *Symposium* through Wilhelm Reich and his sexual-revolutionary heirs, a compelling line of thought holds that if you want people to develop a political consciousness, it's not a bad idea to begin with the erotic—sex, wine, a party. I suppose I'm saying that I hope one answer to the question, "Why is Nino there?" is that he is a dialectically necessary stage Lenù must pass through on her way from being Lila's minder to her own emancipation, intellectual, political, and otherwise. Have I given the novel exactly the kind of telos I said earlier I enjoyed it not having? Well, I contradict myself. I'll admit it: I desperately want true political consciousness for Lenù. *I really, really want her to discover feminism.* I want it for her like you want Sherlock to solve the mystery. I'm not holding my breath for Ferrante to give me what I want. But she has certainly nurtured the fantasy. Lenù needs feminism and feminism needs her. The hazy spoilers that have come my way about the rest of the series have

made me hedge my bets about everything turning out great for these brilliant characters, but in this particular respect, my fingers are cautiously crossed for book 3.

—Marissa

Marissa Brostoff is a writer in New York. She is the Culture Editor at Jewish Currents *and a doctoral student at the CUNY Graduate Center.*

Sacramento, CA
Lili Loofbourow, August 26

Dear Everyone,

I've spent some of this summer searching for my own Lila.

* * *

We're like pipes when the water freezes, what a terrible thing a dissatisfied mind is. You remember what we did with my wedding picture? I want to continue on that path. The day will come when I reduce myself to diagrams, I'll become a perforated tape and you won't find me anymore. Nonsense, that's all.[3]

* * *

My sister erased herself this summer with a gun to her left temple. She didn't give anyone her notebooks; quite the opposite. Her particular disappearing act assumed an electronic aspect of which Lila would have approved: she took a wrench to her hard drives, closed all her email accounts, wiped her iPhone and tablet. Her Myspace page has no connections. Her Pinterest: 0 interests, 0 pins, 0 likes.

All we have left to try and understand her by is a heap of disabled electronics. An irritatingly *material* heap, dull and scratched and mute. The Motorola tablet hidden under the sink was covered with her fingerprints and yet it's dead without them, a glass brick.

* * *

"Mute paper, useless paper" (*TWL*, 348)—Lenù, looking at the French, German and Spanish translations of her book.

* * *

A book was open on my sister's bed. She was reading, I guess, right before she did it. I haven't read that book yet, mainly—I admit it—as a kindness to myself. Also for her, though. I think. I don't want to draw unfair connections. I don't want to assume that reading was as important for her as it is for me. I'm trying not to let the layers of fiction suicide produces completely overwrite my sister. (There are so many, and some of them even have the merit of being true. She was physically ill. She was mentally ill. She was sick at heart. She was wracked with pain.)

It's all too easy to lose her to the black hole that *explains* her—and what she did—by alienating her. Turning her into another Melina. Before we consign her to the ocean of comforting platitudes that help drown out our grief, I'd like to see her clearly as she wished to be seen. Especially since I didn't really try—not hard, not really—to see her for years.

Success isn't the point. I know I'll fail. But I want, more than anything, to see my sister's version of Lila's self-portrait. If Lila erased herself, leaving only an eye and a Cerullo shoe, what parts of herself did my sister want to leave visible, intact?

So we started going through her house. I went straight to her office and started going through her files. I began photographing her phone records, bank statements, all the mundane, irritating packets of paper that now assumed huge significance. They told a story, albeit in numbers. Nonsense numbers, to be sure, the kind Lila dreamed of becoming, but numbers that, fed into the right computer, might lead back to my sister. Numbers it would be our work to decode. Would I look up every phone call? Would I try to track every purchase? I admit it: I was beginning to droop under the weight of that hopeless math.

And then—you can imagine my feelings—I came across a sheaf of paper hidden under desk. It's full of her writing. Her poetry, her life story, and pages and pages on her fear, above all, of having her privacy compromised, of being hacked.

Did I respect my sister's desire for self-erasure and leave the paper alone?

I did not.

* * *

It's emboldening to read about a peculiarly intrusive literary excavation when you're engaged in precisely the same thing. "It wasn't a diary," Lenù writes of Lina's notebooks, "although there were detailed accounts of the events of her life, starting with the end of elementary school" (SNN, 15). Yes, I nod, *this exactly*. My sister's writing is on loose-leaf sheets, not notebooks, but the pages are numbered. Those pages tell the story of her life, but the text is aimed at an audience I can't guess at. Whenever I decide it's a diary, for example, she adds in the kinds of helpful expository parentheses no diarist would need: X *(my husband)*, she says. Or Y, *my brother*.

I've been thinking, in other words, about how and to what extent explanation alienates. Within the affective system Ferrante sketches out in the Neapolitan novels, erasure is an aesthetic as well as an intimate act. Lina is *Lila* for Lenù—if she ever called her Lina (so she tells us in *My Brilliant Friend*) the friendship would be over. I'll respect that—and note that Lina's ability to empathetically enter someone, effectively erasing herself, proves (in Lenù's mind) both her aesthetic and affective superiority.

To the extent that the Neapolitan series has a crisis, it's that Lenù's exposition violates that intimacy. Lenù's betrayal goes far beyond reading and discarding Lina's notebooks. Her decision to reconstruct her friend, to *explain* her, to reveal her in public is an act of violence, especially toward someone who fantasizes about disappearing. Ferrante's is a universe of violent remembrance and tender, even intimate erasure.

These principles mix, of course: sometimes explanation IS erasure. As several of you have said so well, one of the more maddening aspects of Lenù's narrative is the compulsion to *talk* about the brilliance of Lina's writing while withholding the thing itself. Lenù's fulsome praise itself becomes—on this understanding—an exercise in masking. Presenting the judgment without the object obliterates the point of origin: Lila may be Christ, but we are reading the Gospel According to Lenù.

* * *

My sister's life looks very different depending on whose gospel you read. Did a man break into her house every day? No, say the police reports, neighbors, her family. Yes, she writes, and fills several pages with his crimes. "He takes all my eyeglasses and bends the frame, and leaves them bent backwards—visually it's supposed to disturb me. The appearance is violent."

* * *

I've been thinking about Sarah's really brilliant observation about Ferrante's descriptive restraint—what Sarah calls the paucity of detailed physical description in the novels—and how that both spares us from poverty porn and conceptually respects the narrative black hole (Lila's disappearance) from which the novels originate. There's a striking discipline to the lack of visual description. We're taught, I think, to understand that restraint as the writerly difference between Lenù and Lila. Take, as an example, Lenù's account of Lina's notebooks: "The pages were full of descriptions," Lenù says, "the branch of a tree, the ponds, a stone, a leaf with its white veinings, the pots in the kitchen, the various parts of a coffeemaker, the brazier, the coal and bits of coal" (*SNN*, 15).

Lina's writing, we're *meant* to understand, is the opposite of Lenù's: she practices, she's invested in aesthetics, in observation, in accuracy. (Her proficiency at diagramming, at computation, is hinted at here.) Lila is richly descriptive in ways Lenù is not. And yet: Which do *we* experience as more objectively descriptive—the character that emerges from a list of their descriptions of various objects or the detailed description of the objects themselves?

Put to that test, the word *descriptive* dissolves, becomes meaningless. (Which is more descriptive, my sister's list of bank and phone records or her poetry and prose?)

There are echoes here of the childish dialectic Jill points to in her discussion of *My Brilliant Friend*—where the girls organize themselves into the good one and the bad one, the ugly one and the pretty one. Mother and scholar, rebel and conformist: three novels in, dichotomy has become totally inadequate. The muscularity with which the Neapolitan series successively smashes (or dissolves) the borders that once made Lila and Lenù's complementary self-fashioning possible has a secondary, unexpected effect: it proves our narrator's gift as a writer. "Elena Greco's" (quotes are there for a reason) writerly ability is always—to hear her tell it—in doubt. Unlike Lila's notebooks, however, we experience "Elena"'s directly, and by the third novel we have no choice but to admire the skill with which she's created and controlled that progression of Lenùccian perspectives without ever abandoning her *own* point in time. She is always already old. Lila is always already gone. But we experience events through young Lenù and middle-aged Lenù and forget—subjectively, no matter how often we're reminded—that old "Elena Greco" is taking our eyeglasses and bending the frames until we see through her character's mentality as she did during that particular slice of time. The appearance is violent.

"She had an involved way of talking. She chose emotionally charged words," Lenù says, trying to pin down the narrative habits that distinguish her from her friend:

> She described Melina Cappuccio and Giuseppina Peluso **as if** their bodies had seized hers, imposing on it the same contracted or inflated forms, the same bad feelings. As she spoke, she touched her face, her breast, her stomach, her hips **as if** they were no longer hers, and showed that she knew everything about those women, down to the tiniest details, **in order to prove** that no one told me anything but told her everything, or, worse, **in order to make me feel** that I was wrapped in a fog, unable to see the suffering of the people around me. (*SNN*, 98–99; bold mine)

The thing is, those interpolations in bold don't quite hold up—either as true readings of Lina's subtextual intentions or, indeed, as instances of the foggy, unempathetic blindness of which Lenù stands (implicitly) accused. If Lila has an involved way of talking, Lenù is no less implicated. In this passage dedicated to Lenù's fear that Lina has abilities she doesn't—specifically, the ability to narrate by entering the bad feelings of other bodies—Lenù is writing as if Lina's body had seized her own.

Take this passage, in which Lenù is waiting at the university for the editor's son to recognize her and deliver her to wherever she's supposed to be:

> The heat was unbearable. I found myself against a background of posters dense with writing, red flags, and struggling people, placards announcing activities, noisy voices, laughter, and a widespread sense of apprehension. I wandered around, looking for signs that had to do with me. I recall a dark-haired young

man who, running, rudely bumped into me, lost his balance, picked himself up, and ran out into the street as if he were being pursued, even though no one was behind him. I recall the pure, solitary sound of a trumpet that pierced the suffocating air. I recall a tiny blond girl, who was dragging a clanking chain with a large lock at the end, and zealously shouting, I don't know to whom: I'm coming! (*TWL*, 68)

"I remember it," Lenù says, "because in order to seem purposeful, as I waited for someone to recognize me and come over, I took out my notebook and wrote down this and that." The message is clear: Lina's imaginative exercises are serious, whereas Lenù's are ways of masking social discomfort (or worse, angling for social status). And yet: the image of a tiny blond girl trying desperately to catch up to an unseen other while carrying a lock and chain is (for us) deeply meaningful. And yet: a few short pages later, we get this arresting description:

I was struck immediately by a very beautiful girl, with delicate features and long black hair that hung over her shoulders, who was certainly younger than me. I couldn't take my eyes off her. She was standing in the midst of some combative young men, and behind her a dark man about thirty, smoking a cigar, stood glued to her like a bodyguard. What distinguished her in that environment, besides her beauty, was that she was holding in her arms a baby a few months old, she was nursing him and, at the same time, closely following the conflict, and occasionally even shouting something. When the baby, a patch of blue, with his little reddish-colored legs and feet uncovered, detached his mouth from the nipple, she didn't put her breast back in the bra but stayed like that, exposed, her white shirt unbuttoned, her breast swollen, her mouth half open, frowning, until she realized the child was no longer suckling and mechanically tried to reattach him. That girl disturbed me. In the noisy smoke-filled classroom, she was an incongruous icon of maternity. She was younger than me, she had a refined appearance, responsibility for an infant. Yet she seemed determined to reject the persona of the young woman placidly absorbed in caring for her child. She yelled, she gesticulated, she asked to speak, she laughed angrily, she pointed to someone with contempt. And yet the child was part of her, he sought her breast, he lost it. Together they made up a fragile image, at risk, close to breaking, as if it had been painted on glass: the child would fall out of her arms or something would bump his head, an elbow, an uncontrolled movement. (*TWL*, 71)

There is no paucity of physical description here. It's a scene as vividly rendered as any I can remember reading.

So, if Lenù's self-assessment isn't just off but catastrophically wrong, what does it mean for the text as a whole?

* * *

"Today, as I'm writing, that goad is even more essential. I wish she were here, that's why I'm writing. I want her to erase, add, collaborate in our story by spilling into it, according to her whim, the things she knows, what she said or thought." (*TWL*, 105)

* * *

What interests me most about the Neapolitan series, I think, is the fascinating threat that both these women pose to any textual historian. Because the resulting text doesn't consistently conform to either Lila or Lenù's stylistic strategies as they're described.

We know that Nino Sarratore has written articles they've both helped him with. We know that Lina is good at computers. And we know that she's made a very clear promise to Lenù: don't write about me, or else: "I'll come look in your computer, I'll read your files, I'll erase them," Lina says.

"Come on."

"You think I'm not capable of it?"

"I know you're capable. But I can protect myself."

She laughed in her old mean way. "Not from me." (*TWL*, 71)

The Neapolitan series is exactly that provocation to coauthorship: *here I am, disobeying you, preying on your worst fears. Come back, punish me.* I've been thrumming with sympathy for Lenù as she betrays her friend. My sister's greatest fear was being hacked. Well, here I am, hacking.

—Lili

Lili Loofbourow is a staff writer at Slate. *She did graduate work in creative writing at the University of Alabama and in early modern literature at UC Berkeley. She has published in* PMLA, the *New York Times Magazine,* Virginia Quarterly Review, Best American Essays 2019, *the* Week, *and the* New Republic.

Dear Everyone,

When I was seven or eight, my language arts teacher gave us a horribly tedious exercise: diagram all the steps that go in to making a peanut butter sandwich. I'm sure all of us have a memory of a similar assignment meant to instill basic logic, reward finicky attention to procedural correctness, and, it seems to me now, prepare us for a future of inexhaustible domestic routines. There was always another step to be added: one more turn of the peanut butter jar, one more swivel of the knife.

But until reading about Lila's mania for block diagrams—for diagramming "the door opening," "knotting the tie," "tying Gennaro's shoe," "making coffee in the napoletana" (*TWL*, 114)—it never occurred to me that I was also learning the fundamentals of computer programming. Cursory Google research into the history of block diagramming reveals its centrality in teaching how computer systems intercommunicate: where a system's boundary points lie, in which direction information flows, what responsibility each part has in the functioning of the whole.

To create successful block diagrams is not only to understand how a system works, it is also to understand how to make a system grow. In book 3 of Ferrante's Neapolitan novels, *Those Who Leave and Those Who Stay*, Lila has become adept at analyzing and cultivating systems broadly conceived—the intricacies of politics at the Soccavo sausage plant, the language of worker revolt, the System 3 Model 10 card reader at IBM, the data-processing center run by the Solaras. While Lenù feels "pregnant yet empty," Lila, despite being on the Pill, despite her cough, skinniness, and exhaustion, possesses an alarming fecundity that mocks Lenù's inability to write another promising work (*TWL*, 260). None of this is exactly new—Lenù has admired Lila's talents at self-expression since the days of the *Blue Fairy*. But in Book 3, Lenù can no longer fully grasp exactly how—and at what—her friend excels. Sarah wrote of the "dense miasma" that surrounds Ferrante's Naples; Lila's new role as the head of technology appears similarly shrouded to Lenù. One of the novel's feats is to present, through Lenù's clouded vision, technological innovation as most of us perceive it: unintelligible yet fascinating, peripheral yet threatening.

Lenù does grasp that Lila has harnessed a seemingly contradictory set of powers. While Lenù is stuck parroting clichés, Lila can be avant-garde: at once radically abstract and deeply material, occupying a position simultaneously above and below conventional language and narrative. Lila's work at IBM is "incomprehensible jargon" to Lenù, yet it is also alarmingly rooted in visceral reality. As Lila explains to her, "the computer is worse than a stove. Maximum abstraction along with sweat and a terrible stink" (*TWL*, 262). Lenù imagines her taunting, "You wanted to write novels. . . . I created a novel with real people, with real blood, in reality" (*TWL*, 313).

T. J. Clark famously claimed that modernism's two greatest desires were the "recognition of the social reality of the sign (away from the comforts of narrative and illusionism)" and, at the same time, the reversion of "the sign back to a bedrock of World/Nature/Sensation/Subjectivity which the to and fro of capitalism had all but destroyed."[4] Lila, through computer programming, has realized these opposing demands in a postmodern era in which she, unlike her modernist forebears, can enter the capitalist marketplace—the Solaras' data processing plant—without feeling destroyed. A writer that has her cake and eats it too—aesthetic experimentation without sacrificing the grit of lived experience, profit without selling out—Lila represents the possibility of the ideal novel, so perfect that it might only be a single diagram—or, as Lila's disappearance suggests, nothing at all. Some of the anger and bitterness of the Neapolitan novels comes from this sense that their very existence as novels is a problem, an atavism: "Mute paper, useless paper," Lenù remarks (*TWL*, 348).

Lenù's anger at Lila's decision to work for the Solaras also suggests her deeper inability to understand that the communicative systems she participates in—aesthetic, political, sexual—are ones in which revolutionary change is tied up with structures of power and corruption. Lenù happily harnesses the clout of the Airotas to get Lila the money owed her by the Soccavo factory, but she cannot handle the implication that she has herself acted like a Solara: "getting a little money and screwing everyone else over," as Pasquale puts it (*TWL*, 221). Frustration at Lila and Pasquale's lack of gratitude leads to her most baldly self-deluding statement: "Never again, never again would I lift a finger for anyone," uttered on the eve of her marriage to Pietro, childrearing, and housekeeping (*TWL*, 228).

Her refusal to admit contradiction is what makes the feminist tract she is writing both so disturbing and intriguing. She theorizes a female automaton, fabricated by man:

> Eve can't, doesn't know how, doesn't have the material to be Eve outside of Adam. Her evil and her good are evil and good according to Adam. Eve is Adam as a woman. And the divine work was so successful that she herself, in herself, doesn't know who she is, she has pliable features, she doesn't possess her own language, she doesn't have a spirit or a logic of her own, she loses shape easily. (*TWL*, 375)

What's surprising about this idea is not its familiar premise that women are defined by and in relation to men. Rather, its strangeness comes from its profound failure to explain Lila, who, contrary to Lenù's formulation, appears to be fabricating *male* automatons. Enzo—blond, selfless, unreal Enzo—is, in his own words, identical to the computer he operates: "he is me," he explains (*TWL*, 299). And Lila is behind the controls: "I think what she thinks," he tells Lenù (333), who, in flagrant disregard of her own theorizing of patriarchal power, tries to undermine Lila's intelligence based on her wage differential: "if Lina is so good," she teases Enzo, "why do they give you three hundred and fifty thousand lire and her a hundred thousand, why are you boss and she's the assistant?" (299).

What is Ferrante getting at here? That cybernetics are indeed, as Shulamith Firestone imagined, uprooting the biological division of the sexes by undoing the division of labor, an idea that exceeds Lenù's sometimes shrewd but sometimes myopic class-consciousness? Or is Ferrante simply pointing out the inevitable gap between theory and reality that makes writing feel like a futile activity: Lenù's tract cannot give voice to the complexity of her actual experience, another sign of the insufficiency of words. It's hard not to read lines like Lenù's explanation of the subject of her new work—"Men who fabricate women"—as jab at, or a provocation to, readers who speculate about Ferrante's own gender (*TWL*, 361). The pat insufficiency of Lenù's proposition seems to ridicule (or wickedly encourage) readers who smugly assume that one day we will be able to definitively answer: Who is Elena Ferrante?

Lenù, despite her anger at, jealousy of, and malicious response to Lila's block diagrams, punch cards, and data files (vexation that their telephone calls only exacerbate, as if the immediacy of Lila's voice over the wire offers further proof of her abstraction and extension), retains a canny sensitivity to a register of language that Lila's mania for computing risks effacing. Lila is able to both to elevate writing—rendering it poetic, experimental, encoded—and to deflate it, concretizing it into the sweating, stinking computer.

But Lenù desires a way to communicate that eschews the poles of the literary and the antiliterary, carving out a space for that which is neither fully meaningful nor material. She tells one of her early audiences that her first book hoped to capture "what seems unsayable and what we do not speak of even to ourselves" (*TWL*, 64). Throughout *Those who Leave and Those Who Stay* we think we discover what the unsayable might be: Dede's "shriek[s] like a furious little animal," Silvia's "animal cries of terror," and Lenù's own "terrible cries, not words, only breath spilling out along with despair" (*TWL*, 238, 291, 242). Lenù's more potent feminist act may be to let these howls reverberate.

The difficulty with such a reading—in a move that is characteristic of Ferrante—is that we know, by Lenù's own confession, that her reading audience "liked" when she told them she hoped to recount the "unsayable"; after uttering those words, she "regained respect" and began to use them over and over again, a refrain that ensured "a certain success" (*TWL*, 64–65). Do her audiences "like" this refrain because it speaks to a restrictive consensus about women's writing and the female condition—that it is inchoate, formless, indescribable? If so, is Ferrante suggesting that even our unsayables—our cries, shrieks, and howls—are always compromised? Lila's apparent indifference before the novel's opening horror—Gigliola Spagnuolo's battered, bloated body— may in fact bear better witness to the neighborhood's "sandpaper of torments" than Lenù's profusion of tears (*TWL*, 23). Indifference, block diagrams—are these signs of a cold inhumanity or a brilliant appraisal of the real?

—Cecily

Cecily Swanson received her PhD in English from Cornell University and is the director of studies at Mathey College, Princeton University.

A grassy patch adjacent to the Chautauqua Institution
Amy Schiller, August 30

Dear all,

I join you all with admiration, gratitude, and no small amount of chutzpah, at the urging of Marissa, who told me it was appropriate to crash the party. Lenù and Lila have accompanied me on every significant vacation I've had in 2015, which are quickly becoming defined less by destination and more as Respective Reorganizations of Time and Space Around Reading Ferrante. *The Story of a New Name* was my reward for finishing my last major course paper, and *Those Who Leave and Those Who Stay* served the same purpose after several intense months of dissertation proposal writing.

As a political theorist, I find special joy in reading about 1970s Italian fascism and communism and the total collapse of that hoary public-private chestnut in the lives of both Elena and Lila. I really value the specifically Italian flavor of these transnational movements—the feminism here is the Marxist feminism of Silvia Federici, whose "Wages Against Housework" is on my fall syllabus and many others', as well as Carla Lonzi, arguably the Italian answer to Irigaray and Cixous. When Lila, as quoted by Enzo, refuses to lament the loss of welding and other good manufacturing jobs to machines, by stating "humiliating and stultifying jobs should disappear," she reflects in part the philosophy of Autonomous Marxism that originated in Italy with Antonio Negri, alongside Federici (*TWL*, 299). The world is going faster and faster around them, yet the intensity of the times seem to be catching up to, not catalyzing, the passion each of these women has carried since we first met them.

Which brings me back to the public-private folie-à-deux of this epic. Lenù has always pursued the seeming sure thing—education, marrying into a prestigious family—and *Those Who Leave and Those Who Stay* is a fascinating reckoning that not only are her leftist politics out of step with her domestic life but that her entire strategy of advancement is a bit decadent and stodgy. Being a Lila Girl (in my feminist version of the Lennon vs. McCartney debate), I feel a tiny bit of glee that Elena, for all her supposedly emancipatory moves, is in decline from the moment she arrives on the public scene. Her innate conservatism is catching up with her; she bought legacy stock just before the market collapsed, in all respects. She is both the one who left and the one who stayed, stuck in an old framework of hierarchy and advancement within it.

Having said that, I'll allow Elena her rage and jealousy. I too would be pissed if my best friend were a wizard. Lila is a product of both her hiss-dart-bite intellect and her self-reliance, after having to fight for herself even in her own family from a very young age. She adapts because she has to, and she always has an eye for an unanticipated opportunity. Elena, partially because her father was more tolerant of her pursuit of education and her teachers chose to mentor her, learned to depend on existing institutions to contain and reward her ambition.

This is, I think, what Michele is getting at when, at that edge-of-my-seat dinner party, he applauds Lila's quicksilver intelligence and hints that it is superior to Elena's diligence. That moment encapsulates so much about what makes *Those Who Leave and Those Who Stay* particularly significant among these novels: Michele validates and confirms as an outsider what has only been stated in interior voice. Lila's courage and brilliance have seemed almost mythical—she reads first, remains the more natural writer of the two (according to Elena), designs spectacular shoes before reaching puberty, and plays a kind of romantic parkour to avoid becoming a Camorra bride. With one photograph she becomes a renowned model, then dabbles in avant-garde art (to erase the effects of said modeling, as stated so well by Merve[5]), organized and managed several retail operations, adapts to factory work, rallies political opposition, and finally, learns the intricacies of computer technology, all with consistently dazzling aplomb and immediate triumph. I mean, come on. Elena's characterization at times seems absurd and overawed, but with Michele's speech, we now have to reflect back on whether Elena's portraiture has been more accurate than it previously appeared.

With the aging of all our primary characters into adults in *Those Who Leave and Those Who Stay*, the folding of time becomes more poignant, for not only the narrator but the characters themselves are all now far away from those formative moments. That sense of multiplied times that Katherine highlighted,[6] as twelve-year-old Lila and Lenù walk the neighborhood streets, starts to spread, as other characters become part of that nostalgic time-folding enterprise. Think of Bruno reminiscing fondly about the summer in Ischia on the phone with Elena or Lila bringing up the first party at Professor Galiani's, remembering events that previously we only observed through Elena. Manuela Solara probably *did* order the hit on Don Achille—and it matters anew, since now other people are talking about it, not just Elena musing from a distance. These characters perform narrative purposes, retelling and analyzing earlier events, in some ways competing with our narrator, underscoring her own sense of marginalization and irrelevance.

The erosion of Elena's narrative authority, as more characters fill out and articulate the passage of time, is also seen in the evolution of the men of Lenù's world, who seem to undergo much more dramatic metamorphoses than the women in this volume.

I'm intentionally excluding Nino, who I consider to be forever the Marxist Pixie Dream Boy, a perpetually distant crush object, whose actual personality seems reducible to various theory text references. Meanwhile, of the other dudes:

- Michele's devotion to Lila might be some sexual long game, but his rhapsodies about her intelligence and talent make clear that, even to him, this relationship is different and almost secluded from his usual violence.
- Enzo transforms from hardbitten fruit seller—the most village-bound old-world profession—to the most upwardly mobile professional of the men, the one best suited to the emerging knowledge economy.
- Stefano disintegrates from abusive hotshot into a debt-crushed, sulky ghost haunting the neighborhood.
- Pasquale, admittedly a bit of an arrogant dick from the beginning, has gone full-on guerilla bro, condescending and absolutist towards everyone.
- Pietro unravels from Elena's puppyish admirer to a petulant fuddy-duddy who abdicates any domestic responsibility and undermines his wife's writing.
- Rino gains an enormous amount of weight, while losing his rebellious edge, as the Solara payroll starts working for, rather than against him.
- Alfonso's homosexuality is confirmed (and I hope I'm not alone in hoping Michele reciprocates his crush, since the latter's rampant, self-publicized womanizing might indicate some mismatch with his Kinsey score).
- And in my favorite sentimental detail, Elena's father becomes more animated in his affection than we've ever seen once he gets Pietro's company in front of the television. Ah, fathers-in-law.

(As for the other women, compared to secondary female characters like Gigliola, Elisa, and Mariarosa, only Adele seems pretty cool, in a Florentine Emily Gilmore way.)

Even though we obviously know more about our two primary characters' lives, the male characters exhibit far more dynamic and surprising development than we see even with Lila, who evolves pretty much as I could have predicted, upping her badass quotient at every turn. Her skills now match her confidence to such a degree that she can work for Michele without fear; she has likewise conquered her sabotaging family and supports them financially. Meanwhile, Elena is in some kind of goldfish pattern, returning time and again to the publishing house and Nino, respectively, as her instruments of liberation. Even when she admits, "I had decided" to ignite the affair with Nino, she parrots Pietro's direct statement here, after a long stretch of ambivalence and half-consciousness of her actions, rendering her ultimately passive (*TWL*, 386).

I hope Book 4 contains more of a story that turns against Elena—whether through the emergence of more narrative voices, more open acknowledgement of her passivity and traditionalism, or more people defying her earlier impressions and portrayals of them. While I respect Katherine's fraction of optimism that Elena's liberation begins anew on that flight to Montpellier, I'm far more fascinated by the way Elena's own novel ends up decentering her from her own story.

Back to cloud-gazing,
Amy

Amy Schiller is a PhD candidate in political science at the Graduate Center, CUNY, where she is completing a political theory of philanthropy. Her writing can be found in The Nation, The Atlantic, The Daily Beast, *and* New Political Science.

ACKNOWLEDGMENTS

First and foremost, we would like to thank everyone who supported us at Columbia University Press. Matthew Hart, David James, and Rebecca Walkowitz, the editors of Literature Now, first saw the potential for this book in our summer experiment. Our editor, Philip Leventhal, advocated for us at every stage. Monique Briones kept us on schedule, and Jennifer Heuer gave us a beautiful cover. We owe many thanks to our colleagues at Post45, especially Amy Hungerford and Palmer Rampell, who gave us the trust and freedom to embark upon this project in the first place. Our brilliant friends and guest writers, Marissa Brostoff, Lili Loofbourow, Sara Marcus, Amy Schilling, and Cecily Swanson, provided inspiration and encouragement in that first summer. The book's final form was guided by the thoughtful, sensitive critique of Sarah Blackwood and Pamela Thurschwell. Numerous friends, colleagues, and mentors sustained us with conversation and constructive criticism, especially the Feminist Thinking Group at Oxford University, Gloria Fisk, Sophie Gee, Rachel Greenwald Smith, Melanie Micir and the members of C21 STL, Deborah Nord and Maria DiBattista, Namwali Serpell, Dan Sinykin, and Kelly Swartz. We are also grateful to all the fellow readers who followed "The Slow Burn" in its various iterations.

NOTES

INTRODUCTION: COLLECTIVE CRITICISM

1. Elena Ferrante, *Those Who Leave and Those Who Stay*, trans. Ann Goldstein (New York: Europa Editions, 2014), 354.
2. Ferrante, *Those Who Leave*, 354.
3. Ferrante, *My Brilliant Friend*, trans. Ann Goldstein (New York: Europa Editions, 2012).176–77.
4. Carey Kaplan and Ellen Cronan Rose, "Strange Bedfellows: Feminist Collaboration," *Signs* 18, no. 3 (Spring 1993): 547.
5. Sandra M. Gilbert and Susan Gubar, *The Madwoman in the Attic: The Woman Writer and the Nineteenth-Century Literary Imagination*, 2nd ed. (New Haven, CT: Yale University Press, 2000), xv.
6. Elizabeth G. Peck and JoAnna Stephens, eds., introduction to *Common Ground: Feminist Collaboration in the Academy* (Albany: State University of New York Press, 1998), 2.
7. Lorraine M. York, *Rethinking Women's Collaborative Writing: Power, Difference, Property* (Toronto: University of Toronto Press, 2002), 13.
8. Brent Hayes Edwards, Anna McCarthy, and Randy Martin, "Collective," *Social Text* 27, no. 3 (2009): 76.
9. Rebecca Falkoff, "To Translate is to Betray: On the Elena Ferrante Phenomenon in Italy and the US," *Public Books*, March 25, 2015, https://www.publicbooks.org/to-translate-is-to-betray-on-the-elena-ferrante-phenomenon-in-italy-and-the-us/.
10. Ferrante, *My Brilliant Friend*, 301.

11. Cathy N. Davidson, "Critical Fictions," *PMLA* 111:5 (1996): 1071.

12. J. Halberstam, "Between Butches" in *Butch/Femme: Inside Lesbian Gender*, ed. Sally Munt (Washington, D.C.: Cassell Academic, 1998), 63.

I. LETTERS (2015)

1. The original letters were published online in the Contemporaries section of the journal *Post45*. For more information on the journal, see post45.research.yale.edu.

2. Elena Ferrante, *My Brilliant Friend*, trans. Ann Goldstein (New York: Europa Editions, 2012), 259 (hereafter cited in text as *MBF*).

3. Elena Ferrante, "The Art of Fiction No. 228," interview by Sandro and Sandra Ferri, *Paris Review*, no. 212 (Spring 2015), http://www.theparisreview.org/interviews/6370/art-of-fiction-no-228-elena-ferrante.

4. James Wood, "Women on the Verge: The Fiction of Elena Ferrante," *New Yorker*, January 21, 2013.

5. Elena Ferrante, *The Story of a New Name*, trans. Ann Goldstein (New York: Europa Editions, 2013), 159 (hereafter cited in text as *SNN*).

6. W.G. Sebald, *The Rings of Saturn*, trans. Michael Hulse (London: Harvill, 1998), 3.

7. *Patience (After Sebald)*, directed by Grant Gee (Santa Monica, CA: Illuminations Films, 2012) DVD.

8. Sebald, *Rings of Saturn*, 23.

9. Sebald, *Rings of Saturn*, 24.

10. Elena Ferrante, *Those Who Leave and Those Who Stay*, trans. Ann Goldstein (New York: Europa Editions, 2014), 70 (hereafter cited in text as *TWL*).

11. The allusion here is to Rilke's poem, "Archaic Torso of Apollo."

12. See appendix for Lili Loofbourow's August 26 letter.

13. Nanni Balestrini, *The Unseen*, trans. Liz Heron (New York: Verso, 2012), 15.

14. See Appendix for Lili Loofbourow's August 26 letter.

15. Elena Ferrante, *The Story of the Lost Child*, trans. Ann Goldstein (New York: Europa Editions, 2015), 469 (hereafter cited in text as *SLC*).

16. Ferrante, "The Art of Fiction."

17. A phrase coined by Amy Schiller in her August 30 guest letter; see appendix.

18. Eric Hobsbawm and Joan Wallach Scott, "Political Shoemakers," *Past and Present*, no. 89 (November 1980): 86. Thanks to Jeremy Schmidt for directing me to this essay.

19. Hobsbawm and Scott, "Political Shoemakers," 89.

II. ESSAYS (2018)

UNFORM

1. Katherine.

2. Elena Ferrante, *Frantumaglia: A Writer's Journey*, trans. Ann Goldstein (New York: Europa Editions, 2016), 258 (hereafter cited in text as *FR*).

3. Elena Ferrante, *My Brilliant Friend*, trans. Ann Goldstein (New York: Europa Editions, 2012), 38–39 (hereafter cited in text as *MBF*).

4. Jane Bennett, *Vibrant Matter: A Political Ecology of Things* (Durham, NC: Duke University Press, 2009), vii.

5. Bennett, *Vibrant Matter*, xix.

6. Elena Ferrante, *The Story of the Lost Child*, trans. Ann Goldstein (New York: Europa Editions, 2015), 176 (hereafter cited in text as *SLC*).

7. Ali Smith, *Artful* (London: Hamish Hamilton, 2012), 67.

8. Many thanks to Ignacio Sánchez Prado, whose workshop observation that *des-* is even more active a prefix in Spanish than the English *un-* lends credence to these suspicions. This recalls Daniela Cascella's comments on the "destabilizing trick" of the Italian *s-* prefix in relation to *smarginatura*, which felicitously aligns with these meditations on *un-*: "The s-prefix in Italian slips off the margin of the meaning of a word. It's a sibilant un-." See Cascella, "Smarginature: Rebeginnings (Shadows), from her 2016 exchange with Natasha Soobramanien, a project that shares in the spirit of collective criticism: https://writingsoundbergen.wordpress.com/2016/11/19/smarginature -rebeginnings-by-daniela-cascella/.

9. Sigmund Freud, excerpt from *Beyond the Pleasure Principle*, in *The Freud Reader*, ed. Peter Gay (New York: Norton, 1995), 601, 603.

10. Elena Ferrante, *The Story of a New Name*, trans. Ann Goldstein (New York: Europa Editions, 2013), 124.

11. Also, as Cohen and Cohen note, literally "to spend," from *dépenser*. Reading this line, I imagine women, careless shoppers that we are said to be, flagrantly, unrepentantly, joyfully blowing through the miserly savings account of male history, carefully scrimped and hoarded for so long, despite the fact that it's accrued so little interest.

12. Hélène Cixous, "The Laugh of the Medusa," trans. Keith and Paula Cohen. *Signs* 1, no. 4 (Summer 1976): 882.

13. Susan Winnett, "Coming Unstrung: Women, Men, Narrative, and Principles of Pleasure," *PMLA* 103, no. 3 (May 1990): 516.

14. Elena Ferrante, *Those Who Leave and Those Who Stay*, trans. Ann Goldstein (New York: Europa Editions, 2014), 24 (hereafter cited in text as *TWL*).

15. Elena Ferrante, *Storia della bambina perduta*, (Rome: Edizioni e/o, 2014), 161. In Goldstein's translation: "She used that term: *dissolving boundaries*. It was on that occasion that she resorted to it for the first time; she struggled to elucidate the meaning, she wanted me to understand what the dissolution of boundaries meant and how much it frightened her." Ferrante, *Lost Child*, 171.

16. Cixous, "Rire de la Méduse," 876.

17. A. S. Byatt, *Possession: A Romance*, (London: Chatto and Windus, 1990), 551.

THE STORY OF A FICTION

1. Elena Ferrante, *Frantumaglia: A Writer's Journey*, trans. Ann Goldstein (New York: Europa Editions, 2016), 15 (hereafter cited in text as *FR*).

2. Elena Ferrante, *Those Who Leave and Those Who Stay*, trans. Ann Goldstein (New York: Europa Editions, 2014), 90 (hereafter cited in text as *TWL*).

3. Serge Doubrovsky, qtd in Catherine Cusset, "The Limits of Autofiction" (paper presented at the NYU Center for French Civilization and Culture Conference, Autofiction: Literature in France Today, New York University, New York, April 20, 2012), 1.

4. Gerard Genette, *Fiction and Diction*, trans. Catherine Porter (Ithaca, NY: Cornell University Press, 1993), 76; for a useful discussion of fictional selves in contemporary autofiction, see Marjorie Worthington, "Fiction in the 'Post-Truth' Era: The Ironic Effects of Autofiction," *Critique: Studies in Contemporary Fiction* 58, no. 5 (2017): 471–83.

5. Roland Barthes, "The Structural Analysis of Narratives," in *A Barthes Reader*, ed. Susan Sontag (New York: Hill and Wang, 1982), 283.

6. Vivian Gornick, *The Situation and the Story* (New York: Farrar, Straus and Giroux, 2002), 25.

7. Gornick, *The Situation and the Story*, 23.

8. Elena Ferrante, *My Brilliant Friend*, trans. Ann Goldstein (New York: Europa Editions, 2012), 23 (hereafter cited in text as *MBF*).

9. Phillip Lopate, *To Show and to Tell: The Craft of Literary Nonfiction* (New York: Free Press, 2013), 12.

10. Catherine Gallagher, "The Rise of Fictionality," in *The Novel*, vol. 1, *History, Geography, and Culture*, ed. Franco Moretti (Princeton, NJ: Princeton University Press, 2007), 340.

11. Elena Ferrante, *The Story of a New Name*, trans. Ann Goldstein (New York: Europa Editions, 2013), 18 (hereafter cited in text as *SNN*).

12. Elinor Ochs and Lisa Capps. *Living Narrative* (Cambridge, MA: Harvard University Press, 2002).

13. Elena Ferrante, *The Story of the Lost Child*, trans. Ann Goldstein (New York: Europa Editions, 2015), 25 (hereafter cited in text as *SLC*).

14. David Shields, *Reality Hunger: A Manifesto* (New York: Knopf, 2010), 5.

THE QUEER COUNTERFACTUAL

1. Elena Ferrante, *The Story of a New Name*, trans. Ann Goldstein (New York: Europa Editions, 2013), 1. (hereafter cited in text as *SNN*).

2. Elena Ferante, *My Brilliant Friend*, trans. Ann Goldstein (New York: Europa Editions, 2012), 135 (hereafter cited in text as *MBF*).

3. Nina Porzuki, "Language versus Dialect, or Why We're Obsessed with Elena Ferrante," April 11, 2017, in *The Word in Words Podcast*, produced by PRI, podcast, MP3 audio, 30:43, https://www.pri.org /stories/2017-04-07/elena-ferrante-language-versus-dialect.

4. See, for instance, T. S. Eliot, "From Poe to Valéry" *The Hudson Review* 2, no. 3 (1949): 327–42.

5. Eliot, "From Poe to Valéry," 336.

6. Elena Ferrante, *L'Amica Geniale* (Rome: Edizioni e/o, 2011), 1.

7. D. A. Miller, *Jane Austen, Or, The Secret of Style* (Princeton, NJ: Princeton University Press, 2003), 59.

8. Miller, *Jane Austen*, 58.

9. Leo Bersani, *Is the Rectum a Grave? And Other Essays* (Chicago: University of Chicago Press, 2010), 14, quoted in Miller, *Jane Austen*, 4.

10. Miller, *Jane Austen*, 4.

11. Eve Kosofsky Sedgwick, *Between Men: English Literature and Male Homosocial Desire* (New York: Columbia University Press, 1985).

12. See Kristina Busse, *Framing Fan Fiction: Literary and Social Practices in Fan Fiction* (Iowa City: University of Iowa Press, 2017) and *The Darker Side of Slash Fan Fiction*, ed. Ashton Spacey (Jefferson, NC: McFarland, 2018).

13. See Mary Anne Doane, *The Desire to Desire: The Women's Film of the 1940s* (Bloomington: Indiana University Press, 1987) and Henry Jenkins, *Textual Poachers: Television Fans and Participatory Culture* (New York: Routledge, 1992).

14. Jenkins, *Textual Poachers*, 186–87.

15. Abigail De Kosnik, *Rogue Archives: Digital Cultural Memory and Media Fandom* (Cambridge, MA: MIT Press, 2016), 145.

16. Kosnik notes that this term builds off Anne Cvetkovich's theorization of "lesbian public cultures" in *An Archive of Feelings: Trauma, Sexuality, and Lesbian Public Cultures* (Durham, NC: Duke University Press, 2003).

17. Zoe Dinovi. "My Brilliant Threesome." *Wattpad* (storytelling platform), September 19, 2016. See https://www.wattpad.com/story/54226801 -my-brilliant-friend-elena-ferrante-fanfic.

18. heartkeepinghopenhouse, "L'amica crudele" *An Archive of Our Own* (storytelling platform), 16 July 2019. See https://archiveofourown .org/works/17048984?view_adult=true.

19. theoldgolds, "Comments," "L'amica crudele," *An Archive of Our Own* (storytelling platform), 25 December 2018, See https://archiveofourown .org/works/6720628.

20. The Star Freedom, "Gilmore Girls: The Life and Times," *FanFiction* (storytelling platform), 26 November 2016. See https://www.fanfiction .net/s/12248796/3/Gilmore-Girls-The-Life-and-Times.

21. *Contemporaries*, script by Erica Wachs, directed by Aparna Nair-Kanneganti, produced by Jocelyn Wexler, performed by Agnes Enkhtamir, Phoebe Cardenas, Stella Shannon, and Emily Harburg, Saybrook Underbrook Theater, New Haven, 21 April 2018.

22. Lauren Berlant, "On her book *Cruel Optimism*," *Rorotoko*, June 4, 2012, http://rorotoko.com/interview/20120605_berlant_lauren_on_cruel _optimism/?page=2.

23. Carolyn Dinshaw, *How Soon is Now? Medieval Texts, Amateur Readers, and the Queerness of Time* (Durham, NC: Duke University Press, 2012), 31.

24. Sigmund Freud, "Fetishism" (1927) *The Complete Psychological Works of Sigmund Freud*, ed. and trans. James Stratchey, vol. 21 (London: Hogarth and the Institute of Psychoanalysis, 1948), 152–57.

25. Octave Mannoni, *Clefs pour l'imaginarie ou l'autre scène* (Paris: Editions du Seuil, 1969), 9–33.

26. Freud, "Fetishism," 154.

27. For great work closer to this vein of counterfactual, see Paul Saint-Amour, "Counterfactual States of America: On Parallel Worlds and Longing for the Law," *Post45*, September 20, 2011, http://post45 .research.yale.edu/2011/09/counterfactual-states-of-america-on -parallel-worlds-and-longing-for-the-law/; and Catherine Gallagher, *Telling it Like It Wasn't: The Counterfactual Imagination of History and Fiction* (Chicago: University of Chicago Press, 2018).

28. Daniel Philip Todes, *Ivan Pavlov: A Russian Life in Science* (Oxford: Oxford University Press, 2014), 503–4. See also Ivan P. Pavlov, "Conditioned Reflexes: An Investigation of the Psychological Activity of the Cerebral Cortex," Trans. G.V. Anrep, *Classics in the History of Psychology*, March 2001, http://psychclassics.yorku.ca/Pavlov/lecture18.htm.

29. Elena Ferrante, *Those Who Leave and Those Who Stay*, trans. Ann Goldstein (New York: Europa Editions, 2014), 351 (hereafter cited in text as *TWL*).

THE CAGE OF AUTHORSHIP

1. Saverio Costanzo (director of HBO limited series My Brilliant Friend), interview with the author, July 25, 2018 (hereafter all Constanzo quotations in the text are from this exchange unless otherwise noted).

2. Jason Horowitz, "Elena Ferrante on *My Brilliant Friend* Moving to the Screen," *New York Times*, May 26, 2017, https://www.nytimes .com/2017/05/26/books/elena-ferrante-on-my-brilliant-friend -moving-to-the-screen.html.

3. Ferrante, *Those Who Leave and Those Who Stay*, trans. Ann Goldstein (New York: Europa Editions, 2014), 412.

4. Ferrante, *Those Who Leave*, 282.

5. Ferrante, *My Brilliant Friend*, trans. Ann Goldstein (New York: Europa Editions, 2012), 313 (hereafter cited in text as *MBF*).

6. Michel Foucault, "What Is an Author?" in *Language, Counter-Memory, Practice: Selected Essays and Interviews by Michel Foucault*, ed. Donald Bouchard (Ithaca: Cornell University Press, 1980), 113.

7. Elena Ferrante, "Elena Ferrante: 'Anonymity Lets Me Concentrate Exclusively on Writing,'" interview by Deborah Orr, *The Guardian*, February 19, 2016, https://www.theguardian.com/books/2016/feb/19/elena-ferrante -anonymity-lets-me-concentrate-exclusively-on-writing.

8. Elena Ferrante (novelist), interview with the author, September 8, 2018 (hereafter all Ferrante quotations in the text are from this exchange unless otherwise noted).

9. AFP, "TV Version of Elena Ferrante's My Brilliant Friend Debuts in Venice: Watch the Trailer," September 3, 2018, https://www.thelocal .it/20180903/mystery-italian-author-elena-ferrante-tv-adaptation -my-brilliant-friend.

10. Elena Ferrante, "Maggie Gyllenhaal is Filming One of My Books. It's Her Story to Tell Now," *The Guardian*, October 8, 2018, https://www .theguardian.com/lifeandstyle/2018/oct/06/maggie-gyllenhaal -elena-ferrante-film-book.

11. Costanzo, interview.

12. Elena Ferrante, *Frantumaglia: A Writer's Journey*, trans. Ann Goldstein (New York: Europa Editions, 2016), 100.

13. Ferrante, *Frantumaglia*, 100.

APPENDIX: GUEST LETTERS

1. Elena Ferrante, *The Story of a New Name*, trans. Ann Goldstein (New York: Europa Editions, 2013), 21–22 (hereafter cited in text as *SNN*).

2. Jessica Winter, "Selfie Loathing: Instagram Is Even More Depressing than Facebook. Here's Why." *Slate*, July 23, 2013.

3. Ferrante, *Those Who Leave and Those Who Stay*, trans. Ann Goldstein (New York: Europa Editions, 2014), 345 (hereafter cited in text as *TWL*).

4. T. J. Clark, *Farewell to an Idea: Episodes From the History of Modernism* (New Haven: Yale University Press, 1999), 9–10.

5. See Merve's July 30 letter.

6. See Katherine's July 1 letter.

BIBLIOGRAPHY

Balestrini, Nanni. *The Unseen*. Translated by Liz Heron. New York: Verso, 2012.

Barthes, Roland. "The Structural Analysis of Narratives." In *A Barthes Reader*, edited by Susan Sontag, 251–95. New York: Hill and Wang, 1982.

Bennett, Jane. *Vibrant Matter: A Political Ecology of Things*. Durham, NC: Duke University Press, 2009.

Berlant, Lauren. "On Her Book *Cruel Optimism*." Interview with *Rorotoko*, June 4, 2012. http://rorotoko.com/interview/20120605_berlant_lauren_on_cruel_optimism/?page=2.

Bersani, Leo. *Is the Rectum a Grave? And Other Essays*. Chicago: University of Chicago Press, 2010.

Busse, Kristina. *Framing Fan Fiction: Literary and Social Practices in Fan Fiction*. Iowa City: University of Iowa Press, 2017.

Byatt, A. S. *Possession: A Romance*. London: Chatto and Windus, 1990.

Cascella, Daniela. "Smarginature: Rebeginnings (Shadows)." *Writing Sound Bergen* (blog), November 19, 2016. https://writingsoundbergen.wordpress.com/2016/11/19/smarginature-rebeginnings-by-daniela-cascella/.

Cixous, Hélène. "The Laugh of the Medusa." Translated by Keith and Paula Cohen. *Signs* 1, no. 4 (Summer 1976): 875–93.

Clark, T. J. *Farewell to an Idea: Episodes From the History of Modernism*. New Haven, CT: Yale University Press, 1999.

Cusset, Catherine. "The Limits of Autofiction." Paper presented at the NYU Center for French Civilization and Culture Conference, Autofiction: Literature in France Today, New York University, New York, April 20, 2012. http://www.catherinecusset.co.uk/wp-content/uploads/2013/02/THE-LIMITS-OF-AUTOFICTION.pdf.

Cvetkovich, Anne. *An Archive of Feelings: Trauma, Sexuality, and Lesbian Public Cultures.* Durham, NC: Duke University Press, 2003.

Davidson, Cathy N. "Critical Fictions," *PMLA* 111:5 (1996): 1069–72.

De Kosnik, Abigail. *Rogue Archives: Digital Cultural Memory and Media Fandom.* Cambridge, MA: MIT Press, 2016.

Dinovi, Zoe. "My Brilliant Threesome." *Wattpad* (storytelling platform), September 19, 2016. https://www.wattpad.com/story/54226801-my -brilliant-friend-elena-ferrante-fanfic.

Dinshaw, Carolyn. *How Soon is Now? Medieval Texts, Amateur Readers, and the Queerness of Time* (Durham, NC: Duke University Press, 2012).

Doane, Mary Anne. *The Desire to Desire: The Women's Film of the 1940s.* Bloomington: Indiana University Press, 1987.

Doubtless [pseud.]. "The Story of the Returned Doll." Archive of Our Own (storytelling platform), May 2, 2016. https://archiveofourown.org /works/6720628.

Edwards, Brent Hayes, Anna McCarthy, and Randy Martin. "Collective." *Social Text* 27, no. 3 (2009): 74–77.

Eliot, T. S. "From Poe to Valéry." *The Hudson Review* 2, no. 3 (1949): 327–42.

Falkoff, Rebecca. "To Translate is to Betray: On the Elena Ferrante Phenomenon in Italy and the US." *Public Books*, March 25, 2015. https://www .publicbooks.org/to-translate-is-to-betray-on-the-elena-ferrante -phenomenon-in-italy-and-the-us/.

Ferrante, Elena. *L'Amica Geniale.* Rome: Edizioni e/o, 2011.

Ferrante, Elena. "Anonymity Lets Me Concentrate Exclusively on Writing." Interview by Deborah Orr. *The Guardian*, February 19, 2016. https:// www.theguardian.com/books/2016/feb/19/elena-ferrante-anonymity -lets-me-concentrate-exclusively-on-writing.

Ferrante, Elena. "The Art of Fiction No. 228." Interview by Sandro and Sandra Ferri. *Paris Review* 212 (Spring 2015). http://www.theparisreview .org/interviews/6370/art-of-fiction-no-228-elena-ferrante.

Ferrante, Elena. "Elena Ferrante on *My Brilliant Friend* Moving to the Screen." Interview by Jason Horowitz. *New York Times*, May 26, 2017. https:// www.nytimes.com/2017/05/26/books/elena-ferrante-on-my-brilliant -friend-moving-to-the-screen.html.

Ferrante, Elena. *La Frantumaglia, Nuova Edizione Ampliata.* Rome: Edizioni e/o, 2016.

Ferrante, Elena. *Frantumaglia: A Writer's Journey*. Translated by Ann Goldstein. New York: Europa Editions, 2016.

Ferrante, Elena. "Maggie Gyllenhaal Is Filming One of My Books. It's Her Story to Tell Now." *The Guardian*, October 8, 2018. https://www.theguardian.com/lifeandstyle/2018/oct/06/maggie-gyllenhaal-elena-ferrante-film-book.

Ferrante, Elena. *My Brilliant Friend*. Translated by Ann Goldstein. New York: Europa Editions, 2012.

Ferrante, Elena. *Storia della bambina perduta*. Rome: Edizioni e/o, 2014.

Ferrante, Elena. *The Story of the Lost Child*. Translated by Ann Goldstein. New York: Europa Editions, 2015.

Ferrante, Elena. *The Story of a New Name*. Translated by Ann Goldstein. New York: Europa Editions, 2013.

Ferrante, Elena. *Those Who Leave and Those Who Stay*. Translated by Ann Goldstein. New York: Europa Editions, 2014.

Foucault, Michel. "What Is an Author?" In *Language, Counter-Memory, Practice: Selected Essays and Interviews by Michel Foucault*, edited by Donald Bouchard,113–38. Ithaca, NY: Cornell University Press, 1980.

Freud, Sigmund. "Fetishism" (1927). In Vol. 21 of *The Complete Psychological Works of Sigmund Freud*. Translated by James Stratchey, 152–57. London: Hogarth and the Institute of Psychoanalysis, 1948.

Freud, Sigmund. *Beyond the Pleasure Principle*. In *The Freud Reader*, edited by Peter Gay, 594–626. New York: W. W. Norton, 1995.

Gallagher, Catherine. "The Rise of Fictionality." In *History, Geography, and Culture*, edited by Franco Moretti, 336–63, Vol. 1 of *The Novel*. Princeton, NJ: Princeton University Press, 2007.

Gallagher, Catherine. *Telling it Like It Wasn't: The Counterfactual Imagination of History and Fiction*. Chicago: University of Chicago Press, 2018.

Gee, Grant, dir. *Patience (After Sebald)*. 2012; Santa Monica, CA: Illuminations Films, DVD.

Genette, Gérard. *Fiction and Diction*. Translated by Catherine Porter. Ithaca, NY: Cornell University Press, 1993.

Gilbert, Sandra M. and Susan Gubar, *The Madwoman in the Attic: The Woman Writer and the Nineteenth-Century Literary Imagination*. 2nd ed. New Haven, CT: Yale University Press, 2000.

Gornick, Vivian. *The Situation and the Story*. New York: Farrar, Straus and Giroux, 2002.

Halberstam, J. "Between Butches." In *Butch/Femme: Inside Lesbian Gender*, ed. Sally Munt, 57–66. Washington, D.C.: Cassell Academic, 1998.

Heartkeepingopenhouse [pseud.]. "L'amica crudele." Archive of Our Own (storytelling platform), December 12, 2018. https://archiveofourown.org/works/17048984?view_adult=true.

Hobsbawm, Eric and Joan Wallach Scott. "Political Shoemakers." *Past and Present*, no. 89 (November 1980): 86–114.

Jenkins, Henry. *Textual Poachers: Television Fans and Participatory Culture.* New York: Routledge, 1992.

Kaplan, Carey and Ellen Cronan Rose. 'Strange Bedfellows: Feminist Collaboration." *Signs* 18, no. 3 (Spring 1993): 547–61.

Lopate, Phillip. *To Show and to Tell.* New York: Free Press, 2013.

Mannoni, Octave. *Clefs pour l'imaginarie ou l'autre scène.* Paris: Editions du Seuil, 1969.

Miller, D. A. *Jane Austen, or, the Secret of Style.* Princeton, NJ: Princeton University Press, 2003.

Moraga, Cherríe. "La Güera," *This Bridge Called My Back: Writings by Radical Women of Color*, Fourth Edition, ed. Cherríe Moraga and Gloria Anzaldúa, 22-29. Albany: State University of New York Press, 2015.

Ochs, Elinor and Lisa Capps. *Living Narrative: Creating Lives in Everyday Storytelling.* Cambridge, MA: Harvard University Press, 2002.

Pavlov, Ivan P. "Conditioned Reflexes: An Investigation of the Psychological Activity of the Cerebral Cortex." Translated by G. V. Anrep, *Classics in the History of Psychology* (website), March 2001. http://psychclassics.yorku.ca/Pavlov/lecture18.htm.

Peck, Elizabeth G. and JoAnna Stephens. Introduction to *Common Ground: Feminist Collaboration in the Academy*, ed. Elizabeth G. Peck and JoAnna Stephens, 1–10. Albany: State University of New York Press, 1998.

Porzuki, Nina. "Language versus Dialect, or Why We're Obsessed with Elena Ferrante." Produced by PRI. *The Word in Words Podcast*, April 11, 2017. MP3 audio, 30:43. https://www.pri.org/stories/2017-04-07/elena-ferrante-language-versus-dialect.

Rilke, Rainer Maria. *The Selected Poetry of Rainer Maria Rilke.* Translated by Stephen Mitchell. New York: Vintage, 1989.

Saint-Amour, Paul. "Counterfactual States of America: On Parallel Worlds and Longing for the Law." *Post45*, September 20, 2011. http://post45

.research.yale.edu/2011/09/counterfactual-states-of-america-on -parallel-worlds-and-longing-for-the-law/.

Sebald, W. G. *The Rings of Saturn*. Translated by Michael Hulse. London: Harvill, 1998.

Sedgwick, Eve Kosofsky. *Between Men: English Literature and Male Homosocial Desire*. New York: Columbia University Press, 1985.

Shields, David. *Reality Hunger: A Manifesto*. New York: Knopf, 2010.

Smith, Ali. *Artful*. London: Hamish Hamilton, 2012.

Spacey, Ashton, ed. *The Darker Side of Slash Fan Fiction*. Jefferson, NC: McFarland, 2018.

The Star Freedom [pseud.]. "Gilmore Girls: The Life and Times." *FanFiction* (storytelling platform), December 10, 2016. https://www.fanfiction .net/s/12248796/3/Gilmore-Girls-The-Life-and-Times.

Todes, Daniel Philip. *Ivan Pavlov: A Russian Life in Science*. Oxford: Oxford University Press, 2014.

Winnett, Susan. "Coming Unstrung: Women, Men, Narrative, and Principles of Pleasure," *PMLA* 103, no. 3 (May 1990): 505–18.

Winter, Jessica. "Selfie Loathing: Instagram Is Even More Depressing than Facebook. Here's Why." *Slate*, July 23, 2013. https://slate.com/technology /2013/07/instagram-and-self-esteem-why-the-photo-sharing-network -is-even-more-depressing-than-facebook.html.

Wood, James. "Women on the Verge: The Fiction of Elena Ferrante." *New Yorker*, January 21, 2013.

Worthington, Marjorie. "Fiction in the 'Post-Truth' Era: The Ironic Effects of Autofiction." *Critique: Studies in Contemporary Fiction* 58, no. 5 (2017): 471–83.

York, Lorraine M. *Rethinking Women's Collaborative Writing: Power, Difference, Property*. Toronto: University of Toronto Press, 2002.